MW00770559

AMERICAN ALLEGORY

AMERICAN ALLEGORY

Lindy Hop and the Racial Imagination

BLACK HAWK HANCOCK

The University of Chicago Press   Chicago and London

Black Hawk Hancock is assistant professor of sociology at DePaul University. He is coauthor of *Changing Theories: New Directions in Sociology*.

The University of Chicago Press, Chicago 60637
The University of Chicago Press, Ltd., London
© 2013 by The University of Chicago
All rights reserved. Published 2013.
Printed in the United States of America

22 21 20 19 18 17 16 15 14 13   1 2 3 4 5

ISBN-13: 978-0-226-04307-4 (cloth)
ISBN-13: 978-0-226-04310-4 (paper)
ISBN-13: 978-0-226-04324-1 (e-book)

Library of Congress Cataloging-in-Publication Data

Hancock, Black Hawk, 1971–
  American allegory : Lindy hop and the racial imagination / Black Hawk Hancock.
      pages cm
  Includes bibliographical references and index.
  ISBN 978-0-226-04307-4 (cloth: alk. paper) —
ISBN 978-0-226-04310-4 (pbk.: alk. paper) —
ISBN 978-0-226-04324-1 (ebk.) 1. African Americans—Illinois—Chicago—Social conditions—20th century. 2. Chicago (Il.)—Race relations—History—20th century. 3. Blacks—Race identity—Illinois—Chicago—History—20th century.
4. Whites—Race identity—Illinois—Chicago—History—20th century. 5. Lindy (Dance)—Illinois—Chicago—History—20th century. I. Title.
  E185.86.H285 2013
  305.896'073077311—dc23
                    2012044800

⊗ This paper meets the requirements of ANSI/NISO Z39.48-1992 (Permanence of Paper).

For Nana and Ghee with all my love and gratitude.

(Elizabeth "Betty" Warren and Everett "Ebb" Warren)

A . . . major problem, and one that is indispensable to the central-ization and direction of power, is that of learning the meaning of myths and symbols which abound among the Negro masses. For without this knowledge, Leadership, no matter how correct its program, will fail. Much in Negro life remains a mystery; perhaps the zoot suit conceals profound political meaning; per-haps the symmetrical frenzy of the Lindy-hop conceals clues to great potential powers, if only leaders could solve this riddle.

Ralph Ellison

CONTENTS

ACKNOWLEDGMENTS

Originally, writing a book on the Lindy Hop was not my intent. Even after a year of dance education, I never considered the Lindy Hop as a possible topic of intellectual inquiry. In fact, in one of my earliest dance classes, my first dance instructor suggested that I write about the Lindy Hop. I laughed off his remark and never gave it a second thought. As a result, my initial reflections on the Lindy Hop were not instrumentally motivated for research purposes, but instead were an outcome of my passion for the fascinating new world in which I found myself. It has been said that if one intellectualizes one's passion, then the passion withers away. If it were not for all the wonderful dancers, musicians, and other people I met during my time dancing that might have been the case. Instead, their friendship and camaraderie fueled my desire and propelled me into worlds I could never have imagined.

While the pursuit of the Lindy Hop took me from off the coast of Los Angeles to the outposts of Sweden, a word about my home, Chicago, is necessary. While generations of dancers have come up after us and carry on the dance, to be part of that rising tide of the Lindy Hop revival, to help institutionalize it here, makes all the years of working through this project worthwhile. To the bar owners who let us dance in their aisles, to the clubs that would let us clear tables to extend their dance floors, the Lindy Hop resonated deeply with the already rich dance and music traditions of Chicago. While many have moved on from the dance, and several of the best dance venues have shuttered or now bear different names, a more fertile soil could not have been asked for to nurture this dance and watch it bloom.

In order to make an attempt at acknowledging all those who came into my life over the years, it is necessary to retrace some of the major steps of the seemingly circuitous route that *American Allegory* took on the way to its fruition. It is worth recounting some of these seminal moments here, so as to try and account for as many people as possible who influenced me along the way. To all who passed through my life during this journey, and to those who I apologetically have forgotten to mention here, my deepest gratitude.

American Allegory began in the fall of 1997 when, as a third-year graduate student at Wisconsin, I moved from Madison to Chicago, to take classes at the University of Chicago. Without a graduate cohort or concrete institutional support, I was forced to eke out a social existence on my own in a new city. Shortly after my arrival in Chicago, I was introduced to the Lindy Hop subculture. While an academic by day, by night I was plunging myself into the then-exploding world of Lindy Hop and the retro revival culture that came with it. Within weeks of my arrival I had sifted through the dozens of dance studios offering Swing dance, to find Swing-Out Chicago. By the end of September that year I was enrolled in dance classes twice a week and social dancing as often as I could on the other nights. I started taking as many classes as possible and came to know—among others who shaped my initial dancing—Howard Bregman, Dana Cygan, Penny Huddleston, Julee Mertz, Andrew Twiss, Nicole Wood, and Chris Yee. Looking back on those early days at St. Alphonsus Church, I don't think any of us realized just what it all meant. A thank you to John Schmitz for all your support of our dance endeavors there. From lessons to practice session, to performance rehearsals, you were always giving up another fifteen minutes for us to finish.

My academic year at U of C blew by as dance became my all-consuming passion. By June 1998 I had gathered enough skill and fascination that I packed my bags and headed off to Catalina Island for Swing Camp Catalina, where I was to take classes with the greatest Lindy Hoppers from all over the world. It was that summer that I took class with the legendary Frankie Manning, who at the time was eighty-four years old, considered one of the greatest dancers (and one of the originators) of the Lindy Hop. Dancing to live big bands at night, looking out the open windows of Catalina's Casino Ballroom onto Avalon Bay and across the Pacific Ocean, were nights that could only be described as sublime. Thank you to Erin and Tami Stevens for putting together the granddaddy of all American Swing dance camps and for an unrelenting focus on celebrating the beauty and aesthetics of dance in one of the world's most picturesque settings.

Having spent the previous year taking classes in Chicago, I was still obligated to fulfill two remaining courses in Madison. Therefore, rather than moving back, I made the weekly commute from Chicago during the fall of 1998 working closely with communication arts professor John Fiske. It was out of our weekly Wednesday conversations, fueled by the Living Room's most very ordinary red wine, that John and I rehashed my tales of the dance world and the life I was leading far from the halls of academia. It was out of those conversations, which were cross-cut with the canon of cultural studies, that he convinced me that I had already discovered my research project without even knowing it. What would have been considered laughable years before suddenly took hold and the worlds of sociology and cultural studies melded into one. Without the enthusiasm and encouragement of John Fiske, there would be no *American Allegory*. Encouraged by John to get these ideas out into the public arena, I went off to Portland, Oregon, for the Pacific Sociological Association meetings in April 1999, my first professional conference, delivering three different papers on my initial ideas for a study on the Lindy Hop (which at the time was heavily inspired by the work of Bourdieu and covered everything from historical analysis, to issues of social space, to issues of cultural appropriation and embodiment, and the transmission of culture across racialized bodies). Following up on that, at the tail end of that academic year, at Fiske's invite, I traveled again up to Madison, to present what was the first coherent proposal of the overall project to my peers, at the Graduate Student Colloquium in Communication Arts.

Out of the feedback I received from my trip to Portland and the overwhelming constructive feedback from the Colloquium, the summer of 1999 marked what was a cross-continental whirlwind of fieldwork that took me back to Catalina, to Los Angeles to Toronto, to Boston, and on to Minneapolis. During this time I met with all the primary revivalists: Steven Mitchell, David Dalmo, Lennart Westerlund, Eddie Jansson and Eva Lagerqvist, Ryan Francois and Jenny Thomas, Virginie Jensen, Kenneth and Helena Norbelie, as well as spending time with the members of dance troupes the Rhythm Hot Shots and Shout-n-Feel-It! (among others), who set me on my way with their insights and suggestions for my research. A special nod to Steven Mitchell here: from our first meeting with a makeshift mocha and a jaundiced eye toward my initial questions, to those ongoing conversations ever since, in the strangest packages come those who are darker than Blue.

Following through on John Fiske's recommendation, I again made the commute from Chicago to Madison, and sat in on Ronald Radano's Black Cultural Studies seminar in the fall of 1999. It was here that Ron introduced me to the nonfiction work of Ralph Ellison, which proved to be the theoretical turning point in my thinking, and through which everything else was to filter. To Ron I owe an ongoing debt of gratitude for his unending generosity for clearing time for coffee and conversation on spur-of-the-moment trips to Madison over the years that followed. In addition to the intricacies of Ellison's thought, Ron taught me to listen to those elements that other ethnographers only see. If there is any musical quality to my work, it is indebted to Ron. Fall of '99 also brought another trip to Los Angeles, where I studied dance with Josie Say, spent an afternoon on Erin Steven's spacious porch listening to her recount her central role in the Lindy Hop revival of the 1980s, and was escorted around the LA scene by veteran Lindy Hopper and gracious hostess Sophie Lim.

Summer 2000 took me to Herrang, Sweden (population 422), located along the coast at the bay Singöfjärden about an hour and a half from Stockholm to the famous Herrang Dance Camp, where for three weeks I trained, interviewed, wrote, and discovered the reach of Eminem in a global world. To Angela Andrews, Paul Overton and Sharon Ashe, Mattias Lundmark and Asa Palm, Catrine Ljunggren, Rob and Diane van Haaren, my classmates, and all the others that offered your time and your unsolicited opinions about me and my "project" I thank you. Finally, a special thank you to Kenneth and Helena Norbelie, who opened their home, their dance studio, and theirs hearts to me: for showing me Stockholm and the Swedish way to do things—Skål för Fan!

While my entry into the world of Steppin' didn't occur until summer of 2001, almost four years after I started to Lindy Hop, being an expert dancer eased my transition into that scene in ways that may have made a beginner's experience much different. To be able to have participated in one of the most distinctive of all Chicago cultural practices, as Steppin' in Chicago's own particular contemporary stylized form of the Lindy Hop, has made living in Chicago all that much richer an experience. Again, as my immersion into this dance culture was out of my attraction to the dance, and only later was something I drew upon for this book, crisscrossing back and forth between the worlds of the Lindy Hop and Steppin' not only provided an ideal comparative study, it provided a way to expand my dancing repertoire and elevate my dance skills to an entirely new level. A huge shout-out to all the Steppers who took me in, broke bread, showed me love, had my back, and introduced me to some of the finest dance venues and DJs Chicago will ever know: 3G's, Mr. G's, Legend's, and the (old) East of the Ryan. For all your generosity, I hope you find your kindness reflected back here.

I could never have completed this book without the advice of my mentors Chas Camic, Mustafa Emirbayer, Phillip Gorski, Mara Loveman, and Ronald Radano. They were so receptive to such an unusual project and allowed it to unfold with as much leeway as needed. Each one of you brought something unique to the book. I hope you find your support and encouragement echoing throughout.

Beyond these important markers of *American Allegory*, it is necessary to thank all the friends who helped me through the early days of working on this book and talked me down from the bell tower: Gianpaolo Baiocchi,

Brad Manzolillo, Ron Mize, Dan Steward, and Josh Whitford. A special recognition goes out to Tanarra Schneider for her friendship, inspiration, and support. She was a guiding voice in keeping me straight, or at least "straightish" over the years. To Harry Saito, a perfect partner in crime on so many adventures. Julie Siragusa deserves special mention as the greatest dance partner I have ever known, and as a friend who helped me through my darkest days to get the book into its final form, I owe you more than I can ever say. To Paul Stern, my wartime consigliere. A very special shout-out to David Yamane and Big Slappy for having my back since day one—people's for life—your support has meant everything.

Javier Auyero deserves credit for helping me forge my most challenging article, articulating both theoretical and methodological aspects of the ethnographic process into a coherent vision in *Qualitative Sociology* 30 (2007). Thank you for all your guidance navigating those ethnographic waters. Loïc Wacquant also deserves special recognition; he provoked, prodded, and raised the bar in terms of what was not only acceptable, but demanded of good ethnography. From our first meeting back in 1994 to today, his support has been tireless.

Chas Camic deserves special recognition for his unflagging support through my highs and lows, my successes and the failures, along the way. Upon my arrival in Madison, Chas's couch served as my lone point of refuge in an otherwise unrelenting storm of hostility. Despite my sometimes questionable choices, such as that "brilliant insight" I had into the work of Bataille or why Roland Barthes was the greatest "undiscovered" sociologist of the late twentieth century, he never left my side or abandoned his faith in me. Over the last several years it has been his guiding support and wisdom that have allowed me to bring *American Allegory* from possibility to print. During the redrafting of the book, I was asked once why a theorist had such a gravitational pull on my ethnographic work. I responded that if one could undertake historical-contextual work, such as the type Chas Camic does, and wander around the nineteenth century long enough until one found something of significance, then he more than anyone else could grasp and guide a project as mundane as the Lindy Hop.

Two reviewers for the University of Chicago Press provided invaluable feedback that improved the book immeasurably. Finally, a special acknowledgment to the man who provided the backbeat of *American Allegory*, editor-drummer/drummer-editor Douglas Mitchell. Upon our very first meeting, he has not only laid time, but knew when to take the lead and change up the tempo. If a dancer can only express himself within the pocket he is given, then Doug Mitchell is the Jo Jones of editors.

PROLOGUE: THIS STRANGE DANCE

Minstrelsy was the beginning of a long relationship between blacks and whites and black entertainment and white appropriation of it … and this strange dance that we've been doing with each other since, really, the beginning of our relationship in America. It's too close; it's too deep a story, so you have to degrade the relationship.

Wynton Marsalis

Despite his racial difference and social status, something indisputably American about Negroes not only raised doubts about the white man's values system but aroused the troubling suspicion that whatever else the true American is, he is also somehow part black.

Ralph Ellison

•

As I waited in the long line for admission to Club Liquid, the sounds of Swing and jump blues billowed past the red velvet curtains into the dimly lit atrium. Dozens of "Swing kids" clad in fedoras and two-tone shoes awaited entry into the club. Beyond the curtain was an undulating sea of bodies in motion; socialites, dancers, and musicians were ready to dance until the wee hours. Cocooned red globes dangled from the ceiling; their luminous glow was just bright enough to soften the glare of the glittering martini glasses and small white candles that flickered like fireflies across the bar. A thick haze of cigarette and cigar smoke encircled the patrons anchoring the long oak bar along the left side of the club. The barstools were packed and the crowd around them was two rows deep, trying desperately to get the attention of the black-vested bartenders pouring Cosmopolitans and Manhattans. Down at the end of the bar, at the back of the room, lay the brightly lit stage and the vast parquet dance floor, where a myriad of colors and shapes twirled, twisted, and spun. Here, hundreds of Swing kids were dancing the Lindy Hop to the sounds of a dozen musicians beating out the charts from Basie and Ellington to Goodman and Henderson.

Amid the flurry of movement and congestion of people, above the fedoras and coiffed hair, I saw a woman doing the splits as she was lifted into the air, her skirt splaying out around her. Another woman was tossed over her partner's head to wild crowd applause. At the back corner of the dance floor, a group of people bobbing, weaving, and cheering formed a wall with their backs to the rest of the dancers. The main attraction was there in the "jam" circle, where the great Lindy Hoppers held court, challenging each other and demonstrating their latest tricks and turns.

As I made my way through the club, I noticed that all of the tables were completely filled; there was standing room only. Men in pinstripe suits with the "drape shape" and "reet pleats" socialized with women in cocktail dresses and small pillbox hats. Tonight, everyone was here for the Lindy Hop scene. Whether drinker, dancer, or barfly, they all circulated around the Lindy Hop, the original Swing dance that emerged from its more famously remembered precursor, the Charleston, in the ballrooms of Harlem in the late 1920s. This was the dance night of the week at the most popular club in town; tonight more than 800 people would come through the doors in search of Swing dancing and the scene that accompanied the latest craze captivating the nation. That night the club was at a fever pitch of excitement, with every hep cat eyeing each other's latest fashions and dance steps.

At the edge of the dance floor, a barrier of bodies congregated two to three deep in places. They served as a human wall, encircling the dance floor and those dancers inside it. This porous wall of bodies functioned as the intersection of activity in the club; some were drinking, some smoking, some watching silently, others were cheering and clapping to the music with enthusiasm, and still others were waiting to get on the floor when space cleared. Over the top of the crowd, the band was stomping and jumping; their glistening horns trumpeted out swinging jazz and blues as the rhythm section pounded out the heavy syncopated backbeat. The band members' bold geometric-patterned ties and dark suits bopped and swayed in unison as they took the already excited crowd to its peak with an encore rendition of Basie's signature "Corner Pocket."

Bodies jumped, spun, twisted, and glided all over the dance floor. Moving in unison, they did variations of the Charleston, Shimmy, Black Bottom, Boogie, and Texas Tommy and performed all the other variations of the Lindy Hop, the dance that *Life* magazine once billed as "America's True National Folk Dance." The eye-dazzling movement of partners changing places and spinning around each other manifested the physicality, sweat, energy, and excitement of hundreds of people on the dance floor connecting through social dancing. The black and white two-tones, the crisp white shirts, the zoot suits, the pinstripes, the fedoras, the billowing dresses, the lace, the twirling crinoline all decorated the swirling bodies as if this were a large staged choreography. But it was not. I had entered the world of the Lindy Hop, the original Swing dance.

•

This description could have been given by Malcolm X after a visit to the Roseland Ballroom. It could be an account by one of the dancers at the Savoy in Harlem sixty years ago.[1] But fascinatingly enough, this was my initial experience with the Swing dance scene in contemporary Chicago. After moving to Chicago from Madison, I was captivated by this subculture upon my first encounter with it. This fascination has led not only to a PhD dissertation, but also to an ongoing dance education through my personal struggle to master one of the most elusive of social dances, the Lindy Hop. I have never been comfortable separating my personal and professional lives, and the Lindy Hop subculture immediately yielded both a social and a sociologically fascinating world in which I immersed myself completely. There is something both romantic and nostalgic in the sight of hundreds of young people outfitted in suits and dresses, dancing to the music their grandparents called "popular" the first time it came around in the late 1920s, '30s, and '40s. That night at Club Liquid was not a costume party or an isolated special event. This was the subculture of the Swing dance revival, alive and thriving in the city of Chicago, across the nation, and all over the world.

On closer inspection, something unsettling emerges within this beauty. Club Liquid is not an African American club in Harlem, but a contemporary predominantly white club in the North Side of Chicago. What was once an African American cultural practice—forged as an alternative expression of identity against the context of overt and explicit white racism, segregation, and exploitation that defined the American landscape at the time—has now become the tribal call of the privileged white middle class.[2] As Kobena Mercer writes, "In the high energy dance styles that might accompany the beat, the Lindy Hop and Jitterbug traced another line of flight: through the catharsis of the dance a momentary release might be obtained from all the pressures on mind and body accumulated under the ritual discriminations of racism" (Mercer 1994, 431). Ironically, where once whites had to travel uptown to black parts of New York City to Swing dance in the Savoy Ballroom—as the famous Savoy Lindy Hop dancer Norma Miller remarked, "White people had to come to Harlem to learn how to Swing. The Savoy was the home of black dancing; it was the home of Swing"—now African Americans must travel to white parts of town to dance the Lindy Hop to Swing music (quoted in Burns 2000). This ironic twist forces us to think about the relationships among race, culture, and identity in contemporary American society. As Ralph Ellison pointed out seventy years ago, our everyday cultural forms are larger and more important than they appear. Something as commonplace as the Lindy Hop, in its symmetrical frenzy, could hold clues to great potential powers for understanding who we really are. For Ellison, it was in these forms and practices our lives are lived and histories recorded. To come to terms with this irony is to come to terms with what the Lindy Hop is—an American allegory waiting to be told.[3]

LEAD IN: THE COST OF INSIGHT

Perhaps we are able to see only that which we are prepared to see, and in our culture, the cost of insight is an uncertainty that threatens our already unstable sense of order and requires a constant questioning of accepted assumptions.

Ralph Ellison (1995a, 31)

Seven years of experience with the Lindy Hop as an observer, participant, and teacher—and then later, my interest in the Chicago Steppin' scene—resulted in the culmination of this book. This project was not simply one of participation or observation, but involved my immersion in the deepest levels of these communities as an embedded and embodied ethnographer; I participated in all aspects of the Lindy Hop dance culture and became a regular social dancer in the Chicago Steppin' world. The work itself is the confluence of three narratives: (1) a historical narrative of my immersion in and passage through the Lindy Hop and Steppin' worlds; (2) a personal narrative of my own development as a student of dance, as a scholar, and as an individual; and (3) a theoretical and methodological narrative that develops my experiences and approaches in the field to larger studies of race, culture, and identity.

Learning to dance the Lindy Hop was a unique experience. I showed up to my first class alone, without knowing a soul in Chicago. Because I had never danced before, except for a brief flirtation with break-dancing in my youth, I didn't think of myself as a dancer. I never dreamed I would invest years of my life in studying dance, let alone go on to teach and perform it or undertake writing a book on it. As I delved into the Lindy Hop for several years, I spent anywhere from four to seven nights a week dancing, taking classes, teaching, practicing, and performing. Over the years, I watched myself transform from someone uncomfortable moving in his own skin into someone who is fully comfortable with his own bodily movements. This transformation has forever changed me as a scholar and as a person. In fact, without this transformation, the study that emerged could never have been completed.

When I was debating whether or not to pursue an ethnography on this dance culture, I had a memorable encounter with a fellow graduate student. I confided to him that I was uneasy about doing this project because I was initially not a good dancer and feared this would undermine my credibility when discussing the dance. He told me that it was not important for me to be a good dancer because I was there simply to observe and interview people. Most sociologists would not view the mastery of the dance as necessary for writing an ethnography, because dancers are not the sociologist's target audience. The graduate student argued that sociologists would be my audience, and they would not care about my skills as a dancer. His response mirrored the traditional problems that confront researchers in the social sciences about the relationship between insider and outsider status in relation to one's work.

For example, the African American community has long been skeptical of the field of sociology for this very reason. Historically, African Americans have been suspicious of commentators or scientists who claim to be experts on their culture. Their distrust stems from the fact that traditionally scholars, especially white scholars, have been detached; they have lacked the competence and the practical knowledge of African American culture.

This student's comments propelled me in the opposite direction. I felt compelled to become a student of the dance and learn as much as I could, so that my perspective and thoughts would come not from a novice dancer and detached observer of the scene, but from a true student, teacher, and full participant in this culture. In hindsight, the path I chose was the only way I could have proceeded with my project. Without paying my dues and mastering the dance, I could not have had access to the major players or been able to discuss intimate issues and ideas concerning the Lindy Hop and Steppin' scenes. It was integral to the project that I be a practical as well as academic master of my material. My approach of carnal sociology blurred the line between dancer and academic, as my body became both a tool of social analysis and the object under investigation. If I was to embody the very practices I was studying, I had to discipline my body, train, and master the dance from the inside out. This multilayered approach afforded me a level of authority on both intellectual and practical grounds. As an experienced participant in this world, I can now speak with the authority of a sociologist and as a skilled practitioner and teacher of the craft. By becoming an instructor, I raised my level of awareness, my insight into the dance, and my passion and concern for what I was doing. I do not believe one could produce such a detailed study without going through this immersion and conversion. It would be impossible to do an ethnography of the Lindy Hop world without learning to dance and mastering the craft through the body—without understanding this world through bodily experience.

As a student, teacher, dancer, performer, DJ, and promoter, I became involved in every aspect of the Lindy Hop scene. I took classes, went to dances, and attended workshops and out-of-town dance camps. I met hundreds of people, made many friends, and shared many fascinating conversations and wonderful dances. In this sense my immersion was an easy process, because as a student of the dance there was never any question of what I was doing in these places. I traveled from Chicago to a dozen other major cities in the United States and to the global Lindy Hop camp at Herräng in Sweden, where I was able to see the dance embedded in various local contexts. All of these experiences, and the vast knowledge of social dancing gained therein, provided me with the dance skills necessary to later on gain acceptance in the world of Steppin.' Doing an embodied ethnographic study forced a new level of reflexive analysis because the focus for everything I was analyzing started with my own involvement. I was implicated by my very immersion in these scenes as to what I was studying and how I was to make sense of it.

I have gathered and compiled the life stories of dancers, teachers, friends, and colleagues using a number of methods: private conversations, interviews, and informal discussions, as well as watching videos of social dancing, participating in workshops, teaching, and performing, following the newspapers' and popular presses' coverage of the Swing revival, and exploring the websites of Lindy Hop organizations and scholarly material on jazz and jazz dancing. In the summer of 2000 I lived and trained with two of the top Lindy Hoppers and former world champions for two weeks in Stockholm, Sweden, taking lessons, practicing, watching their Lindy Hop performance troupe rehearsals, and attending their performances. I have conducted in-depth formal interviews with more than fifty instructors, as well as more than one hundred informal interviews with dancers and performers. My extensive fieldnotes, dictation tapes, videotapes, and knowledge of the dance and the dancing social scene have allowed me to comprehensively chronicle the Lindy Hop as well as Steppin' scenes.

Although much of this study took place in Chicago, I also drew on my travels to Cleveland, Minneapolis, Milwaukee, Madison, San Francisco, Los Angeles, Palm Springs, Stockholm, Herrang, Toronto, Montreal, and Boston.[1] Chicago is both a typical and an exceptional example of the Swing revival. Since 1997 the city has been a major hub for Lindy Hop; almost immediately the Lindy Hop became widely popular there, and the number and quality of dancers increased rapidly, providing fertile ground for an ethnography. Despite its geographical specificity, Chicago and the Chicago dancers are intimately tied to the larger Lindy Hop scene; most dancers and teachers migrate to camps and workshops and know each other on a first-name basis. As a result of the globalization of culture, there is no specific Chicago style that distinctly separates it from the white dance scenes in other cities. In addition, through the Internet, the Lindy Exchanges (where dancers from all over meet in one city for a weekend of social dancing), and people traveling on their own to social dance in other cities, the Lindy Hop scene is small enough that most dancers know each other. The scene may be dispersed, but it retains a tight coherence. Because the scenes are so interconnected and everyone takes classes from the same elite core group of teachers, the logic and the production of the dance are tightly maintained.

To undertake such a project, I had to confront the unspoken anxieties, uncertainties, and confusions we encounter in the ways that race matters in everyday life. In addition, I had to wrestle out the interconnection between race and culture and the problematic way that each serves as a proxy for the other in our popular consciousness. At the same time, this is a study about the role of popular culture in American society and how the aesthetics of popular culture are always already informed by racial mediations. While academic in its analysis, the other side of this project contends with the people who engage in popular culture, who turn cultural forms into popular productions. These productions are grounded in socio-racial-historical contexts both past and present, of which practitioners are rarely aware. My interest lies in understanding how the concept of the racial imagination works in the most seemingly innocuous of all places, popular culture, with the least of innocuous consequences: those of symbolic and material domination, which perpetuate inequality, misunderstanding, and racial segregation without any necessary intention. Finally this is a book about racial mythologies or, better yet, demythologizing racial myths of race and culture in an attempt to find a way around our current impasses of racial interactions. If we are to address the anxiety-riddled, politically correct stigma of thinking, talking, debating, and understanding issues of race and how race functions in American society, it may not come from the lofty realms of public policy debates, reforms, and legislation, but from someplace much more common, much more pedestrian, much closer to home, and unavoidable—the culture of everyday life.

While this is a story of dramatic conflict between conventional wisdom running up against sociological critique, it is ultimately about my own struggle to understand my own relationship, as part and parcel of me, to these worlds. In doing so, I confront the Ellisonian cost of insight; a price that once paid forever troubles our commonsense understandings of the world and leaves us without a guarantee of ever seeing things the way we want to see them again.

INTRODUCTION: THE LINDY HOP REVIVAL

That night at Club Liquid was not unlike other Swing nights in Chicago or in other cities around the country or even around the globe; from Nova Scotia to Japan, Swing dancing had reemerged from its apparent cultural dormancy. Here in the United States, from San Diego to New Haven, the whole nation appeared to be caught up in a Swing dance craze ("Swing dancing" is the broader colloquial category used to define all forms of dance in this genre, whereas the "Lindy Hop" refers to the specific type of dance and is considered original form of Swing dance out of which all contemporary forms are derived).[1] During the late 1990s its popularity became pervasive throughout mass-mediated culture: in live entertainment (Super Bowl and Orange Bowl halftime shows, *Live from Lincoln Center*), in movies (*Swingers*, *Swing Kids*, *The Mask*, *Blast from the Past*, *Malcolm X*, *Hoodlum*, *Three to Tango*), and in advertisements and the marketing of consumer goods (Gap, Coca-Cola, Haggar Clothing). This Swing dancing revival was in turn part of a much larger retro revival: the resurgence of interest in the Rat Pack and Sinatra, the cocktail nation or *Swingers* subculture of the 1940s and '50s, the cigar and martini atmosphere of indulgence, traditional gender roles, styles, and decadence.[2]

Propelling this movement was a deep, subcultural music trend of punk bands turning toward swing and jump blues music, forming a new musical genre. This new hybrid of rock-'n'-roll and swing, known as neo-swing (a rock-'n'-roll back beat with a jazzed-up melody complemented by a small horn section), caught the attention of fans as disparate as skateboarders and yuppies. With radio airplay and band performances in highly successful films (Royal Crown Revue in *The Mask*, Big Bad Voodoo Daddy in *Swingers*, and the Atomic Fireballs in *Three to Tango*), neo-swing became the backbone and the soundtrack to the retro revival. As these bands rose in popularity and packed musical venues, they provided people a social space in which to dance to the music. Once exposed, Swing dancing quickly captured national attention as the retro revival's most spectacular and athletic manifestation.

Although Swing dancing was the crystallizing spectacle of the retro revival, this misrecognizes both its history and its origins. Despite what has been presented in media reports, Swing dancing did not emerge as an outgrowth of neo-swing music. In fact, the Swing dancing subculture existed below the radar of popular media for some time, and became popular only when these other trends congealed in the national spotlight. Swing catapulted to national attention through the Gap clothing company's major marketing campaign, "Khakis Swing," in the spring of 1998, with music by neo-swing band the Brian Setzer Orchestra. At the same time, Wynton Marsalis had taken control of jazz at Lincoln Center in New York City and was soon to launch a Duke Ellington celebration tour featuring the repertoire of great swing classics, while a new musical was soon to open on Broadway entitled *Swing*, and famous documentarian Ken Burns was starting his massive miniseries on jazz, which would feature swing in several episodes.

The Swing dancing scene is the outgrowth of a dedicated group of teachers and dancers that coalesced into a coherent subculture and scene in the late 1980s and early '90s. In fact, the real swing revival is much more a subtle and complicated story dating from the 1980s, with multiple points of resurgence (New York, Stockholm, Los Angeles, and London), than it is a tale of spontaneous emergence in the American cultural fabric. Yet despite the cultivation of the Lindy Hop in diverse parts of the world, the explosion of interest and popularity that catapulted Swing dancing to a mass-marketed commercialized spectacle was strictly an American phenomenon.[3] Despite Swing dancing catching the white popular consciousness like wildfire, the revival misrecognized its sudden appearance; many of its leaders had been dancing it for almost two decades. A master teacher and one of the original revivalists, Steven Mitchell, once remarked, "I saw this clip on CNN where they were interviewing the band, Big Bad Voodoo Daddy, and claiming that they started this whole swing revival, and I was like, Huh? We've been doing this for years." Tapping into the trend of Swing dancing has afforded capitalist mass media a vibrant marketing tool both because it is exciting entertainment and because it links contemporary culture to a nostalgic, romantic past. Having its roots firmly in African American culture, this popularization appeared to some to be extracting Swing dancing from the historical and racial-cultural context within which it emerged and was cultivated. But what were these "roots" and where did the Lindy Hop "actually" come from? Most important, what did this revival of the Lindy Hop tell us about our ongoing story of forever struggling with our "American" cultural identity?

LINDY HOP HISTORY

In order to fully understand the dynamics of the Lindy Hop revival, it is necessary to examine the historical origins and trajectory of the dance. During the early 1920s, as great numbers of African Americans migrated to New York City, the Harlem Renaissance began to take shape. This massive migration from the south to the north was also a paradigm shift in African American identity. More than a literary movement or a social revolt against racism, the Harlem Renaissance exalted the unique culture of African Americans and redefined African American expression not only in writing, but also in art, music, politics, and dance.[4] This new identity departed from the rural and externally imposed peasant Negro identity in favor of one of urban sophistication—the "New Negro"—and of Harlem, the mecca of urban African American life. This new urban vitality created a sense of community and optimism; in the big city African Americans could eke out space removed from the racial prejudice and violence of the South. This modern urban formation created a novel appreciation for African American culture and artists as significant cultural contributors to American life. Their art provided not only a unique sense of self-defined identity and self-expression, but also a cathartic release from white racism.

Nothing represented this newfound identity and expression more than a new dance, called the Lindy Hop, which was emerging out of the ballrooms of Harlem. Marshall Stearns gives credit to Shorty George Snowden for naming the Lindy:

> On June 17th, 1928, in the Manhattan Casino, Snowden decided to do a breakaway, that is, fling his partner out and improvise a few solo steps of his own. In the midst of the monotony of the marathon, the effect was electric, and even the musicians came to life. Shorty had started something new. At one point Fox Movietone News arrived to cover the marathon and decided to take a close up of Shorty's feet. The general impression that Shorty was out of his mind and his dancing a kind of inspired confusion was gaining currency. "What are you doing with your feet," asked the interviewer, and Shorty, without stopping, replied, "The Lindy."

Dorthea Ohl, in the pages of 1956 *Dance Magazine*, claims that the Lindy Hop arose in a more anonymous fashion with reference to the famous transatlantic flight of Charles Lindbergh, who "hopped" the Atlantic in 1927:

Legend has it that way back in 1927 when Lindbergh made his historic solo flight to Paris, the people of New York's Harlem were just as excited as the rest of the world. Would he make it? When the news that he had arrived was announced at the Savoy Ballroom, Harlem's best known dance spot, pandemonium broke loose. People jumped for joy; strangers pounded one another in glee. One young man, overcome by the thrill, took off over the floor, shouting, "Look! Look! I'm flying just like Lindy." He seized a partner in passing and away they went. The floor soon filled with dancers following his lead, improvising turns and twists on their own, all chanting, "Lindy! Lindy! Lindy!" And so it was born.

Although the development of its name remains obscure, the origins of this dance are easier to trace. The Lindy Hop emerged as a distinct dance form by creating the first breakaway step, known as the Swing Out, whereby partners would separate for a moment for an opportunity to improvise. It was a partner dance that combined the popular European social dances of the day such as the foxtrot and the waltz, as well as jazz steps of the era, such as the Charleston, the Cakewalk, and the Black Bottom, among others (Emery 1998; Stearns and Stearns 1994). By combining these African, African American, European, and Anglo-American steps, the dance emerged as a truly hybridized form—similar to the swing music that accompanied it— called the Lindy Hop.

Situating the Lindy Hop in its cultural and historical origins means understanding it not only as a creative manifestation of the particular urban identity of the Harlem Renaissance, but also within the context of the African American dance tradition and the African American body in white America. As chronicled by dance scholars such as Lynn Emery and Jacqui Malone, among others, dance has always played a central role in African American life. Since the early days of slavery, it has served as a vehicle for communication, solidarity, community, and catharsis.[5] Explosive and dynamic social dancing was an expressive practice of freedom, liberation, self-reclamation, community formation, and creativity against the white racist society within which African Americans were situated. Marshall Stearns highlights the importance of dance for African American identity at the time of the Harlem Renaissance: "The social climate of Harlem was changing in the twenties through the forties. The neighborhood, being in transition, needed a new center of equilibrium for blacks, a replacement for the old world's church to provide structure, a positive influence and a vehicle for advancement. The Savoy and social dancing provided this orientation and center for the community" (Stearns and Stearns 1994, 318). In Harlem a space was established for black entertainment and culture to flourish outside the surveillance of racist white society. Dance became the focal point.

Stuart Hall argues that the body has been central to the identity and expression of African-based cultures because it was often the only capital that blacks possessed and could use. As a result, people turned to the body itself as a "canvas of representation," as the central medium through which they could express themselves. It is this recourse of necessity that was cultivated as a focal point of self- and collective representation; bodily practices and arts such as dance are among its most athletic manifestations (Kelley 1996; White and White 1999). Through this lens we can understand that cultural forms like the Lindy Hop were not only a form of entertainment and pleasure, they were also an escape from wage labor and from the alienation and exploitation of white society. As Paul Gilroy says, when dancing the Lindy Hop, like other expressive African American cultural forms, "The black body is . . . celebrated as an instrument of pleasure rather than an instrument of labor. The nighttime becomes the right time, and the space allocated for recovery and recuperation is assertively and provocatively occupied by the pursuit of leisure and pleasure" (1993, 274). As an expressive practice, this creative cultural labor was a way of reclaiming the body back from wage labor and white exploitation in the form of pleasure and cultural expression for oneself and for one's community.[6] This dynamic display of creativity and improvisation provided a timely metaphor for the state of African Americans in white society.

When the Lindy Hop crossed over into white society in the '30s and '40s both blacks and whites were dancing the same dance—Lindy Hop—while the name may have changed in white circles to the Jitterbug—As Frankie Manning once argued in reference to this difference, "when you're doing the Jitterbug, I'm doing the Lindy Hop, but it is the same thing." White society came to alter the dance in terms of its styling based on cultural differences. Black society kept altering its orientation to the dance, as many saw it as an appropriation by whites and wanted to ensure the dance kept its black identity. As Norma Miller says, "They took everything else, we weren't going to let them take the Lindy, too." Nonetheless the dance was danced by both worlds side by side and only occasionally mixing.

Like other popular cultural formations, the Lindy Hop eventually faded from mainstream popularity. Some say the Lindy Hop decline began in the early 1950s when the great dancer Frankie Manning began working in a post office, or in 1958 when the Savoy Ballroom closed to make room for public housing.[7] And yet others argue that as World War II changed the socioeconomic context of the American landscape, big bands and dance halls gave way to the smaller combos, and the music moved from being dance-

oriented to more experimental and to the aesthetic format of be-bop (Erenberg 1981, 1998; Stowe 1994). As these changes were taking place and rock-
'n'-roll emerged as the popular music of the day, the Lindy Hop was left
behind. But although it lost popularity among mainstream white society,
it did not die; instead, it mutated into other forms of partnered social dancing in African American communities. As Lindy Hop and Swing faded, new
forms of music like R&B and hip hop emerged in African American communities in the 1970s and '80s, and complementary dances arose to fit the music and function of creative cultural labor in the Lindy Hop's place (Boppin'
in Houston, Hand Dancing in Washington, DC, and particularly Steppin'
in Chicago). While all of these dances differ slightly in style and execution,
they still serve as resistive expressive practices that emerged from a common denominator—the original Lindy Hop.

As I pursued the Lindy Hop I was confronted with the questions: What
was different this time around? Was this different from the first times
whites engaged the Lindy Hop when it became the nation's popular dance
craze back in the 1930s? What consequences, if any, did these similarities or
differences have for understanding what was taking place in contemporary
society? Was this Swing dance a revival of a dance appropriated earlier into
white society or was this a revival of the "authentic" or "original" Lindy Hop
as danced by African Americans back in the 1930s?[8]

These questions can be answered only equivocally, depending on the
vantage point and social, historical, and aesthetic contexts through which
we frame our interpretations. In many ways this story of the revival of an
African American art form within white society plays out much like it has
in the past with white society embracing an African American art form
and ultimately changing its style to meet its own needs and preferences.
Simultaneously this revival was peculiarly different from times past in
that the explicit goal of this revival was to revive the "real" Lindy Hop, or
the "authentic" Lindy Hop. Specifically the goal was to revive the version
that was made famous by Whitey's Lindy Hoppers, the performance troupe
from Harlem whose dancers are regarded as the greatest Lindy Hop dancers of all time. They were captured performing in films such as the screw-
ball comedy of the 1940's *Hellzapoppin'*, the Marx Brothers' *Day at the Races*,
as well as numerous concert performances and TV appearances. Whitey's
Lindy Hoppers were and are still considered the true defining dancers of
the Lindy Hop. Whether in the United States, or in other countries where
the Lindy Hop revival was gaining momentum, it was the "original," which
everyone, by watching the clips of Whitey's Lindy Hoppers, tried to emulate. Whether spoken or unspoken it was the "black style" of Whitey's Lindy
Hoppers that the modern-day generation was wedded to revitalizing. The

issues of cross-cultural or cross-racial engagements with the forms of the "other" raises all sorts of issues of race, culture, and identity as the dance was emerging from its dormancy into the national media and popular culture.

American society has moved well beyond the strict segregation and explicit racism of the 1930s and 1940s and the civil rights struggles of the 1950s and 1960s. Today we confront problems of racial and ethnic division that are in many ways far more subtle, complex, and ambiguous than those of previous eras. On the surface, at least, times have changed from the days of legal and routine segregation and bigotry that defined previous eras of racial and ethnic relations. Yet, despite these changes, racial and ethnic inequalities persist at the most basic levels of American society. Just as the times have changed, so have the forms of racial and ethnic inequality that define society and the ways that they operate to organize society and social interaction. It was the tensions between the revival and the past, the implicit and explicit, the colorblindness of American society and the fact that race still matters in American society that made the Lindy Hop revival translucent at best and opaque at worst.

Examining how the Lindy Hop resurfaced in the late 1990s shows an even starker picture of cultural appropriation; the divorce from African American roots was even farther removed through these music and dance transformations. Reviving the Lindy Hop was as if something had been retrieved out of a cultural vacuum. This cultural form was something so archaic to most that it was revitalized unmarked from its racial past, free of its own history of conflict over identity and racial politics. While the presence of both blacks and whites dancing the Lindy Hop during its prime kept a sense of significance of its African American roots alive, the revival in the 1990s served to completely sever it from its African American context. Without addressing this context of the cultural form, a new, more eviscerating form of cultural appropriation occurred. Images of African American dancers and the history of the dance were almost completely absent. This was not simply a reprise of what happened back in the '30s and '40s when large numbers of African Americans were still dancing and African American musicians were still playing swing music. This was a selective revival in a completely new cultural context, not one of segregation and overt racism, but one of multiculturalism and racial diversity. This was not reviving something preappropriated; rather, it was appropriating something in a completely new way in a new context that sets up new particularities and problematics for theorizing cross-racial and cross-cultural contact. Since the dance was now revived from its forty-year dormancy, it creates new opportunities and possibilities about rethinking cultural transmission, cultural understanding, and cultural appreciation.

On the surface, the Lindy Hop revival is a story about a creative subculture deriving pleasure and constructing identities out of the cultural resources of everyday life (de Certeau 1984; Ross and Rose 1994; Scott 1985, 1990). We must move beyond such an uncritical celebration of American dance and self-expression to understand the consequences of this revival, both socially and symbolically, for contemporary American society. In order to do so, we must unearth the material and symbolic representations of race and racial identities performed through the Lindy Hop and what that tells us about the larger narrative of American society.

THE LINDY HOP AND STEPPIN'

In order to understand the Lindy Hop in relation to race, identity, and contemporary American society, it is necessary to relate the Lindy Hop scene to the social dance world—almost exclusively African American—of Steppin'. It is striking that despite the Lindy Hop revival, the Steppin' scene has remained almost invisible to white society. Because Steppin' is practiced solely within African American neighborhoods, it exists apart from white culture and has remained insular to the African American community, with little or no crossover or appropriation. Without cross-promotion or cross-marketing into the media, Steppin' survives in an autonomous African American world, one seldom frequented by whites.

As I began to explore the Lindy Hop and Steppin' scenes, I found myself immersed in a complex social microcosm that would serve as a wonderful laboratory within which to study race in American society. Here were two dances, two outgrowths of the same original Lindy Hop, being danced in the same city, yet in worlds completely separated by race—one world exclusively white and the other black. Within this microcosm, one world was hypervisible with media spectacle, while the other was almost completely invisible in the mainstream media. While mainstream white America was celebrating the revival of the Lindy Hop, across town in the unseen world of Steppin' the tradition continued completely under the radar of white America. When we look past the euphoria over a dance trend and the commodified and commercialized revival of the Lindy Hop, we can approach this cultural form in the very different and often silenced context of its African American cultural history and identity.

Beyond my fieldwork in the Lindy Hop community, I also spent two years of extensive fieldwork as a dancer and participant in the Steppin' community, where I would attend two to three clubs or events per week. As a regular member of the community, I made a number of friends and acquaintances that served as the basis for more informal interviews with dancers, promoters, DJs, and club patrons.

In undertaking the project, I was immediately confronted with a number of methodological hurdles that would prove difficult to overcome. In trying to formulate a project that focused on race, racial identity, and the tension of white dancers performing African American dances, I did not find an easy point of purchase. While issues of race and racial identities dominate the public and social agendas of the country, they are only addressed in coded language and euphemisms. Because of the long and troubled racial history of the United States, no one wants to appear racist, prejudiced, or as a sellout to one's race. This fear of race generates an almost paranoid sensitivity, and consequently people often feel that silence is better. In these multicultural and colorblind times, if race is discussed it is only in "appropriate" or "politically correct" ways. It proved almost impossible to have an open and honest conversation with anyone about race or the research I wanted to do. How does one undertake an analysis of race in America when no one wants to talk about it?[9] How do I handle the tension between wanting to know how people conceptualize race and racial identities and accepting at face value what they say about such a sensitive and explosive topic, whether inside the world of the Lindy Hop or Steppin'? Finally, how would I convey this metaphorical tale of two worlds existing side by side in the same city, sharing a common past, yet no contemporary contact? What would this story illuminate along the way?

THEORIZING RACE IN THE TWENTY-FIRST CENTURY

Traditional sociological approaches to race and ethnicity emphasize themes such as assimilation, discrimination, and prejudice; important as those themes may be, however, such approaches simply fail to see the depths of the issue and fail to grasp the full complexity of how race and culture operate, both in the United States and elsewhere. This necessitates a paradigm shift from whiteness conceptualized as white supremacy (agents acting in conscious coalition toward maintaining racial supremacy and racial hierarchy) to whiteness as the invisible, underlying, unspoken, normalized operation of the racial organization of society.[10] Whiteness is not an individual phenomenon, to be examined on an individual level (as theories of prejudice and discrimination are wont to be). Instead, whiteness is the defining principle of social organization by which white values, ideas, aesthetics, preferences, and privileges are made to appear as the normalized, taken-for-granted basis of interacting and engaging social reality. In shifting the focus of the study of race and ethnicity back onto whiteness and the ways in which the privileges of whiteness are institutionalized and naturalized, we explore how such social organization becomes invisible even to whites themselves. In this way whiteness is not just an unseen system of norms, but also a sense of entitlement and privilege that emerges out of this social organization of resources and opportunities. Whiteness need not be overt, explicit, direct, or conspiratorial, in that the normalized racial operations of society are able to seamlessly absorb whites into the dominant mode of understanding that more often than not is transparent to them due to their membership in the dominant group. As the hegemonic embedded and institutionalized logic of social organization, it becomes a powerful and durable system able to absorb nonwhites into supporting this system, consciously or unconsciously, as well. Finally, whiteness as a mode of social/racial domination is a world into which we are socialized, one that is already the product of naturalized historical construction, where racial-cultural meanings and associations are already in circulation and taken for granted as commonsense assumptions about the normal workings of everyday life.

At the center of this alternative paradigm of racial-social organization is the crucial distinction between whiteness as a system of social organization that structures society in racial dominance and white people as racialized actors within that system. It is important not to essentialize whiteness, to make it into some omnipresent force or metaphysical power, lest we conflate the system of social organization with the actions and intentions of individual people as if they were one and the same. Rather than falling back on a racial essentialism, we must be vigilantly sensitive to the ways that race is situational and intersects and interacts with other categories of classification and organization (e.g., class, gender, sexuality, nation, age).[11] When analyzing the racial categories and racial classifications that are ascribed to people, culture, behaviors, aesthetics, and so on, whiteness can be considered as the underlying structure that gives rise to those mythologies and categories. Since whiteness forms the foundation of our thinking, the racial categories and ways of looking, perceiving, and apprehending the world that emerge out of it perfectly mirror the way that society is organized, since they are products and reflections of the system of which they are constitutive. Therefore, the ideology of whiteness appears seamless and transparent to us in everyday life since it is the bedrock of our taken-for-granted commonsense understanding of the world around us. As a result, our perpetuation of these ideologies is never apparent because our everyday participation in them goes unnoticed. Finally, it is necessary to understand that this paradigm shift to whiteness helps explain why the dominant ideologies of society are so enduring. Since we are all embedded in this dominant ideology it is not just whites that have a difficult time understanding the way that race and culture operate to structure society in dominance, but non-whites too are complicit in the reproduction of these structures.

The separation of whites from whiteness is a necessary analytical and empirical break. Without this break we tend to conflate whites with whiteness, or to infer that whites either reproduce or resist racism, as if this were a matter of simply aligning oneself on one side or the other. The use of specific racial categories—"black," "white"—throughout the book is not to reify them; rather, it is to show how their expressions and movements have been historically situated in specific contexts in the United States that are fundamentally intertwined with the power relationships that import a series of assumptions and myths into them. However, the use of these categories, when moving from colloquial speech to analytic analysis, often leads to a performative contradiction—whereby using them to point out their arbitrary and constructed nature, as well as the complex and shifting boundaries they attempt to designate reaffirms those very racial categories as if they were natural and self-evident. Therefore, their consistent use, that is, "the white use of African American cultural forms," highlights rather than obscures one of the core issues at stake throughout: our attempts to think against racial essentialism or beyond the limitations of those categories of race as natural and taken for granted runs up against the logical and linguistic fact that they are the only categories we currently have to discuss race itself. Put in more theoretical terms, one can ask: How can we talk about race in a way that doesn't reaffirm the very notions we have when all we have are the current categories of race themselves? While we know that racial categories are social constructions without inherent properties or essences, we must simultaneously be aware of our attempt to use them to undermine their taken-for-granted nature; we are simultaneously reinforcing them trapped in "the prison-house" of our own language.

While racism may continue to exist, the fact of racism does not explain how and why race matters, nor does it explain how racial inequality is produced or perpetuated. In fact, it is this conflation that obscures fundamental ambivalences and ambiguities of how people understand and enact race (Hartigan 1999). Since racial identities and racial understandings are always played out in particular places, race is often just one of many or multiple contradictory and competing frames of reference that form our understanding and actions in the world. Race alone does not address all dimensions and forces of oppression, inequality, or marginalization, nor is it essential or deterministic in creating a uniform order of social dominance.

As will be shown, *American Allegory* delves into two dance worlds of Chicago literally side by side, sharing the same dance (at least in its origins), and yet separated from each other by an apparently unbridgeable divide. Using these dance scenes as windows onto these issues to dissect the relatively affluent world of the predominately white North Side and the relatively poorer, predominately African American South Side of the city and takes us beyond the false empirical divisions that situate the Lindy Hop as a white dance and Steppin' as a black dance. *American Allegory* seizes this tension as a unique opportunity to analyze how the white use of African American cultural forms severs those forms from the people that cultivated them, generating and enabling racial domination, while at the same time celebrating those cultural forms and bringing them to the center of national attention. When discussing this contradiction, it is crucial to understand that it was neither the participation nor active inclusion of African Americans that brought the Lindy Hop back to the center of white American popular culture; the centralizing and elevating of this African American cultural form occurred exclusively through white consumption and appropriation of African American culture. As a result, the Lindy Hop is celebrated as a national fad, while African American people, the creators and cultivators of the dance, remain economically, politically, and socially marginalized. By drawing out the dynamics of race and culture against the historical particularities and their lingering effects to understand the contemporary forms of segregation in the city of Chicago, we come to understand how cultural expressions occupy separate spatial realms.[12] In our doing so, separate spatial spheres reinforce racial classification systems that in turn reify and naturalize cultural practices and the bodies that enact them, which define the contemporary conditions of Chicago.

RALPH ELLISON AND THE QUESTION OF AMERICAN IDENTITY

When I began to examine today's Lindy Hop resurgence in the contemporary dance scene, I initially found this to be a quixotic yet fascinating white subculture. Yet I wondered if this was just another cultural fad that garners national attention as an arcane peculiarity. Once the Lindy Hop became a nationwide phenomenon, there was obviously something more substantive at stake warranting serious sociological attention. Interrogating the revival of the Lindy Hop at its deepest levels revealed a fundamental contradiction in American society: African American culture continues to be symbolically central in American culture, while African Americans remain economically and politically marginalized.[13] In order to address this contradiction, of race, culture, and identity, I turn to the work of Ralph Ellison.[14] Over thirty years ago, Ralph Ellison wrote words that continue to haunt us to this day:

Today blood magic and blood thinking, never really dormant in American society, are rampant among us, often leading to brutal racial assaults in areas where these seldom occurred before. And while this goes on, the challenge of arriving at an adequate definition of American cultural identity goes unanswered. (What, by the way, is one to make of a white youngster who, with a transistor radio, screaming a Stevie Wonder tune, glued to his ear, shouts racial epithets at black youngsters trying to swim at a public beach—and this in the name of the ethnic sanctity of what has been declared neighborhood turf?) (Ellison 1995a, 21)

Ellison reveals how African American culture is central to the marketing of images of the American dream as seen in music, fashion, language, expressions, and athletics, and yet the marginalization of African American people is evidenced by the black majority's exclusion from power, money, and resources. Given this contradiction, we must ask a host of Ellisonian questions: How does the simultaneous embrace of African American culture and the marginalization of African American people serve to secure and perpetuate white racial domination? How do cultural forms become both expressions of racial groups and mechanisms of social closure that separate and strengthen those very racial classifications to which those forms are ascribed?[15] How does this blending of identities that occurs through the inherently hybridized world of American society force us to look beyond simplistic binaries of racial identity? And finally, how do the worlds of Lindy Hop and Steppin' allegorically characterize the way that race is played out in American society?

By drawing upon the nonfiction Ellison as an ethnographer in his own right, as a chronicler of the knowledge, meanings, ideas, and the everyday practices of American life, Ellison's rich corpus of thought offers unique substantive insights into race and the place of race in American society, his cross-disciplinary methodological approaches to the analysis of social life, and his theoretical insights into race, culture, nation, and geography in relation to individual and collective identity. Ellison's essays range in topic from art to music to segregation to politics, intervening in a gamut of debates with a myriad of interlocutors, all revolving around the irreducible complexity of life and eschewing all forms of racial essentialism or reductionism. The ethnographic Ellison aids in the development of three central themes: (1) the diverse ways Ellison approached issues of race, culture, music, literature, and politics in relation to the ways they articulate, often in unseen or circuitous ways, the ongoing discussion over the question of what is American identity; (2) the centrality of the seemingly ordinary, those often unheard and unseen aspects of African American, and

American, life more generally, and the power of their import for rethinking our taken-for-granted assumptions about everyday life; (3) the Ellisonian conviction that American identity is of a whole, specifically, that the apparent differences that divide us, from our skin color to our modes of expression that seem to confirm our presupposition of biological distinctness, are in the end so interconnected, both in their composition and their meaning, that they cannot be separated without unraveling the whole cloth of the world. Ellison's enduring relevance can be seen here in the ways that it advances and informs our intellectual and aesthetic perspectives for ethnography.

In doing so, working through these Ellisonian questions requires us to map the racial territory within which these relations unfold. For Ellison, the racial territory of American society is one marked by anxiety and uncertainty:

> Perhaps we shy away from confronting our cultural wholeness because it offers no easily recognizable points of rest, no facile certainties as to who, what or where (culturally or historically) we are. Instead, the whole is always in cacophonic motion. Constantly changing its mode, it appears as a vortex of discordant ways of living and tastes, values and traditions, a whirlpool of odds and ends in which the past courses in uneasy juxtapositions with those bright futuristic principles and promises to which we, as a nation, are politically committed.... Deep down, the American condition is a state of unease. (Ellison 1994, 508)

Despite efforts to find footing on solid ground, the complexity of life constantly eludes stability and certainty. As a result it proves difficult to find direction or definition of what culture is and how it defines the people it attempts to categorize. Because ways of life, with their diverse cultures and histories, are in constant flux, there is no ultimate foundation upon which our understandings of society can rest.

The state of unease of which Ellison speaks manifests itself most viscerally in the concept of race, a concept that has so confounded American society that Americans, especially whites, do not know who they are. When discussing the art of Richard Wright, Ellison notes that the prevailing trends of American criticism have "so thoroughly excluded the Negro that it fails to recognize some of the most basic tenets of Western democratic thought when encountering them in a black skin" (1994, 131). This inability of whites to recognize themselves when presented in a black veneer leads them, especially when engaging in what whites imagine are "black" practices, to confront the irony of American identity. As Ellison comments, "for out of the counterfeiting of the black American's identity there arises a profound doubt in the white man's mind as to the authenticity of his own image of himself" (107). It is this very mixture that defines American identity and yet simultaneously is one of deep rooted anxiety for whites. This anxiety is manifested in the contradiction of both acknowledging and disavowing race simultaneously.[16]

It is this confounding juxtaposition of race that obscures the fundamental realities of life. In a letter to a close friend, Ellison remarks:

> I've come to believe that the real root of many of our problems is not race so much as the contention over power. Of course this is but to say the obvious, since the mystique of race is used to confuse the issue, and none are more confused than some of those who would elect to lead us, many of whom know less about how the country operates than a skilled bell-hop or a quietly observant waiter. Americans are contenders for power and in the contending we often become confused as to how our interests coincide, and thus the common human aspects of issues become clouded in terms of who's black and who's white. It's really a miserable bore, but that's what history has stuck us, and we'll remain stuck until we realize that there's a hell of a lot more to our predicament than race. (1994, 45)

The issue of race for Ellison is one that is central to the conditions of lived experience in American society, and yet simultaneously one of life's greatest fictions. In his collection of essays *Going to the Territory*, Ellison makes his most clear statement about the task of confronting the issue of race. He argues that we must "cease approaching American social reality in terms of such false concepts as white and nonwhite, black culture and white culture, and think of these apparently unthinkable matters in the realistic manner of Western pioneers confronting the unknown prairie" (1995a, 108). Utilizing Ellison's metaphor of rethinking American society without racial terms requires a new imagination—not a *sociological imagination*—but a new *racial imagination*.

A racial imagination requires a new way of conceptualizing and coming to terms with our prevailing conceptual system of classifications that we utilize to differentiate and understand body types, cultures, races, and identities, which in turn naturalizes or makes self-evident the socially constructed connotations attributed to racial categories.[17] The concept "racial imagination" draws its theoretical and analytical power from the ethnomusicologist Ronald Radano, who uses this phrase strategically to tap into an alternative set of ideas in relation to African American studies, American studies, and ethnomusicology. The racial imagination, as used here, also draws from the sociologist Paul Willis's "ethnographic imagination" in the ways that a rich interpretation of everyday life requires both a social and an aesthetic sensibility to illuminate a culture's collective forms of identity, sensuous expression, and creativity in the language, interactions, expressions, gestures, and styles of a way of life (see Willis 2001, 4). By drawing on these two uses of imagination, this provides a way to differentiate the analysis here from the more general "sociological imagination," usually linked to C. Wright Mills, in terms of connecting individual experiences and societal relationships through the categories of history, biography, and social structure by which we "translate private troubles into public issues" (Mills 1959).

The racial imagination, as deployed here, illuminates how cultural practices such as music and dance are understood only after being refracted through the racial categories that come to define them. In order to do so, we must remember that Ellison disdained sociologists during his day for their oversimplifications, stereotyping, and statistical analyses that abstracted and distorted the *lived* experience of African Americans in everyday life.[18] For Ellison African Americans are the product of white construction defined by social scientists' charts, graphs, and other paraphernalia that document their social pathologies, biological, psychological, intellectual, and moral inferiority, as well as their "innate" traits that imply that African American culture is not American. These white fabrications take the place of real African Americans in the popular imagination. "Prefabricated Negroes are sketched on sheets of paper and superimposed upon the Negro Community; then when someone thrusts his head through the page and yells, 'Watch out here, Jack, there's people living under here,' they are shocked and indignant."[19] It is the projected clichés through which African American life appears in the sociologist's mind's eye that threaten to obscure everything else from vision when it comes to African American life.[20] Ellison rejects the sociological simplification of African American lived experience which denies its cultural complexity by reducing and essentializing its differences into canonical measurements and abstract information inadequate to articulate that which gives significance to African American life.[21]

For Ellison there is no one African American culture, nor is there one African American identity. In outlining what Ellison considers African American, he is adamant that it is not skin color. In doing so, Ellison argues:

It is not skin color which makes a Negro American but cultural heritage as shaped by the American experience, the social and the political predicament; a sharing of that "concord of sensibilities" which the group expresses through historical circumstance ... with places of worship and places of entertainment; with garments and dreams and idioms of speech; with manners and customs, with religion and art, with life styles and hoping, and with that special sense of predicament and fate which gives direction and resonance. (1994, 131)

African Americans are not defined by their physiology, by the "racial" category that society imposes upon them, as if there were some inherent nature. What "makes" African Americans is their cultural collectivity and their shared social and historical contexts. These are the circumstances that give rise to the particular expressions, styles, and mannerisms that in turn serve to define the multiple overlapping conditions that produce the *impression* of coherent agreement of a single unified people.

In arguing for this conceptualization of identity, Ellison undertakes the radical move of separating the often commonly held assumption that race and culture are one and the same, or that one serves as a proxy for the other in the popular imagination.[22] By severing the linkage between the two, Ellison opens up a way of problematizing race and culture at both the local and national levels:

The problem here is that few Americans know who and what they really are. That is why few of these groups—or at least few of the children of these groups—have been able to resist the movies, television, baseball, jazz, football, drum-majoretting, rock, comic strips, radio commercials, soap operas, book clubs, slang, or any of a thousand other expressions and carriers of our pluralistic and easily available popular culture. It is here precisely that ethnic resistance is least effective. At this level the melting pot did indeed melt, creating such deceptive metamorphoses and blending of identities, values and lifestyles that most American whites are culturally part Negro American without even realizing it. (1995a, 108)

For Ellison, the melting pot metaphor for American life was successful on the cultural level. To try to separate out who has made what contributions to American society is an impossible task. For Ellison American culture is so diverse and intermixed, its language, styles, music, dances, values, tastes, that there is no point of origin to be found.[23] If whites are also black, then conversely blacks must also be white. If whites are in fact black, at least in part, that undermines the very basis of American social organization. For Ellison this is not just a matter of imagining, or playing at identity, as if one could simply slip on or off a mask, but confronting the deep intertwined nature of blackness and whiteness.

In theorizing our cultural hybridity in such a way, Ellison calls into question two taken-for-granted assumptions about our everyday lives. First is the notion of "authenticity," both in terms of racial-cultural identities and historical-fictitious origins. Second is the notion of the "contexts" (physical, psychical, and institutional) within which the dance is cultivated. Ellison undermines the notion of authenticity through the revealing of the multiple threads of cultures and contributions that run throughout the construction of any cultural form. In doing so, Ellison denies reification and highlights the complexity, if not impossibility, of grounding any cultural form in any constructed or essential identity as being authentic whatsoever. Ellison states:

> I stress American culture because I think we are in a great deal of confusion over the role of creation in our culture. It is so easy to become unconsciously racist by simply stressing one part of our heritage, thus reducing the complexity of our cultural heritage to a genetic reality which is only partially dealt with. . . . You cannot have an American experience without having a black experience. Nor can you have the technology of jazz, as original as many of those techniques are, without having had long centuries of European musical technology, not to mention the technologies of various African traditions. (1994, 445–46)

Just like authenticity, the concept of "origins" is just as problematic for Ellison, since any attempt to trace back to, invent, or reinvent an origin of any sort ignores the complex historical contours and developments in relation to the development of any cultural form. For Ellison, any search for origins, whether cultural or racial, implies the search for a decontextualized myth of invention out of our own ignorance.

For Ellison, it is the role of cultural forms like art, in its widest definition, that offers up the greatest potential for social change.

> You must remember that in this country things are always all shook up, so that people are constantly moving around and rubbing off another culturally. Nor should you forget that here all things—institutions, individuals and roles—offer more than the function assigned them, because beyond their intended function they provide forms of education and criticism. They challenge, they ask questions, they offer suggestive answers to those who would pause and probe their mystery. Most of all, remember it is not only the images of art or the sound of music that pass through walls to give pleasure and inspiration; it is in the very *spirit* of art to be defiant of categories and obstacles. They are, as transcendent forms of symbolic expression, agencies of human freedom. (Ellison 1994, 518)

In its very creation, art has the potential for affecting change. Within art itself lies the inherent potential to both educate and criticize since art has a critical imagination component built into it. Art presents us with the condition of alternative, an "as if" for things to be other than what they are, to inspire us to imagine, beyond just the political sphere, to the sphere of life. Cultural forms cut across racial lines and allow for a counter to race—one that undermines racial essentialism and the conflation between race and culture. Focusing on culture, rather than race, allows us to place race in the context of everyday life.

Looking at the Lindy Hop and Steppin' through Ellison's framework is to see the true hybridity of the dance that usually goes misrecognized. To understand the hybridity of the dance does not deny the dominant African American influence on the dance; rather it serves as the basis of its creative potential as a *cultural*, not racial form. Coming to terms with the racial imagination, we must deconstruct not just the issue of whiteness, but all forms of racializing and racial logic that mediate our ways of seeing, interpreting, and understanding all social interaction. Following Ellison, we must come to understand how culture is embodied and coded through the body and as such come to understand how the racial imagination operates to naturalize and racialize cultural forms.

The fact that the Lindy Hop and Steppin' are situated side by side in the city of Chicago provides me with the opportunity to address these Ellisonian questions. An analysis of the Lindy Hop affords this unique opportunity to analyze how the white use of African American cultural forms severs those forms from the people who cultivated them, generating and enabling racial domination, while at the same time celebrating those cultural forms and bringing them to the center of national attention. When discussing this contradiction, it is crucial to understand that it was neither the participation nor active inclusion of African Americans that brought the Lindy Hop back to the center of white American popular culture. The centralizing and elevating of this African American cultural form occurred exclusively through white consumption and appropriation of African American culture. As a result, the Lindy Hop is celebrated as a national fad, while African American people, the creators and cultivators of the dance, remain economically, politically, and socially marginalized.

In order to fully grapple with these Ellisonian questions, interviewing and ethnographic fieldwork were necessary, yet not sufficient; the most important tool of analysis to answer these questions proved to be what Loïc Wacquant calls "carnal sociology": putting myself at the "epicenter of the array of material and symbolic forces that [I] intend to dissect" in order to acquire the practical knowledge, corporeal schemes, and competences necessary to understand that world (Wacquant 2004a, viii).[24] Dance is an embodied and enacted cultural practice that cannot be fully understood from disinterested observation. Watching and interviewing dancers is not sufficient to fully grasp the logic of the dance without undertaking the necessary labor to master the dance; a full understanding is something that can be acquired only through practical, not conceptual, acquisition. In order to gain insight into the social dynamics of this particular universe, it became necessary to know the world of the Lindy Hop and Steppin' as an embedded participant observer, and, more important, as an embodied practitioner. Cultivating the bodily knowledge available exclusively to dancers opened up a previously unattainable level of reflexivity. I could now analyze these racially marked worlds as they are experienced by the racially marked body—developing an understanding of the dances, the dancers, and the social milieus in which they intersect not only from the outside in, but from the inside out.

CARNAL SOCIOLOGY AS METHODOLOGICAL ENTRY AND IMMERSION

American Allegory is distinctive for taking a "carnal" approach to urban ethnography as codified by Loïc Wacquant in *Body and Soul*, "The Body, the Ghetto, and the Penal State," and "Habitus as Topic and Tool."[25] Carnal sociology requires that we develop embodied practical knowledge to understand our world. Because practical knowledge can be acquired only by putting oneself into the line of fire and subjecting oneself to the social forces under analysis, it cannot come from a detached perspective. Carnal sociology demands not only a new methodological entry into the world, but also a new mode of theorizing the body as both a tool of inquiry and a vector of knowledge. We must, as Wacquant argues, do "not only do a sociology *of* the body but also a sociology *from* the body," in order to make explicit the practical sense of everyday life and the practices that define a specific social context from the inside out.[26]

Carnal sociology differs from autoethnography in that autoethnography focuses exclusively on the researcher's personal experience in the field. Autoethnography focuses on the self, knowledge of the self, the dynamics of personal interest, and the investment of one's own personal experience.[27] Carnal sociology, by contrast, is not about the meaning of personal participation. Rather, it uses full immersion into a particular world of study in order to fully understand the phenomena under investigation from the inside out, a vantage point that is inaccessible to observation alone. In this way carnal sociology also differs from traditional participant-observation, in that carnal sociology is used to "push the logic of participant observation to the point where it becomes inverted and turns into observant participation" (Wacquant 2011, 87). By doing so, the processes of immersion and conversion that the carnal approach affords enables us to unearth the practical knowledge of the internal dynamics of the phenomena in question.[28] Finally, carnal sociology differs from Paul Stoller's "sensuous scholarship" despite their surface similarities. Sensuous scholarship shares one of the aims of carnal sociology in that they both seek to move beyond treating the body as a text to be deciphered and instead incorporate the sensing body— the smells, tastes, textures, and sensations of the agent—into scholarly practices, representations, and descriptions.[29] However, sensuous scholarship retains an outsider perspective to the issue of embodiment in that it offers no methodology for understanding how people feel, no account of how emotions and senses shape everyday embodiment and comportment in relation to their existing conditions, and no descriptive resources to provide an explanation for how embodiment animates social conduct. Following Wacquant, carnal sociology "seeks to situate itself not outside or above practice but at its "point of production" requires that we immerse ourselves as deeply and as durably as possible into the cosmos under examination" (2005a, 466). In doing so, we acquire the dispositions and pretheoretical understandings necessary to negotiate the contours that define the world under analysis. Carnal sociology can, as Wacquant has demonstrated, with varying degrees of depth, empathy, and reflexivity, "go from the guts to the intellect," articulating and translating the understanding one has acquired viscerally into the representational forms required of academic discipline.[30]

The case in question here, dance, is an embodied, nonlinguistic cultural form that cannot be fully understood from the outside. Dance is an art that is learned, understood, and expressed through the body. In order to acquire this knowledge, I could not simply watch and ask questions about the Lindy Hop, I had to reach a point where I could understand the art as a dancer. Therefore, I had to come to understand the dance practically, through my own body. Learning to dance is the process of acquiring the competences of choreography, leading and following, improvising to music, and expressing oneself aesthetically, all simultaneously in time and space. This retooling of the body was a demanding process of inculcation and training, whereby my awkward predance body had to be re-formed and cultivated into an educated fluid dancing body. As with riding a bike, conceptual mastery of dance is of limited use; it is only after the dance has been assimilated into the body through endless drills and repetitions that it becomes fully understood (Wacquant 2004a, 69, 118). This cultivation of the corporeal schema of dance enabled me not only to be a dancer, but to see and comprehend the details and subtleties that remain invisible to those who have not acquired that practical knowledge. In the end, only a carnal sociology of and from the body could render the Lindy Hop and Steppin' fully meaningful.

American Allegory draws upon and extends carnal sociological as both a methodological and theoretical apparatus.[31] By utilizing embodiment as a manifestation and the world of Lindy Hop and Steppin' as a microcosm, this study seeks to explicate larger structures of ethnoracial domination. This study also seeks to understand how the racial imagination operates by refracting, inculcating, and naturalizing the racial mythologies of blackness and whiteness conceptually in our understandings of social life and materially through enactment of cultural practices. As a method, carnal sociology provides a particular point of view as an embedded and embodied practitioner of those practices, as well as how those practices are conceptualized and inculcated. As theory, it offers an analytical framework for conceptualizing how embodied cultural practices become mechanisms of producing and perpetuating racial domination. In this way carnal sociology opens a new window into ethnoracial domination as it connects to the larger Ellisonian thematics of the interconnected dynamics of race, culture, identity, and power that become embodied. Dance itself serves as an allegory for the racial-cultural dynamics that define American society. A carnal sociology approach to dancing forced me to rethink the contingent relationships between cultural practices, racial categories, and notions of identity. This in turn generated two interrelated questions: How do white bodies enact whiteness and blackness through the cultural practices in which they are engaged? How is it that those racial phenotypes may or may not correspond to what they enact or how they enact it? In order to answer these questions, it is necessary not only to consider the ways that race is written onto and enacted by the body, but also to understand how we conceptualize racial identity and how those conceptualizations often reinscribe our essentialized racial commonsense. Commonsense racial categories are objectively defined phenotypes to which interests, aesthetics, tastes, and agency can be attributed. In this way, racial identity is not something one ever escapes, as if self-reflection somehow freed us from its presence in society as a social fact, or loosened the hold race plays on our shared social understanding of the world at a macro level.

This mode of analyzing the racial identity of the body through both its phenotype and its practice enabled me to rethink the contingent relationship between race, culture, and the body. This rethinking was not just a conceptual matter. Rather, I had to understand it through my body, by reexamining all I had learned in order to understand how these racial myths were interlinked with the process of learning cultural practices like dance. What is important here is not the ascribed racial phenotype of any particular dancer; rather it is the way we can come to understand how bodies are both vehicles of racialized meaning through their enactment of cultural practices and racializing bodies in the ways they normalize and naturalize their racialized understanding of the world.

In this way it is not simply the conscious identification of these racial mythologies that frees us from them, as if we could mentally discard them, but to understand how they must be reworked through the very ways we move and understand the world through our bodies.[32] What appears to be the most natural and instinctual of human activities is in fact a highly cultivated and disciplined process of cultural inculcation. There is no necessity to bodies dancing in any particular manner, rather only practices that get misrecognized and enacted as natural to some groups and not others through the symbolic power of the dominant racial mythology. Focusing on the embodiment of racial mythologies, rather than the structural or intention oriented approaches to race, suggests the need for an alternative analysis of how cross-cultural engagement is mediated and enacted.

Acquiring the corporeal schemas of dance provided me with a bodily awareness not only of the practical logic of the dance, but also of interpreting bodily movements more generally. As I scrutinized myself and other dancers during years of training my body through mimicry, drills, and reflexive scrutiny of my movements and those of other dancers, I slowly came to realize how symbolic power and violence are embedded in the very ways that white society interprets, internalizes, and enacts African American cultural forms like the Lindy Hop. As I continued to practice and cultivate my dancing in light of my new understanding, I began to see the process by which my body became that of a dancer. Inculcating the components of dance into one's body, especially a body that had no previous dance training, is an arduous process. By watching this process unfold over time and marking the stages and steps of accomplishment along the way, I began to see how much bodily labor was necessary to learn the dance. Using my own body as the case study, I experienced the limits of how much and how quickly one can accumulate this bodily knowledge and the amount of practice required before it appears natural, as if one can spontaneously and naturally dance gracefully and effortlessly. Only by working back and forth between my own learning curve and watching and asking others about how they felt about their own progress could I see how this racial mythology dominated the way they gauged what they thought and had not thought about in terms of how well they would be able to learn how to dance.

CARNAL SOCIOLOGY MEETS THE ANALYTIC OF
RACIAL DOMINATION

Through this carnal sociology approach, we are able to problematize our own embeddedness by taking the social as primary and explicating the modes of misrecognition, that is, the ways that the meanings and values of any social world, which are always contextually and historically constituted, get taken for granted or naturalized as commonsense.[33] To dissect these taken-for-granted meanings, we must undertake an analysis that connects the misrecognition of racial meanings and values that become embedded in practices of everyday life. To do so, ethnography must work hermeneutically—where the part helps us make sense of the whole and the whole makes sense of the part—to provide us with an understanding of how the individual instantiations examined are always in relation to the larger social-structural conditions that make them possible. This hermeneutic approach must employ Bourdieu's formulation of misrecognition, as well as how it operates in relationship to the "two-fold naturalization of the world"—where racial categories and the racializing logic of the world around us reside both within us, in our dispositions and orientations, and in the world itself so as to appear transparent and natural.[34] This twofold naturalization helps create and perpetuate our misrecognition of race in the ways that the intertwined relationship of racial categories and racial mythologies (a reciprocal process by which racial categories determine cultural attributes and cultural attributes become defined by racial categories) work to inform spontaneous assessments of the world as well as more reasoned reflections. By doing so, we can come to illuminate how race operates in specific times/places and how the mythologies of racial identity become part of the constitutive processes of the practices under analysis; racial mythologies structure both the interpretation of the practices themselves and their modes of enactment through their participants. In turn, this allows us to show how embodied cultural practices serve as symbolic and material mechanisms—as conduits for instilling and reproducing the macro logic of racial mythologies into localized interactions—that generate and reproduce racial domination across the twenty-first-century racial landscape of American society.

By drawing out the interconnection between cultural practices and the racial mythologies of blackness and whiteness that are attributed to them, as in the case of white bodies learning to dance the historically African American Lindy Hop, we can examine two simultaneously occurring processes. First, we can ascertain how bodies come to acquire a practical knowledge of the dance; second, we can analyze how this acquisition also incorporates the racial mythologies of blackness and whiteness that get refracted into bodies, through the schemata of cognitive, emotional, and bodily labor of learning to dance. As a result, cultural practices, and their historically specific forms of expressions and movements, are fundamentally inseparable from the power relationships that have made the racial categories articulated with them—and the assumptions and myths surrounding those categories—enduring sociological concerns.

Whereas previous eras of white racial domination have been characterized by explicit physical or symbolic manifestations, in the post–civil rights period of colorblindness and multiculturalism, white racial domination works "without racists" in an implicit and often invisible form (Bonilla-Silva 2003). What makes the Lindy Hop such a fascinating object lesson is not the cultural form itself, but the dynamics involved in its cross-racial adoption and how racial domination is perpetuated not through racism or prejudice but rather through the misrecognition of the ways that racial domination is perpetuated through the ordinary cultural practices. The carnal-analytic model provides a mode of analytically examining the intersections of race, culture, and the body against the wider mainstream popular understandings of multiculturalism or cultural diversity. Rather than contradictory in form or content, the multiculturalism of contemporary society is interdependent with and mutually reinforcing of racial domination. Multiculturalism and the promotion of diversity often celebrate and promote cultural practices as celebratory panaceas for America's ongoing racial conflicts. These celebrations elide the macro-structural forces that generate racial inequality by isolating them from the racial, political, and economic forces that intersect those cultural forms and practices and therefore go misrecognized even when advocated for with the best of intentions.

Therefore, following Wacquant, we must break from the dominant conceptions of the sociology of race, those he describes as mired in "the logic of the trial" in which judgment parcels out guilt or innocence to participants in attempts to convict or vindicate whites of racism.[35] Rather, by attending to what he designates as an "analytic of racial domination" we can come to unveil the mechanisms that generate, reinscribe, or augment domination. In order to do so:

> We need to forge an analytic of racial domination capable of capturing the simultaneously malleability and obdurateness of racial divisions along with the diversity of symbolic and material mechanisms whereby these are drawn, enforced, and challenged. To do this we must discard the notion of "racism" and its logocentric bias, clearly demarcate sociologi-

cal categories from ethno-racial commonsense, and renounce the urge to
denounce fed by the logic of the trial. (Wacquant 1997b, 231)

Without such a theoretical framework to drive the analysis, explanations
can often fall into pejorative moral judgments rather than scientific inter-
rogations, which simply reaffirm the essential evilness of the dominator
and the inherent goodness of the dominated. This approach does little to
help us understand how race operates and how domination occurs; it col-
lapses different dimensions of racial domination, "obscuring crucial differences, bases, forms, and implications of racial divisions" (Wacquant 1997b,
225). As a result, how whiteness is deployed locally, as well as how it is experienced in distinct locations at distinct times, and even as it is shaped at
national and macro-structural levels, are all simultaneously obscured.

Without understanding how whiteness operates in its particularities,
we cannot begin to grasp how race and culture operate on the ground in
everyday life. We must not allow the paradigm of whiteness or white racism
to become a fulcrum for moral and value judgments by assigning blame or
innocence for unpalatable social facts. Nor can we allow ourselves to analyze racial dynamics solely through the conscious or intentional outcome of
white prejudice or racism. Instead, an analytical framework of racial domination offers a more accurate and powerful explanation of the particular
phenomena under analysis. Whether examining the Lindy Hop as a dance
once historically recognized as black and yet now viewed as white, or conversely to discuss a sport such as basketball, which was historically white
and now considered black, speaks to both the enduring fluidity of racial
identity and cultural forms, as well as to how those changes go misrecognized in the popular imagination.

By illuminating how racial domination works through the interlocking symbolic and material mechanisms that generate and reproduce racial
domination, we can come to understand the perpetuation of the dominant
racial mythology of essential racial differences that are grounded in the
body. Whites themselves can also be oppressed through this essentializing of racial difference as it circumscribes their own possibilities of identity formation. Cross-cultural engagements, like whites learning to dance
a traditionally African American dance like the Lindy Hop, illuminate
the ways that whites themselves are complicit in their belief in these differences. Through an analytical framework of racial domination, we can
differentiate, unhinge, and reassemble the diverse forms that relations of
racial domination assume in different times and places. By drawing on the
racial imagination and the power of embodied cultural forms to undermine
our racial assumptions, we can begin to grapple with the hybridized ways of

living that form the context of cultural engagements and cultural clashes in everyday life. In doing so, this strange dance called the Lindy Hop serves as allegory for the ironies and contradictions that define race, culture, and identity in American society.

CHAPTER ORGANIZATION

The organization of the book is as follows: through an exposition of learning how to dance, chapter 1 dramatizes the bridge between the dance as a cultural category and the processes of embodiment and inculcation of dance as practice. In drawing this out, it demonstrates how even the most "natural" expressions are undergirded by bodily labor. By dissecting four major components of the Lindy Hop (choreography, leading and following, improvisation, and style) this chapter illuminates the centrality of performance in relation to cultural embodiment and racial identities. In conclusion, it discusses those moments of mastery in which the dance becomes seamless and transparent, to the point of seeming instinctual to the outside observer as well as to the dancers themselves.

Chapter 2 examines the dynamics of the white cross-cultural engagement with the Lindy Hop, which is at times a conscious intention and at other times something that goes on without any awareness at all. These engagements are examined through three dominant modalities: minstrelsy, whitewashing, and commodification. By illuminating these modes of engagement, we are able to understand how the negotiation of everyday cultural practices often leads to a complex and contradictory set of positions that serves as mechanisms of racial domination. In order to draw out the "in the moment" dynamics of dancing, the notions of expression and skill are foregrounded, as well as the tensions and contradictions that emerge in direct relation to the general unawareness of the racial origins and associations of the Lindy Hop.

Chapter 3 highlights the lived immediacy of dancing leading to both a simultaneous investment in mastery of those embodied practices and an obliviousness to how those interactions erase the historical conditions of those cultural forms. By mapping out the dominant discourses through which the dance is conceptualized and articulated, I show how the very discourses through which people understand their actions are always subject to those who wield the most power over them. Here, the theme of cultural appropriation in relation to the specificities of the Lindy Hop revival allow the dance to be openly embraced as a cultural form since it has no current grounded racial identity in popular culture. As a result, these discourses provide a window into understanding how the dominant racial logic of

American society circulates even in the most apparently innocuous cultural practices.

Chapter 4 recounts my engagement with the Steppin' scene in Chicago and explores how cultural practice enables the contestation and transgression of racial categories. This approach presents an alternative model for explaining racial identity, grounded in the competencies and embodied knowledges that one enacts in practice, which opens up new antiessentialist possibilities for theorizing race and an antiracist politics based in cultural labor. In doing so, I highlight the nuances of subcultures within the larger African American community by showing the internal differences that exemplify the complexity of discussing a singular African American community in relation to any particular cultural form.

Following chapter 4, the "Lead Out" mirrors the "Lead In" section that preceded the introduction in that it serves as a point of methodological reflection. Whereas the "Lead In" discussed my immersion into the worlds of Lindy Hop and Steppin,' the "Lead Out" considers my own reflections as an embedded and embodied ethnographer in relation to the craft I mastered and the worlds I traveled through on the way to that mastery. This reflection takes stock of my doubly transformative odyssey as both carnal sociologist and Lindy Hopper/stepper. In doing so, this reflection considers ways to establish new inroads into the interconnections between race and culture at both theoretical and empirical, as well as intellectual and practical levels in relation to the allegory of dance as racial-cultural dynamic working itself out within the larger context of American society.

The conclusion reflects on the limitations of cultural appropriation as a viable way to come to a sociological explanation for cross cultural engagement. In addition, I offer some possible alternative orientations that could potentially open up common ground and hybrid space for new possibilities of racial engagement, interaction, and connection that emerge through "positive" racial representations. This is not just an avenue of analysis for the Lindy Hop, but as a model for exploring racial interactions at their localized level of engagement beyond the realm of dance, to all spheres of cultural-racial intersections.

This encounter allows us to reflect on a chapter of our history where racial and cultural issues collide in the popular imagination on a national scale at a particular historical moment. We are also provided with an opportunity to see through this moment into the larger story of our grappling with our American identity, one that is always told through extended metaphors, through dances like the Lindy Hop, which serve as allegories for who we really are and who we might aspire to become.

1 FINDING THE POCKET

Despite their billings as images of reality, these Negroes of fiction are coun-
terfeits. They are projected aspects of an internal symbolic process through
which, like a primitive tribesman dancing himself into the group frenzy
necessary for battle, the White American prepares himself emotionally to
perform a social role.

Ralph Ellison (1995a)

•

It was a warm, humid summer evening in mid-August, and my friend Jayson and I had traveled to a neighborhood in Chicago called Uptown—the
city's renowned entertainment district of the 1940s and '50s. As a new resi-
dent of Chicago, and having recently seen the movie *Swingers*, I was interested in discovering if there was a swing dance scene in the city. A friend of
mine, who was also interested in swing, told me that four neo-swing bands
were performing at the Aragon Ballroom that night. (The Aragon is one
of the most celebrated of the old Chicago dance halls and now serves as a
mainstream concert venue.)

As Jayson and I walked around the corner to the main entrance of the
theater, I noticed how the nearby boarded-up theaters and few remaining
small shops that were closed for the night were juxtaposed with the expansive six-corner intersection that indicated a main artery of the city. This section of Uptown was once an exclusive cultural center for the elite, but is now
marked primarily by prostitution, drugs, homelessness, and panhandling.
The elevated-train stop had appeared threatening, with small groups of
menacing-looking men loitering just outside the exit doors of the station
eyeing train riders as they rolled through the turnstiles in their direction.
The Green Mill Jazz Club, once a speakeasy that boasted such infamous patrons as Al Capone, and the Saxony Inn liquor store and bar were lit up in
the distance and seemed to be the only other venues open for business.

After purchasing our tickets, we raced upstairs to a balcony overlook-
ing the entire theater. In awe, I looked out over the cavernous space below
and saw hundreds of dancers covering the expansive Aragon dance floor.
The band was behind them on the stage, wailing away on horns, while the
people danced wildly, dressed to the nines in hats, suits, dresses, and two-
tone shoes. It was as if I'd stepped into a time warp and been transported to a

dance hall back in the 1940s. I had previously witnessed scenes like this only in old movies or retro pictures like *Swing Kids* and *Malcolm X*, and here it was, a former past world recreated right before my eyes. Just hours before, when I'd been on the phone with my grandmother, she'd said to me, "You know, I danced at the Aragon Ballroom in Chicago when I was your age." I imagined her out there, dancing and enjoying herself among the crowd. The tremendous energy from the ocean of dancers radiated up into the rafters and captivated me—something electric was occurring down below, something that transfixed me. I did not know how to dance, so I stayed up in the balcony and looked down with a feeling of determination. One day I would learn that dance and be out there on that floor.

•

Social dance, as a subcategory of dance, is done by and for dancers rather than for an audience; it is usually informal in nature and emphasizes sociability and socializing, since it can be danced with many different partners. While social dance is practiced around the world, it can also be one of the most misunderstood types of dance, because it is a bodily knowledge that is made tangible or visible only through its enactment.[1] Without costumes or a stage, good social dancers can break into dance without rehearsing, which makes their spontaneous practice appear as if it were innate or natural. As a result, we misrecognize the relationship between culture and the body and assume that dancers are born, that dancing is an innate ability, or that certain groups or races of people are just "natural" dancers.[2] In this way, we mistake "nature" for second nature or the long-term result of practice and repetition of a set of skills.

When venturing into worlds that have been infused with African American culture, from jazz to rock-'n'-roll and beyond, stereotypes of rhythm, fluidity, and expressivity begin to swirl and confuse nature and second nature. Rather than seen as cultural laborers, working on, crafting, stylizing, and perfecting a form of dance, African Americans are perceived as natural dancers. Without exploring the arduous practice that goes into developing any form of expression, we misunderstand accomplished dancers in motion as spontaneous performers. When the misrecognition of bodily labor collides with social categories of race and culture, expressions of any form take on a life of their own—as if detached from any context or conditioning. Without being grounded in their everyday contexts, cultural forms become Ellisonian-like projections by which we believe in the fictitiousness of instinct rather than the reality of learned expressions. In order to dramatize this perpetual misrecognition, we must make explicit the practices and processes of labor that form and shape the body into a vehicle of cultural expression. To do so, it is necessary to step back from the immediacy of dance as a form in motion and understand the constitutive techniques and motions that must be inculcated or incorporated into the body to make it appear as second nature. In order to understand the Lindy Hop as a social dance, it is necessary to demythologize it as a "natural" expression or an innate cultural or racial knowledge and to expose it as a form of expression mastered through the arduous process of bodily labor and inculcation that result in becoming a competent Lindy Hop dancer.[3] In the case of the Lindy Hop, the specific practical knowledge that enables one to be a fluent dancer is something that one acquires over time.[4] In order to parcel out these skills, or "knowledges" of the craft, that define the Lindy Hop as a specific form of social dance, I will discuss four of its most fundamental aspects (choreography, leading and following, improvisation, and styling). By doing so, we can gain insight into the internal dynamics that define this specific cultural form, the tools that any individual must acquire to be a socially fluent dancer, and, most important, draw out those dynamics that lead to the when, where, why, and how misrecognition operates to obscure our understandings of the body and culture.

WHAT IS THE LINDY HOP?

•

I descended from the Aragon's balcony, where I had been watching the dancers, down to the main floor and stood a comfortable distance away from several dancing couples. My eyes gravitated toward one couple whose enthusiasm and dynamism had captured my attention. The man and woman circled around each other, connected only through one outstretched arm. They smiled and focused on each other as she glided into his arms. Her arm rested around his shoulders and his around her hips. He carried her around him in a quick circle as if they were walking hip to hip. Using his momentum and his right hand, he sent her back out away from him so that they were again adjoined only by one outstretched arm. The move looked like a rubber band expanding and contracting in space. The couple glided past each other, then reconnected and turned around together, then separated back to their starting position. They twisted, turned, and traded places over and over, yet each time they did it in a different way. Suddenly the couple broke apart as if a wheel had come off a car, and the symmetrical balance that held them together was broken. Instead of losing their way or falling out of control, they had planned this; each froze for a moment before breaking into his and her own individualized musical interpretations. The man bent his knees and walked past the woman in a kind of weaving motion, as if his knees were buckling under him, while she rotated her hips and twisted around him in a semicircle. Her dress splayed out around her and swished back and forth across her knees as she twisted, while his baggy trousers dusted the floor as he sank into the movement. When she almost passed him, he grabbed her hand and turned her back toward him, and the whole process began again.

•

The circling step that I saw both of them dancing was the Swing Out, which is the "box step" or the basic step that serves as the foundation on which all other variations are built. In the Swing Out, dancers begin apart, and the man acts as an anchor around which the woman moves. As the woman comes in toward her partner, they meet and momentarily connect in the middle of the dance move as they turn around together, and then the man leads her back to where she started by "swinging her out." It is as if she were tethered to a pole, being pulled in and then sent back out to where she started. Like the undulating music of swing, the dance captures a "swinging" feeling with this rubber band–type movement, as the female follower pulls in and out.

The man, who usually leads, begin by bowing down at the opening of the Swing Out. He keeps his torso upright and expands his chest, but lowers himself through bent knees and a tilted pelvis to a lower plane like a bowler would when following through on a toss. This emphasizes and dramatizes the position of the female follower, who remains on a higher plane as she executes her signature "twist-twist" movement. The bowing movement serves a double purpose. Steven Mitchell, the contemporary Lindy Hop master instructor, once commented at a Lindy Hop workshop, "I've had the pleasure of working with Al Minns [one of the great original Lindy Hop dancers from the famous dance troupe Whitey's Lindy Hoppers]. Al said that this movement of the man bowing to the woman was an adaptation of how in the plantation days slaves used to make fun of their masters by exaggerating a bow to them."

Women, usually the followers, are defined by the twist-twist, a sensual step driven by the woman's hips swiveling back and forth as she moves around her partner. The grounded and heavy characteristic of the dance takes its origins from African dance, which gives it a loose and fluid look through constant compression of the legs. The athletic bouncy steps make the dance look more bent and relaxed and distinguish it from other dances that are more upright in posture, such as ballroom dancing styles. Contrary to what the name "Lindy Hop" may suggest, there is no jumping or hopping in the dance; rather, the movement is smooth, solid, and grounded. There is a constant rhythmic eight-count "pulse" and flowing style to the dance and, when well executed, a deep bounce but no hopping.

The defining characteristic of the Swing Out is the "breakaway," in which the dancers find their maximum extension from each other in the Swing-Out figure.[5] Although they remain connected through one arm, this distance offers the space to improvise and display individual interpretations and steps before returning back to dancing with one's partner. The combination of coming together and breaking apart within the partnered framework of the dance is the basic step through which everything else develops. All the elements of the dance are incorporated in this figure—rhythm, timing, individualism, and reliance on and connection to one's partner. Although the move is semi-choreographed, partners cannot merely plow through the choreography; nor can they pull each other back and forth like a rag doll. The dance must be led and followed for it to work correctly.

The Lindy Hop is elusive and difficult to articulate because the dance is based on two intrinsic contradictions of freedom and structure. First, the Lindy Hop is a social-partner dance founded on cooperation and communication through leading and following, yet both partners can do individualized steps throughout if they choose to do so. Since the Lindy Hop has both a closed position (where partners are connected body to body) and an open position (where they are only connected by outstretched arms), the dance is both highly social and highly individual at the same time. Second, the dance is based on a series of choreographed movements and figures; yet at the core the Lindy Hop thrives when dancers improvise steps to the music. Like the jazz music to which it is danced, dancers may "play" with the music so as to dance "on" the beat and "off" the beat, creating syncopated steps and movements that emphasize the framework of the dance as well as its internal plasticity.

As a result, the Lindy Hop has an open-ended structure of creativity that hinges on few formal rules or restrictions other than the structure of the basic Swing steps and the syncopated swing beat that marks the rhythm and feeling of the music. The Lindy Hop is highly individualized, yet both partners are mutually dependent on each other in order for the dance to succeed. The tension between individualism and cooperation, between the improvised solo and the arrangement, is at the heart of the dance. This contradictory logic makes the dance a dynamic interaction as partners communicate and interpret the music together in time and space. It is a personal biographical extension of each individual's aesthetic and identity.

Starting with the basic step, dancers then add an infinite number of variations, twists, turns, and improvised steps. In addition to the swinging motion of the Swing Out, the Lindy Hop also includes variations of the

Charleston—the signature dance of the Roaring Twenties. The Charleston is modified within the framework of the Lindy Hop so that dancers remain connected, dancing together side by side rather than apart as they did in the '20s. In addition, the Lindy Hop offers moments where partners actually separate and perform jazz steps such as the Turkey Trot, Peckin', Shim Sham, Apple Jacks, and the Shorty George (Batchelor 1997, Emery 1988, Stearns and Stearns 1994). On this foundation, dancers add turns, figures, kicks, pauses, dips, aerials, jazz steps, and their own creative interpretations and expressions, limited only by their imagination and the dictates of the music. This aspect of balance between choreography and improvisation is always one under flux and negotiation.

•

Standing along the sidelines at a downtown club, I watched couples switching partners and spinning through a myriad of figures and positions. I could not discern whether this was all haphazard and random or actually choreographed. What I did know was that the dance was fast and almost acrobatic when practiced to up-tempo songs. Watching these Lindy Hoppers dance, weave, and pound the floor was like seeing a mixture of ice skating and gymnastics, a seamless combination of athleticism and grace. Their restrained chaos, somewhere between caution and abandon, characterized the Lindy Hop as both anarchical and poetic.

As the band eased off the up-tempo pace and the music grew more moderate, the dancers adjusted their movements to a smoother, silkier styling. The lights in the room dimmed, and the people on the sidelines turned their attention to the floor. As a social dance, the Lindy Hop reflects a conversation between partners exchanging ideas and expressions about the music through physical connection. As if words are unnecessary, he directs her and she follows under his arm; he indicates a direction and she accentuates his suggestion with a stylized interpretation. Through this process, the dance becomes an extended game of sign language in which the entire body is fair game for expression and interpretation. The dance is both social and personal; its formation and logic are grounded in sensuality, passion, and expression.

•

LINDY HOP REVIVED

While the Lindy Hop was "revived" in the late 1990s, it was not a straight reproduction of the Lindy Hop danced in the past. A variety of viewpoints emerged on how best to cultivate the dance. This diverse set of opinions ran the gamut from those who advocated strict adherence to the classic dance steps or "traditional canon" of the Lindy Hop found in old movies and documentary footage to those who desired to incorporate other dances into the Lindy Hop framework and still others who looked to fuse it with contemporary cultural forms like Hip hop. Examining this multiplicity of viewpoints deepens our understanding of the dance by further defining its logic of practice.

When I first encountered the Lindy Hop, it seemed different from other dances I had seen; it wasn't as tightly centered as salsa or as melodramatic as tango, yet it was freer than ballroom. The Lindy Hop seemed to be completely uninhibited, as the partners sometimes broke away from each other and did individual steps. It appeared to border on both chaos and complete precision and to be more complex and intricate than other dances. The dance strikes a unique balance between dancing alone and with a partner, allowing constant interpretation within its structured framework. While it seems to have its own canon of movements, it also incorporates movements from other dances. As one international instructor told me at a Lindy Hop camp in Palm Springs, California:[6]

> What is so special about Savoy style [Lindy Hop] is that we don't have the prejudice about other dances; to us it's all one dance. We can bring in everything, the Ballroom, the West Coast Swing, the Latin, the Tango, into the dance. With Savoy style, we just want to dance; we want to bring it all in. It all fits. That's why this dance is in the best position relative to other dances; that's why we have the best of everything—because we don't have those same prejudices that other dances have that prevent us from developing the dance and keeping the dance new and alive.

Another instructor offered this opinion at a dance workshop in Boston:

> Since it comes from the Charleston, you have all of that, and then all the different jazz steps and all those things that are basically their own dances that have been adopted into the dance, like the Cakewalk and Truckin'. Think of the traditional figures, like the Swing Out and all of that. And then there are all these people who put Tango or hip hop or whatever into it—it's crazy, but it works. As long as you stay within the dance—I mean within the idea of Lindy Hop—but see to me that is complete freedom. You asked me to define what I think it is—I would define the dance as complete freedom; insofar as you can do it, I say go for it. But I still believe there is a structure to the dance. I think it is complete freedom within the structure that the dance allows, but I think that's what draws people to it. I mean, it's almost a contradiction when you get down to it.

While the Lindy Hop is its own dance, it has the malleability to incorporate other dances and steps into its framework. Since the Lindy Hop has been "revived" and is now being translated into the present, many have raised questions about whether or not the dance we're currently doing really is the Lindy Hop. Some Chicago teachers of the dance who desire a more nostalgic version of the Lindy Hop argue that some instructors, especially those who are more creative with the dance, are not teaching the "real" Lindy Hop. A conversation I had with the most influential Lindy Hop dance promoter based in Chicago reflected a deep commitment to keeping the dance exactly as it was:

> We know what the dance is. You know what Steven [Mitchell] is doing is not real Lindy Hop. We've seen the video clips and the old footage, and Frankie [Frankie Manning, considered by many as the greatest of the original Lindy Hop dancers] is still teaching it. I think we have a real good idea of what they did.

The most important instructor in Chicago responded to the above quote during a formal interview that I conducted at his apartment with a completely different sentiment:

> I hate that. I can't stand that. That I have an opinion on. I mean, Frankie was just one of thousands of dancers at the Savoy and in Harlem in general. To say it's not Lindy Hop because Frankie didn't do this or that . . . how do they know? Frankie has done so much, so it's no disrespect to him, but come on; I mean, there were so many others who created steps and did their own thing. There is this orthodoxy with some people that kills me, because it's like if Frankie didn't do it then we shouldn't do it. I mean, what about all the other great dancers like Al Minns and Pepsi Bethel and whoever, and what about all the women that never get mentioned? I mean, look at all the members of Whitey's Lindy Hoppers; they all had their own style. There were so many dancers back then, we have no idea exactly what is or isn't Lindy Hop when it comes down to it.

Rather than fossilizing the Lindy Hop by preserving exactly what was done before in a rigid and nostalgic way, some of the leaders of the Lindy Hop revival have made a concerted effort to undermine that nostalgia by pushing the dance forward so that it will have a future as a social dance and cultural form.

For many instructors, keeping the Lindy Hop alive as a social and cultural form meant keeping the dance fresh by cultivating new steps and ideas within the logic of the dance. While strict reproduction to a particular logic was rejected by most, many defined their views along degrees of adherence to the original choreography. As one master teacher commented during an informal conversation in San Francisco,

> You know, I've talked to Norma [Miller, one of the great female dancers from Whitey's Lindy Hoppers dance troupe] about this and she says, "been there, done that; we did that fifty years ago. Is that all you can do? What else can you do?" So you know, it's not just about doing the same old steps; we know how to do those backwards and forwards. The key is, where are we going to take the dance now? I mean, when Norma says that, she's right. We must come up with something new—we must develop the dance and take it somewhere. The best way to honor the dance is to develop it and keep it alive. If you don't develop it, what is the point? Why are you trying to do it? It's to keep it fresh and alive as a living, breathing art form.

While I was at the Herräng Lindy Hop camp in Sweden, another instructor commented on it this way:

> People are too purist about what they think Lindy Hop is. I think that Lindy back in its time is not how it is now. I see people in San Francisco and they play really slow or mid-tempos, whereas when you look at the Rhythm Hot Shots and other performance groups, they play fast music where it's all fast and kicking out, like in *Hellzapoppin'*. So it's really all across the board. Everyone can't dance to the same tempos or in the same ways. You see, Lindy is a dance form. It's going to evolve or it will die. So you need to add other elements so that other people can get into it. Lindy Hop is creative. I know some people like myself who have been influenced by the tradition of calypso and reggae; I try and bring that in 'cause that's what I know. I know others that like hip hop, and other people put together tango with Lindy. But really Lindy Hop is about the soul; you've got the framework, but then you've got to give it something, and that's what they're doing. But I do think there comes a point where people start to go too far, and there is a point where you go too far when you forget the basis. So there is that element out there, but I haven't figured that out yet.

One pair of instructors interviewed at the Catalina Lindy Hop camp, on Catalina Island off the coast of Los Angeles, responded with the most comprehensive overview of the issue:

Well, there are several camps to think about. I mean, there is Steven, who is really far out with all the ways he is constantly innovating and bringing other things to the dance, and then there are the Rhythm Hot Shots who do just the "classic" moves from the videos like *Hellzapoppin'* and *Day at the Races,* and then I guess there are people more in the middle like ourselves who I think do a little of both, but we lean more toward the classic material, and then maybe Ryan and Jenny [two of the elite international instructors], who lean more toward Steven's approach. But as far as where the dance is headed, I think it is Steven that really attracts the new people and who is the energy of where the dance is going, at least for the way we think about it. Because really, the dance has to keep going. Everyone has sort of their own niche in a way and they all fit together, it is all still Lindy Hop. I don't think any of the top teachers look at each other and think what someone else is doing isn't Lindy Hop. I think as long as you work within the things that make it Lindy, then it's still Lindy Hop. I think the instructors need to make that clearer to the students, because I think they get confused and think that one style or another is "correct," and that makes it harder on the next instructor when they come into town to teach.

In this way, the logic of the Lindy Hop is defined by both its jazz structure and its social nature. Since we have so little video footage of people dancing the Lindy Hop socially (most of the preserved dance footage of the Lindy Hop from the '30s and '40s is of choreographed performance routines or short sections of dance choreographed for Hollywood movies), we often mistake choreographed performance for informal social dancing. During an informal interview in Pasadena, California, Steven Mitchell argued,

> We have so little footage of people social dancing from back then, and besides there were thousands—thousands of dancers who danced the Lindy Hop, so to reduce it to a few video clips makes no sense. It's the small-mindedness I hate—this whole thing about is this or isn't it Lindy Hop when you do something. That's what I love about Hand dancing, they just do it, they don't talk about whether it's "okay" or not okay. That's not even an issue for them—it's not even an issue.

In another interview, while in Sweden, he revealed,

> What I want to do for Lindy is keep the improvisation alive, the house dance of it—not the performing part of it, but the social part of it, the part that you don't see on the films, when you're just dancing.[7]

This dynamic between strict reproduction and open-ended creativity, between preserving the Lindy Hop and turning it into a new dance, makes the cultural form a constant point of contestation over its cultivation. Despite the lack of consensus over the direction of the dance is taking during the revival, the Lindy Hop, like any other cultural form, is always the subject of contestation and conflict and always only settled through bodily labor.

BODILY LABOR

•

After I had been dancing for about a year, I was out social dancing at a club one night. I was walking to my chair for a break when a man sitting at a nearby table reached over and put his arm on mine, saying, "You make it look so natural—so easy. I mean, I watch you dance, and man, it looks so natural out there. We were watching you out there and man, you are smooth, real smooth." The idea that others saw me as a smooth and natural dancer was quite unexpected; I still considered myself an awkward beginner. I laughed and thought I had fooled him—either that, or he hadn't seen much Lindy Hop before. The fact that he mistook me for a natural dancer, whose body looked smooth out on the dance floor, led me to think more seriously about these issues of the body and how learning to dance is a matter of labor and practice and has nothing to do with naturalness.

•

Dance is an embodied practice in which the dancer strives to reach a point where the dance becomes second nature.[8] Because the Lindy Hop is such a complex dance, this process of acquiring practical mastery is never settled; the body must constantly refine and cultivate itself in order to retain its "feel for the game."[9] The dispositions and competences associated with the Lindy Hop are elusive and true "mastery" of the dance almost never happens. The body's ability to synchronize itself with the game via the "practical sense" of the game enables advanced dancers to make adjustments to the dance as they go.[10] Those who have greater mastery of the dance can trust more completely their dispositions or feel for the game than those who are just learning.

Beginning dancers will necessarily bring to consciousness those situations that for an expert are transparent; they are not able to adapt the changing dynamics of the dance as it is unfolding and they are incapable of generating the appropriate responses in a seamless manner. When a dancer can acquire practical mastery, by seamlessly and instantly anticipating the

dance and constantly adjusting to its changing conditions, he becomes like
"a fish in water" where the dance appears as self-evident.[11] In the case of
the Lindy Hop, how exactly is this practical mastery acquired? It is acquired
through internalizing the defining components of the dance: the skills of
mastering choreography, leading and following, improvisation, and style
through training and inculcation. Skilled dancers eventually acquire the
ability to learn informally, by watching someone on the dance floor and
picking up a particular step or move, by sharing techniques or ideas while
out at a club or social dance, in the act of dancing itself by trying out new
ideas or improvising on the spot, among others, but this is only after having
mastered a solid foundation within which to understand and incorporate
aspects of the dance in this way.[12]

In breaking down these four components of the Lindy Hop, it should be
noted that these are analytical distinctions in order to isolate these separate aspects of the dance; one is learning all of these components simultaneously as one learns to dance. In addition, I will focus almost exclusively
on the dance studio, either dance classes or workshops, so as to present the
most direct and explicit cases of bodily labor and training to document how
one learns to Lindy Hop. While this may appear to "formalize" the dance,
making it more rigid or distorting of the musical aspects of the dance, my
approach here resonates with what master Lindy Hopper Steven Mitchell
has discussed when I approached him about the current state of teaching
the dance:

> No. No. No. People get that all wrong. It's like scaffolding, especially for
> people who are new to the dance. You can't just expect someone to just
> dance. It's like anything else, you have to build a foundation and build up
> from there. Especially since the dance is so new [in the revival stage, in
> terms of its contemporary return as a popular social dance]. You have to
> put the dance on the body, not the feet. But that takes work. Hard work to
> get people to get that. You know? We tend to just count with the feet and
> not the body; we have to get to where the body counts, how your body
> moves in the rhythm, how your body feels. Because in the end it's all there,
> it's not like you learn to move your feet and the body follows—you move
> your body and guess what the feet go with you.... Without that it's just
> steps not dancing. For me it's trying to get people to get that whole pack-
> age that is the dance.

As Mitchell points out, it is building a foundation upon which to work that
is essential in learning how to dance, and at the center of that foundation is
the body and bodily labor. It is to these topics that I now turn.

FOUR ASPECTS OF SOCIAL DANCE

•

As I looked around the dance classroom that summer evening, it was evident that labor was taking place: some people toweled off their faces, a couple of men left the room to change their shirts, a few dancers sat on the window ledge to get fresh air or leaned against the wall to support their tired bodies. Still others practiced the dance routine silently or by walking and talking it through step by step. Whether it is through repeatedly doing exercises with partners, asking teachers questions about a step, or practicing on their own, this dedication demonstrates an overwhelming desire to master the dance. Despite the fact that it was the middle of summer in Chicago and the day's temperature was pushing into the mid-nineties, this Lindy Hop class was sold out, and some people were turned away at the door. As the beads of sweat ran down my own face, I began to think that the Lindy Hop was really closer to boxing than to a pristine ballroom dance.

•

When one imagines the Lindy Hop, one must imagine it in motion. To hear a random song on a crowded dance floor and lead or follow another individual in time through a series of moves and patterns, to then improvise your own steps on a breakaway and add your own styling and interpretation of the music, while always complementing your partner as you move together among other bodies on the floor—this is the Lindy Hop. All aspects must be synchronized and executed simultaneously in order for the dance to be a seamless flow of movement that attains the ideal goal of blending into the music like an instrument in the band. Truly embodying this social dance form requires much more than the common eye perceives.

This struck me one morning when I entered the hotel ballroom where a Lindy Hop workshop was being held. It was just before nine o'clock and the room was full of students like me, rubbing their eyes, stretching out, and nursing cups of coffee in preparation for the workshop. The fluorescent lights were surprisingly bright and the music loud to motivate everyone after a long night of dancing. As my classmates stretched out and warmed up by dancing with each other, I thought about how different the room had looked just hours before, when these same people were tearing up the dance floor in a frenzy of movement. In the bright light of day, all of the labor, effort, and training were revealed. But during last night's late-night dance, any trace of labor was hidden: the lights were low, and everyone was dancing the moves and forms that they had practiced.

When one observes a crowded dance floor from the outside, it may appear as if everyone is a skilled dancer, with all the moving bodies swirling around each other at the same time. But, in fact, when we turn to analyze the dance from the inside, there are many different levels of practical mastery occupying the same social dance space. The goal of dancing is to make all of these movements appear as second nature. This requires the dancer not only to master all the components of dance, but to keep them all balanced and working together harmoniously. There are four mechanisms of socialization—choreography, social dance, improvisation, and style—by means of which such inculcation and embodiment occur. By following the trajectory of learning how to dance from the introductory choreography to leading and following, improvisation, and styling, we can make explicit the processes of bodily labor that make up the "natural" dancer, who appears to move spontaneously and effortlessly to the music.

Choreography

•

It was around nine o'clock on a cool fall weeknight in Chicago, and the dance studio windows were steamy with body heat. This class, like the one before it, was sold out with a waiting list. Young adults, some still in their work clothes, others in sweats, had come out in droves to learn Swing dancing. The room was hot and humid, and some couples talked while others practiced their dancing; some were loudly complaining that they didn't understand a certain dance step. Still others feigned indifference as they waited for the next person in line to rotate and dance with them. My dance partner had gone for a water break. I glanced hesitantly around the room, trying not to attract any attention as I awkwardly replayed over and over in my mind what the instructor had just said and done, but the simple task of getting my right foot to move slightly forward and to the right of my left foot befuddled me as I tried it again. Self-consciously, I took tiny steps in place so I wouldn't bump into the couple standing next to me in line. It all seemed so easy theoretically, but it was the *doing* part that was difficult. If I could only make it through that night without embarrassing myself and looking like a total fool, I would be grateful. I wondered how much longer would this class last? How did I ever get involved in the first place?

My partner returned and we attempted the routine again, trying not to run over the couple next to us. I had no idea what I was doing. I had never social danced before. Although I'd played sports all my life, my athleticism seemed useless here. It was frustrating and embarrassing to feel this lack of control over my body; I couldn't make it do what I wanted. But then, fortunately, practice time was over, and the instructors called our attention back to the center of the room to clarify some points and continue on with the lesson.

The room was packed with people; I felt like any way I turned, I would run into someone. As I stumbled and bumped into my partner, I apologized profusely for my unending mistakes. The instructors came around to my partner and me and physically moved us through the routine like parents disciplining little children. I watched the instructors move on to the next couple and force them into the routine. As one instructor offered to do the steps side by side with the couple, the other one yelled out, "Rotate!" and we all exchanged partners. Finally, class was over, and I walked to my car feeling frustrated, confused, and more insecure with my body than I'd felt the week before. Was it really this hard to dance? It was just a matter of moving your feet one after the other . . . how difficult could that be?

•

This class was held in a cramped classroom–turned–dance studio on the third floor of a Catholic school on the Near North Side of the city. The location offered cheap rent and several spaces, so there was the option of taking more than one class a night. Other classrooms on the third floor were used by performance groups such as comedy troupes, theatrical companies, and other dance groups. With its dusty plywood floor and large mirrors along one wall, the dance space was sparse and uninteresting. The effect of being in a school made the idea of dance class seem more formal than necessary, especially since this was a social dance class, for fun. The instructors arrived from their workday just as the students, and while they changed their shoes, they discussed what they'd be teaching that night. I gazed around the room and saw one guy working through the steps of last week's class by himself; he walked it through over and over as other couples worked together on the steps. This was a beginner-level Lindy Hop class, where the goal was to accomplish three basic moves: the Swing Out, Circle, and Swing Out from closed position. We partnered up and made four long rows of couples, with all the leaders facing the front wall so no one would hit each other when we began the choreography.

Choreography is a balance between executing formal, predetermined steps correctly and precisely while making that precision appear relaxed and effortless. Learning the basic choreography means learning the most basic elements upon which all other aspects of the dance are built. Choreography serves as the basic anchor of the dance, whereby a dancer executes set patterns, figures, and steps with her partner. By synchronizing these movements, both dancers understand where they should go and where they should end up in any given pattern. It is helpful to think of choreography from a bird's-eye view, to understand the patterns as outlines that dancers trace on the floor as they move. Because the movements must be coordinated and dancers must be correctly oriented to each other, much of the initial stage of social dancing is the memorization of basic positions, steps, and movements. Entering into the dance for the first time requires not only an immersion of the body in new knowledges, but also a retooling of the body at the most fundamental and imperceptible of levels.

The foundation of all Lindy Hop choreography is the basic stance and posture: feet are shoulder width apart and flat on the floor, with the dancer's weight slightly forward on the balls of the feet; knees are bent to ensure maximum stability and balance. This posture is maintained throughout the dance, and when done properly with feet directly below the torso, it is referred to as "using one's center" whereby the dancer keeps a solid and balanced body position, as in ballet or modern dance. When one first begins to learn any social dance, it is key for him to understand how far he actually moves his feet and how far he should move them. Beginners think they are taking tiny steps when in fact their steps are enormous. As the body becomes aware of itself and its surroundings and gains fluency in the dance, the steps become smaller and more precise. Because the Lindy Hop has a history in African American movement, the bounce or the compression of the body into the floor is counteracted by the way the top half remains, by contrast, still and motionless. This separation of the compressed lower body and the relatively calm upper torso allows the Lindy Hop to be both an expressive syncopated jazz dance and a social-partner dance. The amount of space maintained between partners is important; keeping an "imaginary center" between the partners provides a sense of togetherness, and dancing without this form results in recklessness and loss of control.

The learning of basic patterns often can become tedious, preventing one from seeing the forest through the trees, or the dance through the motions.

•

That night we went over the Swing Out through numerous exercises and drills. One of the instructor's most interesting exercises was to separate the men and women so we could practice the basic figure and steps of the Swing Out on our own. The drill was to practice the basic step by orienting ourselves on a line so that each time we turned we marked off 180 degrees, which would be like trading places with our real dance partners. In the Swing Out, the man is like a ballast and the woman moves around him, as if they're forming two concentric circles moving simultaneously one inside the other. The focus in this class was to help us get the "line" and "shape" of the figure, something I would later learn is the direction of movement and the basic positioning and steps that our bodies utilize to make the dance what it is.

That night we put together all three moves—the Swing Out, the Circle, and Swing Out from closed position. The instructors reminded me of drill sergeants as they called out the routine over the music. But eventually their screaming faded, and they left us to our own reconnaissance to work it out on our own. We repeated the same steps in a sequence over and over. Finally, after six weeks of classes and practicing these steps repeatedly, either here or at my apartment, I was putting all the figures together. Then the instructors began counting the music, and all sixty of us danced at the same time. From above it must have looked like amateur synchronized swimming or a mangled line of chorus dancers as we attempted to move in unison. While this may have been the social dance that everyone wanted to do, it looked nothing like the spontaneous and creative dancing I'd seen on that first night I watched the Lindy Hoppers at the Aragon Ballroom. Here it was all routine and formalization.

•

Social-dance choreography is inculcated through techniques that socialize the body into performing these patterns and positions. First, the moves are broken down and isolated into distinct individual movements so that students can practice the mechanics—the nuts and bolts—of the dance. Second, choreographed patterns or routines of steps—usually several basic steps with a variation in between—are set to music. The basics serve as a resting and regrouping period to set up the next variation. Instructors begin teaching choreography using music with slower tempos; then they increase the tempo to drill the steps into the students. These methods for learning choreography rely on the technique of mimicry; learning to dance is about learning how to reproduce the visuals you see before you. Sometimes one will dance behind the teacher to learn a step, watching and repeating what the instructor does. The goal is to learn set movements and to socialize your body to move through a symmetrical process the way that you see it being taught in front of you. There is a tension in choreography, in trying to make it second nature, which exists between the deliberate execution of the patterns and the need to make those movements appear unrehearsed.

A common technique for teaching choreography is to use numbers to isolate the movements within a particular figure: left foot 1, right foot 2, left–right–left on 3 and 4. By counting out the music and applying the parts of the pattern to a count in the song, the body can learn the steps through a "paint-by-numbers" approach, in which certain movements must occur at a specific time and place in the music. As one Lindy Hop instructor remarked during a Lindy Hop workshop in Cleveland,

You can use the numbers—I use the numbers for people who want them or need them to be explained in that way—it's just how you use the numbers that is important. I can say 1–2–3–4–5–6–7–8, but I will say it according to the melody or in terms of the music so that every number isn't given the same stress of feeling. That's the problem when people rely on the numbers in teaching—it just loses all its feeling in the process.

Being strict with the steps and counts is often necessary and helpful when learning the basic structure of the dance, yet if taken to the extreme it becomes too perfunctory and one risks flattening out the dance and the expression in the music.

In social dancing there is no formal mandate for practice time. The dedicated practice time at the beginning of the process is not communal; it is individual. When I was first learning how to dance, I would come home, turn on some swing music, and drill the basic steps over and over to various tempos. Later I told my students that when I was starting out, I would pull the shades down so my neighbors could not see me practicing in front of the mirror. A fellow student told me that when he was first learning how to dance, he would practice at work by pushing around a wheeled office chair that he pretended was his partner. Another student held a broom in his left hand and danced around it as if it were his partner.

The result is that one learns the basic choreography both in class and through individual practice, but at this point these movements are still far from being a social dance. One knows what to do ideally, but there is not yet a "social" aspect to it, as people are just working through the choreography for themselves at this point. In addition, since everything is scripted and there is no spontaneity to the dance yet, the dancing still looks perfunctory. Each of the individual's moves can be clearly seen in his or her own enactment of the patterns as each step is brought to consciousness with little blending from one step to another. Because it is all choreographed at this point, it is still just individuals dancing patterns without any real social interaction.

After completing the beginner class, one has learned the basic concepts of Lindy Hop dancing. However, at this stage the dance is still raw and uncultivated; it is only through hours and hours of practice that it will become inscribed in the body. In order to move to the next level of dancing, from class novice to accepted social dancer, one must master these essential basics and embody them as second nature. Once this has occurred, a dancer can establish himself on the social dance scene as someone who goes out, dances, and has a firm grasp of the basics, making the transition from beginning dance student to someone who is accepted and acknowledged as a social dancer, someone who is developing a feel for the game.

Leading and Following

•

Standing at the edge of the dance floor, I leaned back against the wall of the crowded bar, careful not to stick out or look too eager. I avoided any gestures or eye contact that might suggest I wanted to get out there and dance. I tried to make small talk with a few people around me while scanning the room for someone from my dance class, someone who might have felt like I did, nervous and intimidated. I wondered if I should have even come here. If I went out on the floor, would I freeze up and stop dancing for fear of forgetting what to do? The last thing I wanted to do was to embarrass myself and prove my incompetence in front of the very people with whom I eventually wanted to dance. I could only do about six steps, and it felt like I had to count out the steps verbally when I did them, so I wouldn't get off beat. I couldn't wait until I didn't have to do that anymore! Suddenly I recognized someone at the end of the bar. I decided to go hang out with him until I was more comfortable; this was just too intimidating. I'd have a drink and watch from over there. That way there was less chance of being asked to dance.

•

Leading and following refers to the basic communication between dance partners. It is the basic action and reaction whereby dancers listen and respond to each other's bodily cues, which convey information about where, when, and how to move. There is always a tension between anticipation and comprehension, between knowing when and how to respond in the moment, that must be balanced against the knowledge of the possible figures that precede it. As dancers develop better bodily communication, they must also work to make their choreography transparent. What makes the dance so dynamic is the ability to act and respond by executing the choreography in an infinite number of combinations, to strike a balance between communication and anticipation, between the predefined steps of choreography and the openness of partners communicating. When the balance between leading and following is not achieved, the conversational aspect of the dance is blocked from being realized.

•

All eyes were focused on the center of the room as the instructors demonstrated the next figure, going through the motions of the step several times. Once they had broken down the choreographed footwork, they demonstrated the "lead and follow" technique, in which the partners execute physical signals and cues to indicate direction and timing. After we spent several minutes practicing with different partners, the instructors stopped the music and pointed out the excessive movements of the flailing students around them. They called our attention back to the center of the room, aiming to correct our mistakes by demonstrating the figure over and over again, emphasizing what we were supposed to do and how. Several utterances of "It looks like this" and "Try to move this way" or "Get your body here, so she can go there" were repeated. The instructors said to the leads, "Make sure you lead the followers," and to the followers, "Don't anticipate. Make sure you feel the lead before you go." Doing the steps seemed hard enough; now we also had to think about doing them to the music while leading and following.

•

The transition from the classroom to the social dance floor is difficult. At this awkward stage, students have mastered the basic choreography—they know how to do the steps—and they must next learn how to actually lead and follow these steps in the dance. This stage can cause major tension between partners; this is when the dance advances to a new level and becomes more about communicating with one's partner. As both a student and an instructor, I would overhear couples literally arguing with each other on the dance floor about whose fault it was that they missed a step or a lead, throwing them off track. "She helps too much." "He doesn't help enough." Women yelled at men and men yelled at women. I, too, experienced this frustration when I was a student. I would find myself wondering, am I leading too much? Not enough? Is she actually following my lead, or is she just doing what they taught us comes next?

Almost all Lindy Hop veterans agree that the most important part of the dance is its social aspect: not how many moves or tricks one knows, but one's ability to lead and follow and enjoy dancing with another person. One instructor that I interviewed in San Francisco defined leading and following as the most important of all the components:

> It is the lifeblood—the heart of the dance—the meat of the dance—the feeling. It is so important to get the feel for your partner's skills and abilities—how they feel in your arms, how they move their bodies—how they respond to you. Are they light or heavy, strong or soft? You have to get a feel for them and let them get a feel for you, so that you can find that pocket of the music together, so you're on the same page about this. Don't just start in and do all of your tricks and try to impress her, because then you're not dancing with her—then you're not focusing on her; you lose the

connection. Then there's nothing there, and she might as well be dancing alone. You must establish the connection; you must keep the connection the whole time you're dancing—it must be consistent. It is the life blood, the heart of the dance—it starts here and runs through my arm, through her arm, into her. We share the same blood—we share the same heart— what I feel, she feels, and what she feels, I feel. We are together—we are connected here—and that's the meat of the dance that makes it so special.

The connection between partners occurs on three levels. First, it occurs between the partners physically, as they must learn to listen, respond, and assist each other in the dance. Cultivating this kinesthetic awareness is necessary to anticipate and feel the movement of other bodies in motion around you. By learning to apply pressure with the hands or to respond to pressure or the feeling of a body in motion, one can learn to "hear" or communicate without saying a word. It is this ability to sense each other, to feel shifts in weight and direction, that is crucial to leading and following. This idea of "connection" between a leader and a follower is the nonverbal communication that lets one's partner know how and when to move. Second, partners must cultivate a mental connection, by focusing on each other and being present for the other person. This deep mental awareness makes the dance intimate, as people must become aware of each other in new ways. Third, there is a connection between partners as they try to enjoy and interpret the music together. In order to master the dance, both partners must work together physically and mentally while simultaneously responding to the music. Virginie Jenssen, Master Instructor and dance partner of Steven Mitchell, expressed these concerns about connection in this way:

> When the guys start putting in all this fancy footwork, it ends it, because I don't know what they are doing half the time, you are supposed to be dancing with your partner, you are supposed to be connected and that doesn't just mean holding hands. You and your partner are supposed to be connected through your minds and your soul; if you feel him going one way, and as a follow I'm waiting, and he doesn't do anything I just stand there. If you want me to come toward you, you have to use some leverage and pull me towards you. I don't mean rip my arm off like some caveman, but use compression, it's physics, if you want me to come forward you need to indicate that, if you want me to go away you have to push me away, I mean we can put all those fancy steps into the dance, that's fine, but let's get back to the reality of what this is about. Why dance if you feel no connection. I might as well go stand in the corner.

These three levels of awareness must become so ingrained that they are forgotten, so that one can dance without reflexivity and self-awareness and instead focus attention on the music and the interaction with one's dance partner. This social aspect cannot be perfected through formal training alone; it is the result of time and labor, of practicing with many different partners on the social floor.

Learning to lead and follow comes from repetitious exercises that teach a dancer how to respond to a partner. Although the dance is "semi"-choreographed, it must be led and followed. Dancers cannot merely "do" the choreography for the dance to be and feel correct. One must labor to complement, listen to, and understand the other person through physical connection. Both participants must work to establish the tension between their bodies that enables them to communicate back and forth, to be led and followed in a constant state of assessment of oneself, one's partner, and the music. Once dancers are able to lead and follow at even a basic level, they will get asked to dance all the time. Two veteran social dancers explained during a dance workshop in Chicago,

> The difference between being an accepted social dancer and just a beginner is you go from people running *from* you to running *at* you, to fill their dance card or ask for reservations for dances that night—they want you to save them a dance. Where you first start as a follower it's more like a rollercoaster, because you don't know what's coming next. But once you become a social dancer, you feel in control and can respond and don't need to know what's coming next; you can play off your partner. There's no longer any anxiety and it's much more fun.
>
> As a leader you move from having to think it through all the time—ahead of everything—so that you plan everything out. When you get to be thought of as a social dancer, at that stage you've done it enough where you can just enjoy dancing without all the thinking, because you're focused on listening to the music.

One thing that instructors do agree on is that Lindy Hop is about social dancing. Despite the concern for technique and nuance, it is still a social dance, not a professional activity, and is meant to be enjoyed. This social emphasis comes through in dance classes as teachers urge their students to go out dancing; one instructor bluntly says

> It's of no use to you unless you go out and use it, otherwise you won't remember what you've learned. Just because we're showing you this in a

workshop doesn't mean you only do it here. That's the whole point about social dancing, what we do in here is to help you connect better with people out there; but we can go over and over it, but if you don't get out and practice it with different people you won't really understand it. We can show you, but it's up to you to use it—not in here—out there.

An aspiring Lindy Hopper must constantly condition himself and practice the steps, movements, and leading and following to such an extent that it becomes second nature through time spent social dancing. While one can work on dancing alone, there is no substitute for the actual experience of social dancing.

At the leading and following stage, the dancer is able to balance the anticipation of leading and following, the bodily communication, and the predetermination of the choreography and scripted steps. By developing this aspect of the feel for the game, a new practical sense emerges whereby the dancer can move to the next level of the dance and concentrate on interpreting the music and improvising. Once a person becomes a solid social dancer and has mastered the choreography, attention can be turned toward mastering other aspects of the dance.

Improvisation

•

I remember being on the dance floor with a particular female dancer who was much more advanced than I was at the time. Right in the middle of the song, she stopped following me and started dancing her own steps. I couldn't believe it. There I was, leading her through the song, trying as hard as I could to impress her with what I'd learned, and she suddenly decided to improvise on her own. She looked at me and said, "It's a break . . . you're supposed to let me play here." (A "break" is a period in the dance that allows the dancers to improvise and create their own individualized interpretations. Usually this is where the leader offers space, both physical and temporal, for the follower to show off or "play" with the music, or where the leader performs his own creative break.) I stood there, dumbfounded. What was I supposed to do? What did she mean by "play"? I was trying to lead her, but she had decided that something else was going to happen. She encouraged me, "Keep moving; don't just stand there. Improvise!" What? Improvise? "I don't know how to improvise," I yelled back over the music. I tried to mirror her steps, but this obviously did not please her. She frowned and derisively let me know that I was not supposed to do the same thing she was doing; the point was to improvise on my own. I knew the basic steps, and I could lead and follow, but what was this improvisation stuff? No one had ever taught me this.

•

The balance between choreography and leading and following generates a new level of tension when we consider the next crucial component of the Lindy Hop—improvisation. This component of creativity and scripted spontaneity, whereby dancers must express themselves individually instead of just repeating patterns, requires balancing the individualism of improvisation with the structured framework of partnered social dance. At this third stage of the dance, after mastering and balancing the knowledge of choreography and the leading and following, improvising within the framework becomes the most important component on which to focus. This new challenge requires managing self-expression while working within the established framework. When this occurs, the dance takes on a new level of intricacy and playfulness, as the dancers can now dance together while also interpreting movements and music in different ways that are no longer dependent on each other. Dancers, much like skilled jazz musicians, must come to learn how to maintain a delicate balance between autonomy and partnership which when brought into alignment is one of the most difficult challenges to master.[13] If these components are not all balanced against each other, like the music for jazz musicians, the dance for dancers constantly breaks down. Constant practical self and group awareness is required to maintain this cohesion and avoid letting the dance become too individualistic, too improvisational, placing one individual outside the structure of the collective on one hand, and too formulaic or repetitious, leading to a mundane predictability on the other.

I once asked Lennart Westerlund (one of the founding members of the famous Swedish performance troupe the Rhythm Hot Shots, and one of the most improvisational and rhythmic dancers in the Lindy Hop world) about how he mastered the improvisational aspect. I told him how hard it was for me to learn and wondered if he could offer advice. He laughed and said he asked the same question of Frankie Manning:

> I asked Frankie about how he made up his steps. I asked him to show me once, and he said, "I don't know, I just make them up on the spot." This is very foreign to the way we as Swedes think about the dance today. We are so cerebral . . . . It is something that I work on. I spend a lot of time working on the rhythms of music in my dancing, listening to the music, and trying

new ways of emphasizing it. It certainly does not come natural to me. I suppose it does for some people, but certainly not for me.

Although the Lindy Hop has basic choreography, the central impulse behind the dance is to improvise and interpret the music. It is the tension between the patterns and improvisation, knowing how and when to improvise within that structure, which makes the Lindy Hop the signature "jazz" dance. The improvisational aspect occurs at almost any point in the dance during which each dancer has the ability and freedom to interpret the music. Improvising requires understanding the music and navigating time and space as one moves around, not only with one's partner but with other couples on the dance floor. Only by cultivating this practical sense, through knowledge and experience of the game, can one be in tune with the rhythm of the dance in order to improvise correctly (Bourdieu 1990a, 75). This means, for example, knowing when to break, when to Swing Out, and when to accentuate an instrument in the song. It means being able to manipulate time through the anticipation of future possibilities, combining different steps, breaking with time in terms of syncopation, interpreting the music, and keeping the balance between two people dancing as individuals and dancing together without breaking the flow of the dance (Bourdieu and Wacquant 1992, 128). This ability to improvise to break out in a spontaneous creativity, interpreting music on time and as if one was not consciously thinking about it. As one expert Lindy Hop dancer expressed that he felt this was the pinnacle and most important aspect of the dance to master:

> It is all about improvising, to be able to make up what you want to do, there is nothing better. Anybody can just do the same old patterns, but when you can do your own thing, that's the true sign of a dancer. I find so much of it so boring and confining sometimes, like I have to do this move or that and I just think I want to do it my way, screw the "framework" and all the rest of it. I look out and I see somebody doing their own thing, just doing whatever and I think that's what the dance is about, that ability to do your own thing, but still be doing the dance.

Another influential International instructor echoed a similar theme:

> I guess I'm probably in the minority here, but I think we need less structure in the dance. That's the thing with this dance, it is so free-spirited, it's like a Hell's Angel on a bike. It wants to go where it wants to go and you

can't tell it not to; you can't control it. It's jazz. It's creative by nature. You can try, but really who is to say what the rules are anyways.

To be comfortable improvising means that the dancer has mastered the basics to such a degree that the dance is no longer simply an amalgamation of steps or individual pieces. The dancer generates improvisation by producing the "correct" action and is able to anticipate future possibilities within the current social constraints in which the body exists, where the dancer and the dance are completely aligned and the dancer displays his or her true feel for the game at its zenith (Bourdieu 2000b, 139).

Improvisation is one of the most elusive and misrecognized aspects of dance. It is the extemporaneous ability to create movement and interpret the music in that moment, without calculation and without predefined routines. Executing movements by way of certain figures, patterns, and steps is never an arbitrary or spontaneous outburst—it is always undertaken within the framework of a bodily knowledge that informs the possibility of such movements and the parameters within which these movements can occur. It is only when this bodily knowledge is misrecognized as natural, when bodily movement appears spontaneous and uncalculated, that it appears to emanate seamlessly from the dancer without the need for conscious reflection.

When I started dancing, I watched others and marveled at how they knew to do specific movements or how they knew that the music would pause or change. The dance seemed too free and extemporaneous for it to have a set structure. How did the dancers improvise all of that? Learning to improvise is one of the most ironic aspects of the dance, because improvising is, in the end, always constrained within the structured framework of the dance. This practical mastery of the game appears random and unrehearsed, but in reality it is the cultivation of years of experimentation and experience with the game (Bourdieu 1990b, 61). Dancers begin by undertaking the bodily labor of mimicry by copying the breaks and syncopations of more experienced dancers; they also spend time learning the structure of the music they are dancing to and even memorize the canon of songs played at dances, down to the nuances and accents in particular songs. In fact, the trained eye can immediately spot advanced dancers because they just seem to know, or anticipate, when the music will break or change before it actually does. As one top dancer, known for his incredible improvisation skills, told me during an interview in Chicago:

It's just practice. Look at how long I've been doing this compared to you. I just know more; I've spent hundreds if not thousands of hours social dancing, just trying stuff out. You just come to learn it after a while, what goes where, what you can and can't do, what fits and what doesn't. You just keep trying stuff; sometimes it works, sometimes it doesn't. But it's not some magic secret or anything; it's just the experience of a whole lot of time out there just doing it. I know I put a lot of work into it.

Improvisation is acquired and practiced through the cultivation of the body into a naturalized appearance of spontaneity, which belies a carefully disciplined bodily knowledge that has become internalized and partially unconscious.

Mastery of improvisation comes at the point when so much of the choreography has been embodied that a dancer surprises himself by what he can do and when he can do it. At this point, the dance is second nature, and it is easier to let the body flow well all night. Now the dancer is able to dance and relax at the same time. Having this embodied understanding of improvisation takes dancing to the next level of complexity and frees the dancer from having to consciously consider the choreography or the leading and following, which are now part of the dancer's established feel for the game. This allows the dancer to focus only on interpreting and playing with the music.

While mastery of improvisation is a massive accomplishment, balancing this competence with the other components of the dance is often not achieved. Many dancers take the ability of improvising too far; sometimes people forget about the partner-dancing aspect and improvise all the time. One instructor commented on the tendency for dancers to overdo improvisation during an interview I conducted with her in Stockholm:

> To us it is like disco dancing. I can't follow any of the leaders because they aren't leading. They are just dancing by themselves. I think they expect me to know what they are doing. So I just stand there. That isn't social dancing to me—not Lindy Hop, anyway. It's like we're not even in the same place or dancing to the same song. Yeah, we think it's like disco dancing, where you dance by yourself. I think that it gets boring if you dance with someone and they do the basic all night, but at least you're dancing with them. I mean, I would rather do basic for the whole song than try and dance in that style. It just doesn't make any sense to me.

When the dance misfires and becomes overly improvisational, it is no longer a social dance that is led and followed. Often, too much showing off occurs, and everything about the dance becomes tricky and complicated; there is no longer any basic step or pattern to be followed. The dance then folds back in on itself. Another instructor has lamented this on numerous occasions. During an interview on Catalina Island he remarked,

People get so wrapped up in doing all these moves that they don't allow the dance to breathe—they go for the kill right away—and the music doesn't say that; the music builds and flows. But people miss that in an attempt to show off to their partner or to others by bringing out all their tricks right at the beginning. You've got to build and relax, so that when you do tricky things it means more and fits into the dynamic of the dance—without that you're just doing a bunch of steps, so what's the point then? There is too much going on now. Everybody is doing their own thing, everybody wants to get all this movement in it and all these tricks. They don't let it swing, it just doesn't swing anymore.

In a different interview, conducted in Cleveland when we were discussing what appeared to be a growing trend among dancers toward overimprovisation, he commented,

It's about the feeling, the connection; the rest of it's extra—it's not in the tricks; it's in the basic. We've lost the feeling that makes it swing. It's here in the Swing Out. If you get bored with that, then that is something inside of you, not with the dance. If you get tired of that or bored with that, it's on you, 'cause that's what makes it swing. If you forget where you came from, you lose everything.

What the great dancers achieve is a masterful balance between the ability to improvise and create and the limits of the framework of partner dancing. They appear to be dancing freely all the time, to be embodying the feel for the game in its fullest potential, even as they remain within the structure of the dance.

Style

•

About fifty of us were circled around the instructor. As I looked around, I reflected that it was strange to be in a dance class without a partner, in a room filled only with men. I could see the others exchanging glances, expressing the same uneasiness about what we were supposed to be doing. This was a men's "styling" class, held in Denver, and we were here to focus on the aesthetic of our own individual movement.

Styling classes serve two purposes. First, they try to help dancers become more comfortable with their own bodily movement. Second, they cultivate a more "swinging" form of expression through a dancer's movement. As our instructor said to us that day,

The dance is about expressing yourself through the movement. So many of you guys dance so small, so restrained. It's so tight. I want you to open up your dancing, to open up your movements, to let them breathe. Everyone is so focused on what they have to do that you don't relax; you hold it in. You hold back and don't let yourselves fully commit to the movement. There's no follow through. You've got to follow through. I want you guys to focus on that—following through all the movements.

The instructor ran through a series of simple jazz steps that most of us knew and asked us to watch closely the way he moved his arms, torso, and hips. He encouraged us to notice all the shapes and lines that he made with his body as he executed the steps. After we learned the short routine, he asked us to extend ourselves by doing the steps in bigger and more exaggerated ways. Then, after warming us up through these exercises, he introduced a completely new routine, telling us to follow along as we'd been doing. These new steps were not traditional Lindy Hop moves at all; they seemed more like modern dance or even hip hop. Looking around the room, I could see other dancers struggling with the steps—some looking as if they were out of control, others restrained to the point where it looked as if they were barely executing the routine. These awkward movements were forcing me into positions I couldn't ever recall dancing. How could I follow through the movements when I couldn't even *do* the movements? The purpose was to work on our styling. How was doing this going to help my style?

•

Style is the most elusive Lindy Hop category to discuss. This is where bodily labor reaches its greatest payoff, as the body itself becomes aestheticized, like a personal signature—your own way of interpreting the dance that people can identify. The process of developing style requires the dancer to reach a balance between the poles of mimicry and eccentricity, between copying the way another dancer moves and therefore being simply derivative of someone else, and at the same time working within the aesthetic framework of the dance that defines the movements of the Lindy Hop. Style is not something extra over and above the dance, nor is it something autonomous or separate; in fact, it is present in the very basic steps—in the very leading and following of the dance. Style is not just a few moves or individual steps that a dancer creates, but the way his or her body is consistently carried throughout their dancing. When one reaches the level at which one can focus solely on style, all the pieces of the dance meld together and one generates a distinctive identity, a unique mode of self-expression and creativity.

Style, like improvisation, is an act of mimesis, or mimicking the instructor as he demonstrates what is correct and proper. This act of mimicking steps is as much about doing what the teacher says as it is emulating what the teacher does with his body. One must physically replicate what the instructor does and then also replicate the way he did it by inculcating what is "good." Teaching the body how to move in the "correct" way (any number of dance competences can be noted here: posture, stance, fluidity, rhythm, and being on time with the music) directly shapes the way the body moves. At this stage, it is no longer the steps that people are watching or seeking to emulate; instead they desire the instructor's manner—what it is that makes him unique and, for those elite masters of the dance, awe-inspiring to watch. Discussions of style among dancers often lead to arguments over which or whose style is "the best." As one instructor remarked during an interview in Chicago,

When people get into the whole styling thing, it really is just personal choice. I don't think there is one style to the dance, it's just who you like; there is no one style. If you look at the elite teachers, you have everything—it's all across the board. They run the whole spectrum. You have all these different periods, in a way. The Rhythm Hot Shots—groups like them are great because they keep the old-school classic stuff that defined Lindy Hop in its day—but that's what they do. And Ryan and Jenny, they bring their own style; it's not classic, but they have this clean style that's big movements and very crisp. And then there are people like Frankie who is strong and powerful, and then people like Steven who is so creative and improvisational. So I mean, all of the very elite teachers have their own styles that are very distinct, but it all works, I mean, it all fits within the dance.

During an interview in Los Angeles, another veteran dancer commented,

I understand it [the debates over style]. You copy the top dancers; they're the best. They teach the master classes, why wouldn't you? You learn to move, but when you don't know how, you have to start somewhere, you have to model someone. I think that's the biggest influence, who you start learning from, and that's why it's so important to take classes from all the top instructors, so you can see all the differences. But everyone has a favorite. I think that's okay. That's how you learn. But to say that one has a better style or that the dance has to be danced a certain way is absolute craziness. Once people get beyond that stage, they start to open up and then they start to find their own identity in the dance. My view of the Lindy Hop isn't to be just like, you know, what it was in the '40s or '30s or whatever. Because you know, when they were inventing the dance, they weren't saying, "I want it to be looking just like this." They were saying, "Let's make this something that no one else does"; each dancer was working out their own interpretation. That's why there were so many styles, because there was that spirit of individualism of expression. It's about expressing yourself in the dance. And I think that's the spirit we should have.

Learning in formal classes is about replicating what the instructors do; this learning by mimesis entails the replication of movement the way the instructor is teaching it. Because the dance is learned body to body, it is never entirely about what intentionally goes on in people's heads; dancers don't necessarily know their bodies well enough to understand how to define their own style or expression through the dance.

Learning by mimicry also creates a certain handicap that can undermine a dancer's quest for self-expression. During an interview at a dance camp in Chicago, one instructor commented in frustration:

> What works for one person doesn't work for everybody. What one person does looks great on them, but then you see others do it. It comes from the top. The top teachers set the tone. Everybody picks one of them, whoever, and then they copy them. Everyone is a disciple of someone. The dance has become homogenous because people make themselves carbon copies of other people, because that's what they learn, to imitate. I don't think they realize it. The top instructors probably don't see that as a detriment, but I do. The dance has lost its spirit of originality. Look at Whitey's Lindy Hoppers on film. Frankie is the only one doing that "bent over, lean out" thing. He's the only one that did that. He did his thing. Every one of them is different, but when you look in a classroom situation and these camps today, everybody looks exactly the same.

Another international instructor I interviewed at Herräng shared this perspective on the issue of mimicry:

> I feel honored that people want to be like me. I like the way I'm dancing. I'm satisfied with my style, and if someone else likes it, that's good, but you shouldn't copy people 100 percent. You should pick what you like and then make something that's your own, even if you're like Mickey [Mickey Sayles, one of the great dancers from the Whitey's Lindy Hoppers dance troupe]. I don't look like her, but I've tried to do what I like about her. But I'm not doing exactly what she does. Because if you try to be someone else,

that's not honest; you are not someone else. You should keep this feeling that it's my way and do what fits you best. Even in the performance group, we don't have the same background, even style-wise, because we have our own personality. I think that's really important.

This tension between mimicry and individualism is a never-ending battle. On the one hand, since we learn bodily, a dancer has to learn by modeling herself on someone else; we are shaped by the bodies we learn from no matter how conscious we are of that fact. Yet too much imitation leads a dancer to have no identity of her own. One veteran instructor/dancer expressed this sense of too much imitation:

It does bother me. It Ahh! It kills me when people say, "Well, Frankie [Manning] said this," or "Frankie said that," and therefore that's the way it is. Ahhh! It kills me when people say that because I'm like Frankie was one of thousands of dancers out there and just because Frankie says so doesn't mean it is right. It makes it Frankie's style. I love his heart and I love the way he dances, but I don't dance like Frankie at all. I don't want to dance like him, even in his time I don't necessarily think it was Frankie's style over everybody else's styles. You know Frankie is clean and powerful, I'm not clean and powerful; I'm messy and creative. Not to take anything away from Frankie, but to say that his style is the way to dance is just ridiculous and it kills me because it just kills the whole style of the dance overall, because everyone thinks Frankie's way is the only way.

This mimicry creates a limitation whereby the logic of the dance as an artistic expression is lost because the dancer has no voice of her own. This incongruity between learning the dance and being able to express oneself individually prevents dancers from reaching the highest levels of the dance. The inability to master this tension leads to a constant discord, because dancers do not develop their own expressive capacities or cultivate their own emotions through their bodies.

Style is not a matter fundamentally of conscious choice, because when one learns the dance one is learning the style of the dance at the same time. Ironically, this works for a dancer in this way: he learns to dance the way he has been taught by his initial instructors. But then, once he masters the basics, he must develop and learn to adapt and perceive subtle changes that need to be made to the specific way his body dances. In regards to developing this practical sense, one instructor commented in an interview in Palm Springs,

What helps is when you do something else like jazz or ballet. It makes a difference to take other types of dance classes to stretch your understanding
of your body. Doing different dances is so good for that. We get so locked
into what we think we are doing, and we lose our awareness. People need
to learn to watch and train themselves; they need to analyze for themselves how they dance, like when my old partners and I would repeatedly
watch videos of ourselves dancing. Usually I have to teach by actually moving people; if you determine everything, that's no fun. They have to learn
by imitation to start, but you have to express yourself your own way in the
end. We can show you the movements, but we can't convey the emotions.
You have to learn to feel, and that can only come from you.

Style means developing an eye for the dance, a practical sense; style means
being able to interpret movement and evaluate the quality of that movement. This cultivation of the practical sense is where one learns to see
angles of the body, body positioning, and bodily shapes. Developing this
practical sense enables dancers to monitor their own dancing and to cultivate the dance in themselves through their own self-scrutiny. In learning to
stylize one's movement, dancers have a number of strategies to assist them.
They videotape themselves dancing with a partner in order to scrutinize
their movements, often by freeze-framing and slowly advancing the tape
so each step can be examined and each bodily position inspected. Dancers
also spend a great deal of time in front of a mirror, rehearsing their steps.
In the process, they see themselves dancing and develop a bodily awareness
through their own self-critique. This fine-tuning of the corporeal schema
enables dancers to see the aesthetic minutia of other dancers as well as of
their own bodies. Through a highly tuned bodily awareness, dancers can
constantly monitor and adjust their bodies to produce the most aesthetically pleasing presentations.

CONCLUSION

•

The band was really swingin' tonight—in fact, it was the best I had ever
heard them sound, and I felt like I was dancing at my best as well. After
dancing more than a dozen songs with different partners, I finally located
Julie, the one woman I wanted to dance with, across the room. As the song
ended, I made a break for it and intercepted her before she was asked to
dance by someone else. I had waited all evening for this, and I was thrilled
that I had finally caught up with her. We did the Swing Out several times to

get a feel for each other. Dancing with her was elating; she was an expert and made me feel as if I could do no wrong. We moved symmetrically across the floor, as I led and she followed; we mirrored each other like mimes, effortlessly turning and circling each other. Each movement led into another as the conversation of dancing was elevated to a new level: I sent her in one direction and she played off that movement, suggesting new possibilities, and I responded in turn as we exchanged ideas. We danced as if it were purely instinctual, as if we knew ahead of time what the other would do, constantly creating and improvising off each other as we hit all the breaks, syncopations, and accents in the music.

This feeling of seamlessness between a dancer, his partner, and the music is when a dancer becomes completely absorbed in the dance, feeling as if the music were written just for him and his partner, as if the dance floor were his alone. Dances like these evoke feelings of flying through the air, where everything is transparent, creativity is unbounded, and nothing else matters. Here, in this moment, the artistry of the dance is realized: we are expressing our own thoughts and interpretations of the music through our bodies, and yet we work effortlessly together, complementing and elevating each other's dancing. These moments in which two bodies meld together in time and space, where all the poles of the dance come together, where the choreography, leading and following, improvisation, and style are all in complete alignment without misfiring—these are the moments that enable dancers to reach the pinnacle of personal and aesthetic expression. It is this elusive connection that dancers strive for in every dance and only rarely achieve. This one dance with Julie—this partner, this music—made me truly fall in love with the Lindy Hop, as I tasted its finest fruit for the first time.

•

The complexity of the Lindy Hop as a cultural form makes its mastery elusive. Each of the four analytic categories requires constant labor to maintain and refine. What makes the Lindy Hop so dynamic is what also makes the dance so liberating when it is done correctly. Throughout this analysis, I have focused on the labor required to learn the dance. Analytically, this is much more easily dissected than the dancer dancing perfectly in sync, because the complexity of the dance leads to constant missteps or discordance between dancers and the dance. Master execution is under constant threat from the breakdown of one of the four components; one of the dancers may not know the choreography, one partner may not be communicating or listening well, one dancer may be too individualistic and thus limit the creativity of his partner, or they may have different styles that do not complement one another. All these tensions must be balanced for the dance to work and be executed seamlessly. So much can misfire that there is rarely a time when one is completely seamless with the dance.

When a dancer finally reaches the stage at which he can pull all these elements together, it often comes as a surprise; he has worked so long and so hard that he has actually forgotten all that he has learned and internalized. Since all components of the dance have been socializing the body at the same time, focusing on the cultivation of one component does not necessarily lead to the exclusion of the other. When all these aspects come together on a certain night of dancing, when someone has danced so much that it all becomes embodied and natural, the practice can feel qualitatively different. The dance can flow freely from the body as if the dancer was unconscious, making him feel as if the dance were truly natural or instinctual. An expert Chicago Lindy Hop dancer and instructor put it this way: "Oh man, there's nothing else like it. It's why you love the dance. I mean, when you get in that zone, when it all flows, everything is right there in the music and you can do no wrong. It's just like total freedom. It's like you can't even put words on it."

Dancers have several different ways of describing this experience. All of these descriptions try to articulate the underlying harmony between the body, the dance, their partner, and the surrounding spatial-temporal context within which the dance takes shape—the feeling of complete transparency and ease of action in the field, the complete alignment in the moment. Many describe this feeling of seamlessness as being "in the zone," a popular expression used by many athletes. Here in the zone it is possible to do anything: one can create on the spot, interpret the music, and enjoy the pleasure of dance on a different level. Here in the groove anything works and one feels free—a sensation that some dancers refer to as a feeling of "flying." What makes the cultivated dancer live for more dancing, as if it were a drug, is the completeness and the fulfillment of being able to find unity in the synchronicity of music, rhythm, and body.

Here in the zone the choreography, the timing, and the counting are let go, and the music makes sense in a new way. Similar to realizing that he is fluent in a language, with confidence and ease the dancer can open himself to new modalities of expression. The feel for the game that has come through endless repetition and accumulation over time produces progress without being able to measure those results precisely. In the moment, the realization of the body comes before one's full mental cognizance of what has been learned. This "cultivated instinct" allows the body to respond and to adjust to new developments in the field without mediation as it understands, judges, and reacts all at once. Responsiveness and adaptability come through the embodied dance sensibility, which is not through calculation but rather rooted in the dance disposition that has been inculcated.

The dance comes without struggle and without consciousness; dancers often describe this in shorthand with the expressions "feelin' it" or "being on." These expressions work to describe both a previous dance, "We were feelin' it," or a sense of seamlessness: "I'm on" or "We were on during that song." There is the full dynamic of partner dancing, where dance is more like a conversation; the more fluent one is, the more in-depth and complexly one can express one's thoughts. The interaction of complementing and relating to each other—being together in the moment in a comfortable relationship—defines dancing, as partners exchange ideas and interact, expressing themselves to each other through the dance.

When one is dancing in the zone, the most useful metaphor that teachers employ as an aid in learning the music also depicts that sense of seamlessness. Many describe this sensation as "being an instrument in the band" or "playing inside the music." Like a musician, the dancer is playing within the structure of the dance, improvising both in time and in key. This melding of two bodies in time and space is a knowledge that cannot be completely described, only felt and understood through the dancing body. It is here in these moments where all the interrelated components of the dance meld together in a synergistic whole. Here the practical sense of dance that has been acquired allows the dancers to move to the music and with each other as if they knew what was to come next, as if they could anticipate both music and movement. As Steven Mitchell responded to my interview question on the synthesis of the dance:

> I think that is one of the things we don't do enough of and I think we need to strive for better integration of that, to really work with the musicians on this, too ... to get that collaboration between everyone, that give and take, that conversation, if we could get more of that in the scene it would be ... ooooh [smiling, clenching fists and bringing them close to his chest] because it is all part of one thing, there's no difference, it is just parts of the whole. And that's all of it, when you get everybody in that groove, in that pocket, I mean that is what it is all about. Man, when the band is in the groove and the dancers find the pocket and it all sets in ... I mean when it really sets in, when everybody is working, you know working together, it just takes it (the dance and the environment of the dance) to a whole other level. That's what Savoy style is.

When you, your partner, the music, and the dance all converge in time and space, cultural forms like the Lindy Hop are not superimposed upon the dancers nor are they following explicit rules or formalized techniques learned in the past; rather, culture is enacted through the body. The dancer and the dance become one and the same.

Here we can see how the consciousness of dancing is not the same as the consciousness of learning the dance. It is of a different form and understanding of the body. It is a new relationship to one's body. Undertaking the process of becoming a dancer shows us about practices, inculcation, and the relation between body, theory, and practice, to get at bodily knowledge that is outside the immediate realm of consciousness. Socially fluent Lindy Hop dancers have embodied a disposition of temporality of movement and music, as they become adjusted to the field and able to flow with the music while provoking and responding to each other without verbal expression. Skilled dancers take in the music and work through it as a medium to which they are attuned, maximizing their skills and sensibilities to and with each other in time. Dance cannot truly be studied from the outside since it is by nature something that unfolds in time and plays with time—to take it out of time is to distort and take out of context. Only by analyzing the Lindy Hop in this way can we come to understand how all forms of social interaction are the synergistic interaction of multiple techniques and skills that come together in the moment without our conscious awareness.

As we will see, it will be these very issues of consciousness and conscious awareness that take on a very different life of their own. As the opening words of Ralph Ellison at the beginning of this chapter portend, dance is an activity that may look one way to one set of eyes and very different to another's. While the movements may look the same, their symbolism may convey something altogether different depending on one's awareness. It is to these aspects we now turn, taking Ellison's words as our point of entry.

2 CAUGHT IN THE ACT OF APPROPRIATION

Despite their billings as images of reality, these Negroes of fiction are coun-
terfeits. They are projected aspects of an internal symbolic process through
which, like a primitive tribesman dancing himself into the group frenzy
necessary for battle, the White American prepares himself emotionally to
perform a social role.

Ralph Ellison (1995a)

•

One evening, at the end of dance class, all the students gathered around in a
group and sat on the floor of the studio. One of the instructors had brought
a copy of a 1943 *Life* magazine to class; the cover was titled "The Lindy Hop"
and featured a photograph of two young white dancers doing the Lindy
Hop. Inside was a photographic essay, "The Lindy Hop: The American
National Dance," with a statement underneath the accompanying photographs that read, "The Lindy Hop; A True National Folk Dance has been
born in U.S.A." Our instructor diligently showed us the pictures page by
page, noting how each of the photographs documented one of the "classic"
steps of the dance. As he worked through the photos, I noticed that there
were ten pages of photographs of the two white dancers from the cover and
four pages of photographs of a pair of African American dancers. Excited
over our enthusiasm for the Lindy Hop, our instructor said that the goal of
our dance company was to "keep this dance tradition alive" and "to promote
the Lindy Hop as the national American dance."

I later discovered that the white dancers on the cover of the magazine
were two seventeen-year-old Broadway performers (not Lindy Hop dancers of any reputation), while the African American dancers were Willa
Mae Ricker and Leon James, two master Lindy Hop dancers and members
of the most famous Lindy Hop dance troupe in the world, Whitey's Lindy
Hoppers. Thinking about that issue of *Life* made me wonder: If this was a
dance that came from Harlem, and these were two of the greatest Lindy
Hop dancers, why were they buried inside the magazine while white dancers were featured on the cover? What did this say about the dance's Afri-

can American origins and history? Did this presentation of the "American Dance" simultaneously erase the dance's African American identity? Was this simply the racial politics of 1943? And what did this say about the way that we understood race and racial identity in America today?

•

As I pursued the Lindy Hop, both as a dancer and as an academic, I became increasingly interested in the history of the dance. I came across a fascinating documentary titled *Call of the Jitterbug* that was made in 1988 (Sorensen, Winding, and Ross 1988). The film discussed the origins of the Lindy Hop, documented some of the best Lindy Hop dancing from its zenith in the 1930s and '40s, and interviewed some of the great dancers and musicians of that period, including Norma Miller and Frankie Manning. Since this was made long before the Lindy Hop revival exploded and became a popular cultural phenomenon across American society, the discussion focused on the significance of the dance for African Americans back in the '30s and '40s. Their memories were not of the celebration of the "National American Dance," but reflections about the dance's importance in the African American community and the social conditions within which it was danced. Norma Miller discussed the Lindy Hop's popularity at its height:

> It was our ballroom that opened in the heart of Harlem. I didn't know it in those days, but when those doors opened in 1927 blacks walked through those doors like whites. Whites came to our ballroom. Everybody came to the Savoy Ballroom. It was the home of black dancing. It was the home of Swing, and everybody wanted to learn Swing. You had to come to the Savoy Ballroom. It was the dance that was created in Harlem. (Sorensen, Winding, and Ross 1988)

Norma also reflected on the racial conditions outside the ballroom, where segregation and racial violence were omnipresent:

> I was traveling with Ethel Waters, now we were traveling with two cars and a bus, a Lincoln and a Lincoln Zephyr, and a bus with two chauffeurs driving. I mean, we were talking about big-time show business and we couldn't eat at a White Tower, a White Castle, I mean a White Castle—they told us all to get the hell out—at a White Castle on the highway. Ethel Waters could have bought both of them, could have bought the whole damn block and we couldn't get a hamburger.... When people would refuse us, we would laugh. It did not have the effect that racism has today; it did not

bother us because we were insulated. It wasn't like you were traveling by yourself and you couldn't get a drink of water. You'd be surprised how inventive you become, how you steel yourself against, you grow an armor, people refusing you.[1] I say, "You refusing us," I say, "We're better looking than anybody in that place, what are you talking about." I mean people welcomed us to come somewhere—we weren't a bunch of scruffy people on the highway, we were the biggest show out there. But of course you ran into problems. (Sorensen, Winding, and Ross 1988)

In another documentary, I found an additional interview with Norma, one that was made in 1993 for PBS and chronicled social dance in America, entitled *Dancing New Worlds: Popular Dance in American Society*. In this film she again discussed the significance of the Lindy Hop for African Americans and white America's attraction to the dance:

A lot of people wanted to do this dance. But, you see, we had an edge. We felt like we had an edge, and I think that's how we danced. This will be something you do not do better than we; I don't care who you are. We wanted our tempos fast and the white dancers didn't like that. So that was always—it was always a battle, because we didn't want them taking our dance. They had everything else so we couldn't allow them to take the Lindy Hop. . . . I love the fact that the kids today want to do it, they want to know about it, they want to be part of our history. We sweated for that, we busted our butts to get that the way it was. And that's ours. We created it. It came out of the blood and sweat of Harlem. (Grauer 1993)

As I watched these documentaries, I was struck by the incongruity between the way that the history of the dance was being "remembered" today and the reality of the blood and sweat of Harlem out of which the dance emerged. It was as if the history and the people that created and nurtured the dance, and the segregation and racism under which the dance was formed, were completely unheard in the clamoring contemporary celebration and embrace of the Lindy Hop.

This silence contrasted sharply with what people were doing on the dance floor. How were we to make sense of this silence while at the same time white bodies were dancing steps with names like the Black Bottom, Cakewalk, Pimp-walk, and other movements based around the twisting and swiveling of the hips, shimmying, and shuffling, all undertaken with a wide stance and low center of gravity—all markers of African based dance?[2] These were not movements that emphasized the upright and more formal stance of

European-based ballroom dances, but movements that came from a tradition of social dancing far removed from traditional white society. With people laboring to learn the dance in classrooms and going out social dancing African American dances to African American swing music at clubs every night of the week, this incongruity suggested something sociologically fascinating—but something that I could not yet articulate. One evening at one of our dances, this issue was brought into perspective:

•

At the height of Swing dancing's popularity here in Chicago, a dance was held once a month at the Boulevard Ballroom on the North Side of the city. This was one of the highlights of the Chicago scene and was always the best attended of the Lindy Hop events, as two to three hundred Lindy Hoppers from around the Chicago area would gather to dance. One night I brought an African American friend of mine who was a graduate student in the Afro-American Studies Department at the University of Wisconsin. On numerous occasions we had discussed my growing interest in the Lindy Hop as a dissertation project and how I was exploring issues of cross-cultural engagement as a way to interpret what I saw unfolding around me. I was excited for him to come to a Lindy Hop event and anxious to get his reactions. As we made our way through the entrance, we found the place packed with dancers; the entire ballroom was a whirlwind of bodies in motion. We worked our way through the crowd and made it upstairs to the balcony to get an overview of the entire scene. As we stood there and looked out over the crowd of dancers, I commented that it easily could be said that this revival was just another chapter in the white "appropriation" of African American culture. He turned to me and replied, "I don't know, all I see is a bunch of white folks dancing." I stood there dumbfounded. At first I was incredulous that first as an African American, and second as an academic, he did not immediately grasp what I felt was happening. While we had completely different perspectives on the scene in front of us, in the end we were both right: white folks dancing was the entire point.

•

CONTRADICTIONS CONSIDERED

The whites, looking out at the activity in the yard, thought that they were being flattered by imitation and were amused by the incongruity of tattered blacks dancing courtly steps, while missing completely the fact that before their eyes a European cultural form was becoming Americanized, undergoing a metamorphosis through the mocking activity of a people partially sprung from Africa. So, blissfully unaware, the whites laughed while the blacks danced out their mocking reply.

Ralph Ellison (1995a, 223–24)

As Ralph Ellison drew our attention to the question of American identity, he captured the historical complexities of the white engagement with African American culture, which has never been straightforward; in fact, this interaction has been a complex, contradictory, anxiety-riddled process of negotiation by which whites have simultaneously embraced and rejected and have desired and disdained African American culture within the constraints of the dominant racial order.[3] This anxiety emerges out of the racial tension between proximity and distance of whiteness and blackness, over white identity and black identity of what one is and what one is not. In addition, this anxiety generates a tension that is worked out through various ways of cultural engagement. Whether defined by reticence, self-consciousness, or enthusiasm, these engagements occur within a spectrum of emotional and psychological orientations and dispositions. This anxiety is not always a conscious awareness; rather it exists mostly below the level of consciousness without direct awareness of how people interact with cultural forms (Bourdieu 1990a, 2000a, 2000b). Cultural engagement itself is never unidimensional; there is no one particular reason or frame that explains all investment or involvement. As a result, modes of engagement range from strategic utilization to unaware complicitness, and therefore must always be seen as ambiguous, contradictory, and overdetermined. This contradictory complexity defines not only the ways that groups interact, but it also defines any one individual, since our motives range from conscious intentions to unconscious desires that are never fully brought to our awareness. This equivocal relationship has generated a particular racial logic through which whites have conceptualized African Americans and enacted African American cultural practices, often times resulting in minstrelsy, whitewashing, and commodification. Even in today's "multicultural" and "color-blind" society, this racial logic continues to define the interactions and cultural-racial politics of white society. As a result, white interaction with African American culture must be situated against the larger sociohistorical context of racial domination in order to break from the liberal myth that cultural appreciation serves to generate social equality. Whereas white attraction to, identification with, and enactment of African American cultural forms are often undertaken either in an explicit resistance to white societal norms and aesthetics (gangsta rap) or explicitly, or implicitly as a symbol of multicultural unity (the Lindy Hop). In either case, cross-cultural consumption ultimately works to affirm and perpetuate racial domination, despite intentions, through the simultaneous marginalization and domination of African American people. This is not to argue that cross-cultural engagement is racist, therefore conflating and confusing whites with racism. This assumption is not only counterproductive to explaining the nuances of everyday life, but it also undermines the potentials and possibilities for reconfiguring social relations. Cross-cultural engagement is just as able to destabilize notions of race as it is to reinforce racial domination. However, because of social position and through selective engagement, whites are afforded the luxury of "playing" black through cross-cultural consumption, while simultaneously never having to endure the consequences of being black in white America.[4] Therefore, cross-cultural engagement can never be seen as insignificant or neutral, but rather as a crucial ambiguous symbolic and material mechanism in the production, circulation, and consumption of racial meanings and racial divisions in American society.

This chapter explores the racial imagination, the ways that we reconstruct history through the notion of a revival, and then moves on to discuss three particular modes of engagement through which culture, bodies, and race intersect: minstrelsy, whitewashing, and commodification. By illuminating these particular modes of engagement, we can come to see how racial domination is produced and operates not only through conscious intentions and actions, but also through the misrecognized practice of cultural forms in everyday life, as black and white bodies enact, consciously and unconsciously, notions of blackness and whiteness. As a result, this cultural engagement not only oppresses African Americans, but also simultaneously (and ironically) dominates whites themselves as they remain trapped in their own essentialized whiteness.

THE RACIAL IMAGINATION

It is through the racial imagination, our prevailing conceptual system of classifications, through which we apprehend and appreciate the world that we use to classify and conceptualize ethnoracial differences. In doing so, we come to differentiate body types, cultures, races, identities, and practices to which we attach socially constructed attributes that become naturalized over time. These differences cohere together to establish our imagined concepts of racial divisions and racial differences.[5] The racial imagination is not a lens layered over our existing ways of comprehending the world; rather it is part and parcel of it, forming our taken-for-granted racialized commonsense (Bourdieu 2000b, 181). By interpreting the world through this framework, racial differences are embedded in a biological nature that is itself a naturalized social construction.[6] Because the body is the intersection of race and culture, it becomes the anchor of natural and absolute differences (physiological, racial, or cultural) between blacks and whites and simultaneously serves as a mechanism to mask and reinscribe that very system of racial oppositions of which it is a product (Bourdieu 2000a, 23; also see Bourdieu 2000b, 128–63). Beyond simplistic commonsense notions of "stereotypes" and as a result, culture, the body, and race become fused when we try to explain its actions in everyday life: racial differences explain cultural differences (what is culture, ownership, authenticity), and cultural differences explain racial differences ("acting white," "acting black") as race and culture become reciprocal tools to articulate the ways we conceptualize difference (Radano 2001, 2003).

The search for racial identity in American society, whether black or white, has always been a quest for a foundation or a guarantee as to what race really is. Ellison calls our attention to how this search is founded upon a joke, a joke in which both groups share—that American identity is one without past foundations, is something homegrown, all the while pretending it is not, without either side wanting to admit it.

> When the white man steps behind the mask of the trickster his freedom is circumscribed by the fear that he is not simply miming a personification of his disorder and chaos, but that he will become in fact that which he only intends to symbolize; that he will be trapped somewhere in the mystery of hell (for there is a mystery in the whiteness of blackness, the innocence of evil and the evil of innocence, though being initiates, Negroes express the joke of it in the blues), and thus lose that freedom which, in the fluid, "traditionless," "classless" and rapidly changing society, he would recognize as the white man's alone. (Ellison 1994, 107)

This denial of history manifests in white people's delusion over the true interrelatedness of whiteness and blackness. When whites attempt to "counterfeit" black identity, this play of putting on a mask instills a piercing doubt as to whether the purity of identity (of race) is actually true as they want to believe (implicit in Ellison's writing is also the converse of this statement). It is this doubt which obscures an understanding of African American life as it imposes particular psychological attitudes which "leads to misjudge Negro passion, looking upon it as they do out of the turgidity of their own frustrated yearning for emotional warmth, their capacity for sensation having been constricted by bourgeois society. The Negro is idealized into a symbol of sensation, of unhampered social and sexual relationships" (Ellison 1994, 137). These psychological impositions construct an image of African Americans, one that exaggerates and distorts African American expressions and behaviors. In relation to what whites perceive as their own "coldness" and rigidity, African Americans are projected as the excess of sensuality and sexuality. It is these types of mythologies, while obviously caricatures and social constructions, which affect how people understand and structure the worlds within which they live (Bourdieu 2000a, 11).

In the case of African Americans, the black body has traditionally been mythologized as innately and essentially exotic, sexual, expressive, and naturally rhythmic; this sense of blackness is constructed as exterior to whiteness, whereas the white body is marked by its rationality, restraint, and rigidity.[7] As scholars such as Ronald Radano have pointed out, the concept of "black music" emerges in the antebellum period of the southern United States, when representations of slave performances became the hegemonic representations of African American culture.[8] At this time "black music" became defined through a natural or innate creativity grounded in their ascribed racially marked differences, which was itself a response to previous historical characterization of African Americans as incapable of creativity due to their barbaric qualities (Radano 2001, 464). In addition to the rise of intuitive aspects of musicality, a romanticized folk characteristic also took hold that highlighted the similarities of melody and harmony that marked European musical conventions.

By the 1870s and 1880s, melody gave way to rhythm as the defining origin of blackness, a quality that was thought to be a primordial impulse. By the turn of the century, blackface minstrelsy and colonial depictions of Africans as savage and exotic transposed onto African Americans were transformed into an ideological discourse of primitivism that informed discussions of black music's appeal and its simultaneous threat to the social order. With the turn into the early twentieth century the emergence of "hot rhythm" became the sign by which black music was recast to reflect the changing economic and social order alongside mass migration. This characterization of blackness with its primalism and violence linked it to the destabilization of this social order for white which further solidified a new blackness that was based in modern urban areas.[9] Black urban migration and the "New Negro" accompanied this black migratory population and reflected its new displacement in its varying rhythmic character as ragtime, blues, jazz, and Swing, whose center was a black essence. As rhythm became the defining characteristic of black music into the jazz era, it now took on connotations of precivilized and primal sound, which predated music as defined by traditional European form as such. This innate characteristic of rhythm, one that defined traditional European logic embedded itself as an innate characteristic of the racial other, became a defining marker in marking, maintaining, and legitimating racial differences (Radano 2001, 474).

While these associations that inform our contemporary everyday understandings have a deep history that reaches all the way back to the days of
plantation slavery, the naturalizing of blackness and rhythm came as recently as the turn of the twentieth century.[10] As a result, the racial imagination interprets and mediates cultural forms in terms of their aesthetics,
dynamics, and movements. African Americans are then seen as natural
dancers, while whites are considered naturally awkward and arrhythmic.
The racialized imagination creates a set of expectations about competencies. African Americans are perceived as "natural" dancers not simply by
physiology, rather through the racialized cultural category of dance that
imputes capacities such as the ability to quickly learn certain types of dance
or looking good doing certain types of dance. As a result, whites often misrecognize dance as an inherent racial knowledge. The Lindy Hop is therefore often viewed as an innate African American knowledge or as some sort
of racial essence rather than as a historical urban cultural formation.[11] The
naturalization of race and the racialization of the body and culture reciprocally perpetuate each other and reinforce belief in the prevailing system
of classification of the natural differences between "blackness" and "whiteness."[12] The racial imagination predetermines the way people understand
the intersection of the body, culture, and race. The racial schemata through
which we see the world overrides all other criteria of explanation. The racial imagination becomes not only the lens through which our dispositions,
orientations, and perceptions are formed; it also generates expectations,
imposes characteristics and abilities, and mediates the ways people are understood and treated, based on their racial classification.

The racial imagination is not something that only whites have in conceptualizing race, but all racial groups conceptualize others through the dominant logic of the racial order; this works for African Americans as well as for
whites. What is key to understand is that it enables us to understand how we
are all complicit in perpetuating racial essentialism and the normalization
of racial differences without our conscious awareness or intention. Through
the workings of the racial imagination in society as a whole we see how the
twofold naturalization of racial difference in categories and in social structures is not the action or outcome of white racism, but the working out of
the very understandings all racial groups have of race in everyday life.

THE RECONSTRUCTING OF HISTORY THROUGH
A REVIVAL

The racial imagination operates on many levels; one of particular interest
here is the way that we construct the narrative of history. In order for there

to be a Lindy Hop "revival," there had to be something dormant to revive. What is central in the analysis here is not the "originary" meaning of the dance, rather it is the processes of preservation, transformation, subversion, and legitimation through which cultural forms like the Lindy Hop become reconstructed in the present. Much like the discussion of the body, history ascribes racial attributes to cultural forms that become invisible over time.

At the initial stages of the revival, when the dance was soaring into mainstream popularity, one of the "original revivalists" who had been dancing since the mid-1980s, Steven Mitchell, told me:

> The dance is so young in so many ways now. We've been doing it for a lot longer, but the whole explosion of the thing is crazy. Where now everybody is teaching it, everybody is an expert, and it makes you wonder about where it is all going to go. I say it in classes, and I'll say it again now—if you respect the Lindy Hop, you must protect the Lindy Hop.

Pushing this individual to elaborate further on this issue, he confided:

> You have to look at people's reasons for doing it. You have to look at their motivations. Part of the problem is people's motivation for dancing. Why did you get into this? Most people are doing it because they saw *Swing Kids* or the Gap ad; people are doing it because it is the thing to do. That Swing is back is not enough, you know; you have to think, what are you representing here, is this a commercial thing or are you trying to get at the heart of the dance? If you have never had feelings like this before, it's hard for me to convey to you and have you move to the music in that way—if you don't know what that feeling is. I mean, we didn't create these dances for nothing. Black people created these dances to express the pain and the blues of growing up in the hood.

Because of the "newness" of the dance and its almost overnight skyrocketing to national popularity, this left little to no critical time to reflect or establish distance from what was happening. As a result, the dance, and the racial connotations attributed to the dance, drew upon those deep historical racial mythologies as if natural inclinations. David Dalmo, a world-class dancer and choreographer, explained to me:

> I think there is definitely an image in people's minds, of being sexy, or being cool, or whatever descriptive you want to use. There is some image out there in people's minds of what they should aspire to look like, what they

feel they need to look like. I would shy away from saying that people want to be black, since I don't think most people would say that, but I believe deep down that it is really the way that black dancers dance. I think this is not something most people would say, but I think that is very much part of what we are all trying to do. I mean who wants to dance white!

Dalmo's interpretation of the Lindy Hop revival was not uncommon. When I interviewed another of the principal Lindy Hop revivalists, expert dancer and teacher Lennart Westerlund, he explained the relationship between race and the dance accordingly.

I think that blacks are more uninhibited and the whites are more inhibited, so I think that that is probably the reason is because this is their dance so when they get out there they are just dancing. They don't have any reservations about what they are doing. I mean if they want to shake their hips, they go ahead and shake their hips. Generally a white person, since it is not their dance, so in picking up a black dance I think they are a little bit leery of what they are supposed to do, so some of them feel hesitant about shaking their hips as much as you will find black people. I think that insecurity may one of the main differences we see in the dancing today.

In this case, it is precisely because those two individuals were exceptional dancers that their words carried even more weight than others in that they were two of the primary teachers leading the dance revival. Their instruction weighed heavier on the dance community, as mentors and exemplars, than any random dancer selected who would have made a similar statement.

While the perspective of elite white dancers and instructors yields us one vantage point, the perspective of an "average" African American dancer may yield another. One night I brought an African American female friend to one of the clubs. She had taken a few dance workshops but had never gone out dancing socially. She was interested in learning the dance and wanted to check out the scene. After having several dances with different partners, she returned from the dance floor exasperated. She told me,

I felt like a fly in the buttermilk. Just because I'm black doesn't mean I actually know how to dance. Why is it that I get all these guys coming up to me assuming I can dance Lindy, and then when I go out there and can't do it that well, they're shocked? Why? Because I'm not dancing like a black person is supposed to.

One of the few African American female dancers responded in a similar fashion when I asked if she felt that people assumed she could dance well because of her race.

> I love to dance. I love the Lindy Hop, but I'm not like most of the hardcore dancers. I want to go out and have a good time and all, but I don't need to be the best dancer. And it's like, I mean, I get this feeling, not from everybody, but from a lot of the guys, that I should be a lot better than I am. And I really do think it's because I'm black. I just can't imagine guys being disappointed if they danced with a white girl; it would be like, "Hey, that's cool, you dance at this level." But with me I feel like there's all this extra pressure in some way. It doesn't stop me from going out, but I just have to ignore it, you know?

In projecting these notions of rhythm and naturalness as the "essence" of African Americans, we can see how the racial imagination imposes a set of assumed characteristics and competences that, when not upheld, create confusion as the racialized commonsense is violated.[13]

This expectation of competence creates awkwardness and self-consciousness among many African American dancers. In an interview one African American dancer and instructor at the Herräng dance camp in Sweden lamented this feeling of being viewed as different simply because of her race:

> There's only a few of us anyways, that puts us apart from the get go. I feel like a tourist attraction here. "Look, a black person." It's really sad. I mean, look at the nighttime dances; all the blacks line up against that far wall. Like we are on display, me and Dawn and Frankie, and people just stare at us like we're supposed to do something, like we're there to entertain them.

The most central African American in the entire Lindy Hop community, master Lindy Hop instructor and dancer Steven Mitchell, echoed this sense of self-consciousness over white expectations, not only in the Lindy Hop community but throughout society:

> You know, it's like that all the time. I guess I get used to it in a way. I mean, you can't let it bother you, but it's tiring, it's really tiring being black. When I'm out and dancing with some white girl, and I mean anywhere, not just the Lindy Hop community, but just out, and people say, "Hey, what are you doing with that white girl, oh you're just dancing with her, you're a

dancer, oh well then that's okay." But it's even worse when there's a couple of us [African Americans] out somewhere in public. When I'm out with Angela or Janice, or some of the others, everyone looks at us. It's like we're the entertainment for people. Wherever we go, people look at us: "Oh so that's how they dance; that's how they move." It's always a show, like we have to perform, like we're on stage.

This sense of self-consciousness serves as a window into seeing the essentialized racial categories through which we understand the world. African Americans are conceptualized as inherently good and natural dancers and therefore desirable to watch by white society. As a result, this self-consciousness in African Americans works reciprocally to reinforce the differences between blacks and whites.

•

As I stood at the edge of the club's dance floor, my teacher, with whom I had been taking dance classes for several months, approached me with a pleased and fascinated look on his face. He pointed to one particular dancer—the only African American male in the club that night, a fellow student named Riley. Given that the two of us had started dancing at about the same time and were both taught by the same instructor, I was puzzled to see our teacher so enamored of this particular dancer. He leaned over to me and said, "You know, he really dances like the old-timers … just like them." I thought about this evaluation and wondered what it was he saw that reminded him of "the old-timers" (this was shorthand for referring to Whitey's Lindy Hoppers, the greatest of the Lindy Hop dancers from the 1930s and '40s). His comment struck me as strange for a number of reasons. First and foremost, the African American dancer had, like myself, only been dancing for a short time and could hardly be considered a master of the dance. Since several of the performances of Whitey's Lindy Hoppers have been preserved on video, which many avid Lindy Hop dancers watch for inspiration, I wondered how watching video clips of Whitey's Lindy Hoppers related to one of the very few African American dancers in today's Swing scene. Did our instructor consider him a great dancer not because of his skill, but simply because he danced like the old-timers? Because he was black like them, or because he could dance like them?

•

As I became more embedded in the Lindy Hop community, I pursued the question raised by this interaction. I began to ask several of the female dancers what they thought of dancing with this particular African American male dancer. As if on cue, almost all the women I spoke with described him in a particularly stereotyped way. Rather than discussing his leading or his style, the dominant theme they used to describe his dancing was one of rhythm. One dancer remarked, "I can't follow him at all. But I love dancing with him, though, because he is so rhythmic." Yet another follower defined his dancing this way: "It's so different dancing with him than with the other leaders. I can't explain it; it just is. He's so musical and so rhythmic."

Some women even equated his abilities with the very best Lindy Hop dancers in the world. One female dancer told me, "You know, dancing with Riley is so much like dancing with Steven or Ryan [the two master Lindy Hop instructors that define the dance today, one African American and the other black British; both have been doing the Lindy Hop since the mid-'80s]. It's just like they *dance*. I know that sounds weird, but it is." Another woman confided, "I think he's the best dancer in the scene here. He dances like Steven and Ryan. He's got that rhythm just like they do."

Yet when I asked a skilled African American dancer how she perceived this dancer, she responded:

I'm not sure what his experience is but it has nothing to do with blackness or Soul. He's black, like I'm black, but I know lots of people who wouldn't even begin to pretend that he's an authentic dancer. To look at him there is nothing about the black experience that would lead you to believe there is much soul going on. I've danced with him and from a dance perspective I don't really think he understands the music, there's no evidence of a relationship to the music he's dancing to, at least I couldn't feel it. I don't get it. That guy tries to act all black and yet he's one of the whitest dancers here. . . . If you are talking about soul and feeling anyway. I have no idea why so many followers think he so amazing. No idea.

Filtering our appreciation and interpretation through the racial imagination forces our thinking through essentializing categories that conflate competence, culture, and race. An analysis of the racial imagination enables us to understand the underlying unquestioned racialized commonsense through which whiteness and blackness are interpreted. This orientation shapes not only the expectations and assumptions about people's competences and abilities based on race, but also the very ways that people are disposed to act based on those racial differences.

While the focus of this study is to understand how whites come to apprehend and understand race through cultural practices, African Americans are just as prone to seeing whites through the same racialization of cultural forms. While there are very few African American dancers in the Lindy Hop scene as a whole, they still assist in perpetuating the racial imagination. As one dancer expressed to me:

> Black people don't have to try and dance authentically, we just do. It's who we are. I think it's really just white people who think about it, I guess because they have to. It is something they have a hard time with. I mean we have natural ability. We don't have to count the beats. We just dance. They don't have the rawness, it's just not in them, so I think they dance [the Lindy Hop] in a way that makes them feel comfortable. I mean that's cool and all, but it's like they don't want to be threatened with anything else.

Two other dancers echoed this sentiment:

> I think most black folks wouldn't even recognize the dance when they see white people dancing. It's not like seeing Eminem out there, he moves and flows like a brother so it's very different. But with the Lindy Hoppers, it just doesn't register, because it's just different. The aesthetic, it not only looks different, it isn't even in the same vicinity.
>
> Just look at all the great dancers in tap or jazz; they are all black. It's just that black people excel at that, it is not a racist thing, but look at who is the best in football or basketball—the players are always black. How do you explain that?

To reiterate, the dominant racial logic operates not only in the minds and dispositions of whites in society, but of all groups simultaneously interpreting and interacting with each other. In this way we can see how it is not just how whites view themselves and African Americans, it is also the ways that African Americans view themselves and whites. As a result, this is not a false consciousness by which everyone is under some misconception of how the world "really is," which would simply be thinking through stereotypes that could simply be proven wrong. This is about the deeply embedded orientations that all groups have been socialized into and live out in everyday life as they confront issues of difference, identity, skill, aptitudes, and cultural forms. Since this study focuses the white racialized orientations and their modes of engagements with the dance, it is to those issues which I now turn.

MODES OF ENGAGEMENT

Analyzing the modes of engagement by which whites have taken up the Lindy Hop opens up a way to consider the ways that the racial imagination influences the ways that cultural practices are conceptualized and enacted (Bourdieu 1990a, 69). Only by analyzing how understandings of race manifest themselves in and through the body in practice can we come to understand how bodies enact the racial imagination. This in turn will allow us to consider how the body is not just a site of expression, but an embodied *history* of meanings that have been socialized into it, that offers a window into the way that race and culture are conceptualized, interpreted, and practiced (Bourdieu 1990a, 2000a, 2000b).

As the symbolic boundaries of blackness and whiteness are negotiated, the racial imagination leads to particular modes of engagement with the Lindy Hop.[14] The practices that belong to one (racial) group, which appear natural and are encouraged, are simultaneously forbidden or discouraged as inappropriate for other (racial) groups. This provides a useful framework for understanding how this process of racial negotiation unfolds (Bourdieu 2000a, 25). This boundary maintenance is the process of defining the "limits of the thinkable and the unthinkable" by which one racial group distinguishes itself from another. It simultaneously serves to naturalize these identities and contributes to "the maintenance of the social order from which it derives its power" (Bourdieu 1990a, 108).

While these boundaries serve as essentializing racial divisions between blackness and whiteness, they simultaneously serve to generate the desire for that excluded otherness. From the days of minstrelsy, to Elvis Presley and rock-'n'-roll, to the wiggers and Eminems of today, white society has always imitated and emulated African American cultural forms.[15] Historically, as has been discussed by critics like Lott, Radano, Roediger, and Gubar, whites have entered into an engagement with these forms because they have provided whites with a resource of expression normatively denied to them.[16] As discussed previously, these cross-cultural engagements provide a space within which whites can transcend, at times knowingly and at other times unknowingly, however fleeting, the constraints of their whiteness. These engagements with blackness have been undergirded by essentialist and romantic notions of African American cultural practices and people as naturally more instinctive and sexual, less inhibited, and more expressive than whites, who have been conceptualized as emotionally and culturally vacuous.[17] Consequently, whites have used, borrowed, and appropriated African American culture as a surrogate vehicle to express their own rebellion, sexuality, and pleasure, denied by the social constraints of white society (Deloria 1997; Fusco 1995; hooks 1992b, 1994). This white desire for blackness is always a process of negotiation, between desire and disdain, embrace and rejection. This enables whites to consume African American cultural forms, while at the same time rejecting African Americans as people (Lott 1995; Radano 2001, 2003). This dynamic of negotiation enables us to understand how everyday cultural practices like the Lindy Hop are articulations of much larger structural issues of racial domination.

In order to fully unpack the symbolic and material consequences of the white embrace of the Lindy Hop, we must examine the ways that dancers conceptualize, embody, and enact the dance. This requires us not to make aesthetic arguments over whether whites are good or stylish practitioners of the dance, but rather to undertake a more objective analysis of the racial schemes through which this cross-cultural engagement is mediated and enacted. This negotiation in the pursuit of the Lindy Hop leads to three dominant modes of engagement (minstrelsy, whitewashing, commodification) that serve as mechanisms for generating and reinscribing white racial domination in society.[18]

By conceptualizing the emptiness of their own whiteness in relation to the natural richness of blackness, whites reinscribe racial essentialism in society, dehistoricize the dance as a cultural formation of a particular era, and conflate race and cultural competence. Thus it is not only African Americans that are dominated through white cross-cultural engagement; whites themselves are dominated by these racial cosmologies as they are locked within their own essentialized racial identity that prevents them from a full understanding and cultivation of the dance. Exposing these mechanisms enables us to understand that these are not natural or inherent outcomes, but rather contingent social constructions, opening up possibilities for alternative modes of engagement.

MINSTRELSY

white engagement with African American culture generates minstrelsy, by which the desire to perform African American culture "authentically," or correctly, leads to an overexaggerated caricature of African Americans in style, mannerisms, or motion. This supports and furthers white racial domination. I argue that the tradition of minstrelsy continues in the Lindy Hop revival, in a new form under new social conditions.[19] Like previous forms of minstrelsy, neo-minstrelsy relies on structural relations of domination and control and the selective use of African American culture by white society. While this new incarnation of minstrelsy has shed its blackface paint, it continues to be a racial ventriloquism that is at once a racial embrace and a racial distancing, enabling whites to work out their attraction to African American culture while simultaneously distancing themselves from blackness through an implicit degradation. Since this new form of minstrelsy works through the racial imagination that has normalized meanings of blackness and whiteness, whites enact their understandings of African American dancing without self-conscious reflection on the symbolic meanings generated by their performances. As a result, neo-minstrelsy is able to continue its historical function of maintaining racial essentialism and racial domination not only in the staged performance of the dance; it also comes through in everyday social dancing, in the cultivation of the dance through teaching, and in the more general form of the ways that whites conceptualize how African Americans act.

As a mode of engagement, minstrelsy is not something over and above the dance or something added to it; rather, it is constitutive of the dance's enactment. By excavating the implicit understandings of blackness and whiteness that come through in the performance of the dance, when we are able to examine these embodiments in action.

•

"Sing, Sing, Sing," the signature Benny Goodman dance number, came booming over the PA system, and almost instinctively all the dancers flocked to the center of the dance floor. They congregated in a "jam" circle, a ring of people forming a showcase space where dancers strut and perform their flashiest and most complicated tricks for the audience. One after another, couples burst into the center of the circle and tried to outduel each other for the status of best dancers. As the song is lightning fast, the couples had only a short time to dazzle and impress the onlookers. As I stood amid the crowd, taking in the spectacle of twists and turns, one particularly admired couple leaped into the circle and captured everyone's attention. They immediately began to execute extremely complicated moves. After a few partnered moves, the couple broke apart and performed individualized steps; the male dancer paraded around the female by strutting and waving his hands, while the female dancer started into the "crazy legs," where the woman wobbles her legs as if to appear out of control. The crowd went wild over this display, and instantly another couple jumped into the circle to outdo them and earn the applause for themselves. One after another, couples entered this self-constructed fishbowl of performance, seeking the attention and acclaim of the dance community; as couples attempted bolder and more ostentatious moves, the dance became more and more theatrical. The crowd's expectations rose with each improvisation. Yet the more ostentatious and burlesque the Lindy Hop becomes in these "jams," it only seems to garner more mutual enthusiasm, respect, and applause among the dancers.

As I turned away and walked off the dance floor, I wondered if these displays were taking the Lindy Hop into a realm of interpretation that we as dancers should be working to avoid. At what point do these performances top out? Was the boundary between dancing and minstrelsy becoming blurred, or were they in fact one and the same, as the desire for an ever more ostentatious display became the defining logic of the jam session?

•

Removing the burnt-cork greasepaint, which defined the black mask of minstrelsy, makes it harder to document these caricatured performances of what whites imagine African Americans to be like—now the minstrelsy is no longer so explicit. But we still must be sensitive to the mode of engagement that defines this new minstrelsy. Whereas the stereotyped language and racialized speech of the minstrel stage shows, such as racialized songs and poems, provided easy access to documenting the minstrel performance, today's minstrelsy continues to signify the racial difference without those explicit forms. While these cross-cultural engagements can appear merely literal, we can also read the visual vocabulary of these performances as enactments of stereotypes of African Americans as wild, primitive, and out of control. As these notions of blackness are worked out as vehicles for personal and group expression, they become over-the-top spectacles of racial performance undertaken within the controlled and localized community of the Lindy Hop scene, serving to reinscribe racial essentialism.

While this minstrelsy is enacted through imitation, it is also cultivated through teaching the dance. This is illustrated to me many times when working as a performer.

•

When I worked for a Lindy Hop performance company, we were often hired to give performances and teach dance lessons to middle and high school students. One engagement took us to a wealthy all-white high school in the north suburbs of Chicago. The owner of the company had hired me to assist her in two short dance workshops for the school drama class. We first did a demonstration of the Lindy Hop, and then we were to teach the students a short lesson in partner moves and a few individual jazz steps. After showing them the basic step and a couple of turns, the company's owner moved on to the individual steps. She said to the class, "I want all the guys to pay attention to me. Girls, you can relax for a moment. Okay, now I want the guys to do a 'pimp walk.' Do you guys know what a pimp is? And do you know how a pimp walks? I'll show you." (The owner, who was a slender white female, hunched over and started to swing her right arm from side to side as she lazily strutted across the room, leaning to one side in a mimic of the "pimp" stereotype.) "Now guys, I want you to do it like this; make sure that the girls see you strutting your stuff, so they check you out. Show them how cool you are. So try it, just pretend you're a pimp." She turned to the girls. "Now girls, when the guys do their thing, I want you to do what's called a fishtail." (She bent over and started to swivel her hips, walking backward in lunging steps.) "And girls, when you do this, I want you to really stick it out and give them something to look at. While the girls do that, I want the guys to pimp walk around them and check them out—really show your stuff, guys, and girls, I want you to check them out ... get ready, I'll count you in with the music." The students were thrilled and took to the steps without missing a beat, as if they were veteran dancers.

•

As they acted out these parodies, the visual image of the hypersexualized pimp and the fishtailing of the women's posteriors served as titillating entertainment for the high school students. Within the safe confines of this elite high school auditorium, I had to wonder what myths of blackness were being reinscribed. As this dance workshop was unfolding before me—as I watched these youngsters enact the steps according to the visuals we had provided them—I wondered if they were making a connection in their minds to a racial other, absent from the room but implicitly there as they enacted these movements with gleeful abandon. Since the students so easily grasped the movements, I had to wonder if this visual imagery was already socialized into them, already buried in their subconscious as a perception of what black folks are supposed to be like. The minstrelsy that circulates throughout the Lindy Hop was not just occurring in the elite spaces of the jam session. It was finding its way through all modes of enactment, even in the teaching of the dance. While these exaggerated and overdone stereotypes were being offered up by the instructor, their easy embrace suggested that these myths of blackness were already somewhat in circulation, merely needing someone to activate them.

When considering minstrelsy in relation to the Lindy Hop, we must examine the ways that the dance is inculcated with a series of racial mythologies implicit in its movements. The "Twist-twist," the defining female movement of the Lindy Hop, is an all-encompassing bodily rotation that emphasizes the hips, thighs, pelvis, and feet. The female dancer rotates her hips back and forth in a twisting motion, which serves as both a dance step and a ready position for the next move. This twisting motion emanates a particular stylized and sexual dynamic by emphasizing the buttocks and hips in its gyrating display. Mastering the Twist-twist is essential in order to develop a feeling for the dance and to capture its aesthetic. The Twist-twist movement also allows individualization and stylization; no two women will twist exactly alike, as each tries to stamp her signature or personality on the defining movement. Yet, like all art forms, the fundamentals are always the most elusive and difficult things to master, requiring constant practice and revision.

•

Late one afternoon in July, at the Herräng dance camp in Herräng, Sweden, I was taking an advanced Lindy Hop class from Angela Andrews, a black British woman who is one of the leaders and revivalists of the dance in England. We were working on the basics of Lindy Hop, including the Twist-twist, when suddenly Angela started yelling, bringing the class to an abrupt halt: "Stop! Stop! Stop! Okay, all right. I didn't want to have to say this, but I have to. Ladies, what is this?" She demonstrated the follower's basic step in an overly dramatic motion, with her buttocks way out behind her as if she were about to fall over. "All right, I'll tell you. It's ugly. In your face, it's ugly! Be ladies! This is not ladylike. Okay, now I didn't want to say this, but look, I know a lot of you are trying to copy me and stick your bums out when you dance, but it's ugly; don't do it. Look, this is God-given. I am not trying to stick it out. Dance with your bum under you; don't stick it out! Be a lady when you dance. Don't try and make your body do something it can't do."

The class stood there stunned, uncertain what to make of this. What did she mean? "What is she saying?" one woman whispered to me, as I stood there, speechless. Had she just said what I thought she said? I was shocked; the women were embarrassed and confused. Wasn't this what they had been taught as long as they'd been doing the dance? Wasn't this how the step looked in the old black-and-white movies? Didn't this step require them to extend their buttocks out in a twisting motion? How or why would the women do anything else if this was what they were taught? Here we were in the backwoods of Sweden, learning Lindy Hop in a class with some of the best dancers from around the world, and everyone looked around at each other like they had never heard or even thought of this before. What exactly was the problem? Was it simply that they were sticking their butts out too far, or was there something more?

•

Angela was pointing out something so subtle, so implicit and unspoken, that they could not see it. Yet it was so offensive and significant to her that she had reached her boiling point. Ostensibly this was about mere body movements, not the movements' literal meaning. But what was really happening was that Angela was treading on taboo ground, articulating the unspoken racial tension of the Lindy Hop—the unspoken and seldom-acknowledged minstrelsy that pervades and dominates the Lindy Hop revival. The ugliness that she pointed out came not just in body positioning, but in the minstrelsy that posture signified. It was the imitation and the representation that had angered Angela, the imitation of black physiology according to how whites envision it. Its ugliness came not in white bodies dancing a black dance, but in the grotesque overexaggeration of the body in motion. This was not about the superiority or the aesthetic of the white versus the black body; it was about dancing within the limits of your own body, not in an imitation of what the white racializing imagination perceives that a black female body must look like.

Later that week I interviewed Angela, asking her if she saw this as a problem:

> Oh, I do think it's a problem. Nobody wants to talk about it; no one ever does, because when you do. . . . But I had to say something. I mean, it really is offensive in this white perception of black physiology that they are trying to do but won't acknowledge. Look at the girls, they're trying to dance with their asses way out, in what they think is the way black people dance! But look, I don't stick it out. I've got a big bum, but I don't stick it out; it does that on its own. But for some of these girls, it looks so outrageous, so I had to confront them on that. I don't even think they realize on a conscious level how offensive that really is.

Here was the underlying problem of the Lindy Hop revival that was never articulated, never confronted, never even spoken, yet constantly present: this white obsession with black physiology, an unspoken and maybe even an unconscious mimesis in whites' performance of the dance that is illuminated here in Angela's words. It is here in this confrontation that the white racializing imagination is made visible, as it produces and cultivates minstrel performances that are knowingly and unknowingly symbolically racist. The performance of the dance, the way it was done, represents something that whites have normalized and accepted. Minstrelsy is subtly at work, and yet it more often than not escapes the white consciousness, since that is not their intention. This contradiction was made apparent when I followed up with one of the women from Angela's class later that day. When I inquired about how she felt about what happened when Angela interrupted class, she responded:

> I really don't understand what she was so mad about. I don't think anybody meant anything by it. We were just trying to dance like her. I wasn't trying to stick my butt out. I mean, how are you supposed to learn how to dance

with style if you don't model the teachers you are taking the classes from. They are the experts, right?

The minstrelsy being illuminated here is a performance that is socialized, not just last week, but from the very beginning, as it is woven into the fabric of our racial imagination and the culture we inherit. This was not a class of beginners; these were advanced dancers from around the world who had danced for years and traveled all the way to Sweden to attend one of the world's best Lindy Hop camps.

Even when not dancing, the racial engagement with African American culture was present. It was not just the dance alone that reproduced notions of racial essentialism; it was circulating through everyday culture and affected all the African American cultural forms that whites engaged in. The following anecdote reconstructed from my fieldnotes proved useful to the extent that it was not just the Lindy Hop that was at issue here, but rather all forms of African American culture that whites engage:

•

Outside the building where the workshop was being held, I leaned against the wall and watched the dancers return from their lunch break. I was talking to Steven, an African American instructor, when two white dancers in their early twenties walked by. When they saw Steven, they greeted him with a dramatic "Whasssssup," the colloquial greeting recently made popular in a national Budweiser advertisement featuring several twenty-something African Americans. Steven laughed and greeted the two men as they passed him. Then he turned to me and said, "I understand it—and it's cool that they want to be a part of it—but it's just so much sometimes." These two young men were prime examples of neo-minstrelsy, staring us in the face. I asked Steven if the exchange had bothered him. He replied, "This is my job. This is their party; this is not my party. But I do what I have to do because I'm a professional, and this is my job." I asked, "Is everything okay? You look a little shaken all of a sudden." He looked at me and said, "They kill it for me. No, I don't even want to go there, I don't even want to go there, I can't."

•

This sense that all African American cultural forms are enacted without people recognizing the significance of their actions was something brought to light in my interviews. A Lindy Hop master who had been one of the principal revivalists described his feelings about the sometimes-awkward outcomes when whites participated in the dance:

For most people it becomes artificial. You don't believe it at all, really. It's the same sometimes when you see people that dress up in their zoot suits and things; most people can't wear them, it just hurts when they come into the room—they can't even walk in them. I think you need a certain attitude to carry such a thing, and it's the same with the dance: you need a little bit of an attitude to carry off such a thing, to bring it to a certain level, and most people, they don't have that attitude or that inside feeling for it. It's only when you have that attitude that it can become part of you. If you look at it critically, at least to me, it's a little bit pathetic. It can be like a big masquerade, something like that—something artificial, I can't touch it—it's something false—it's a bit off, but I don't know if you can put your finger on it. It's a lot of big hats and costumes walking around, and there's no one inside them, really. But then you see that some people are able to do it, and it's normally the black people. It seems to be their thing, because for them it's so natural.

This sense of something happening in the dance, something that cannot be articulated, seemed to me to be the very issue of the way the racial imagination generated these distorting modes of engagement. While it exists, most often below the level of consciousness, it continues to shape and inform the ways that whites engage the dance.

However, when forced to reflect upon their understanding of the dance, dancers can articulate, if only in part, how they see their engagement with the dance. As one dancer, I asked directly, said:

When I think about dancing and the style I like, I mean it's the way that the old-timers did it, like in the videos [referencing Whitey's Lindy Hoppers from the 1940s]. You asked me about the race issue, but I don't really think about that. Isn't mimicry the best form of flattery? And if that person is black, am I mimicking a black person or their style? I think it is their style that I try to emulate, the way they dance; if a white person danced like that I'd imitate them, too.

This separation of style and race was a common theme when asking dancers about how most dancers desired to dance. Another dancer told me

I just think of it like acting. You have to play the part. I'm not saying acting black like you suggested, but I think there is a level of imitation. They defined the style of the dance, so to be good you have to dance like them if that's what you're getting at. So yeah, I would say I try to dance black, but I don't think that means anything bad. It just means you're trying to get better.

When addressing the same issue of whites "emulating" black style, with an African American instructor who I met at a dance camp in Los Angeles, she said:

I don't see any white dancers who can dance that way, except David. He is the only white dancer I would say has it. I don't know how but he feels the dance, he just understands it. I think that maybe is what it is, but he is the only one, everybody else really is just a bad copy of the dance to me. I'm not saying I don't want people to dance, but as to your question about race, it doesn't translate to me.

At the same camp, another African American dancer from Los Angeles expressed a very different point of view about the dance translating and how whites imitate black style. In referring to a particularly popular African American male dancer at the camp:

I see what you're getting at [minstrelsy], and yeah, I think there is some of that going on. He just uses the fact that he's black like he is some sort of "down-ass brother." It's him using his blackness as a form of boundary maintenance, like he is the *only* one who can really understand the dance. The way he acts, the way he dances, the way he acts around other dancers, is actually kind of pathetic. Yeah, you talk about the minstrel tradition. There you go. Like he is some sort of authority figure, like he is the authentic black experience. Maybe I'm more sensitive to it being an African American woman. He takes himself seriously, but it's like he is playing to an audience. I'm not going to say serious cooning, okay, I already said, but please, it is some serious posturing on his part that makes me embarrassed.

In my very first interview with Steven Mitchell, I asked how he felt about the racial aspect of the Lindy Hop scene being predominantly white. I asked him how he felt as one of the few black males teaching a predominantly white audience. He answered, "Sometimes I feel like there's an Amos and Andy aspect of this, when I use words like 'flava' and 'bootray' to communicate when I'm teaching. I mean it when I say it, but then I look around and I see the audience and I wonder." His words belie a sense of self-consciousness that the very language he used in instruction could be turned around and used in possibly distorting or misleading ways. In another interview he commented more generally about the state of the dance, lamenting that despite his efforts to control the way the dance was being inculcated, the situation could not be remedied by direct instruction:

> I'm trying to get them to understand that it's a dance. That's why I had [you and your partner] demonstrate in class, because [you] were dancing, [you] were keeping it a dance. That's the problem—people have taken it so far out, it's not even dancing any more. It's just sex out there; it isn't a dance anymore, and that's what's killing it.

These statements all resonate with the fact that there is something larger, something beyond just the literal, which defines and shapes how the Lindy Hop is engaged and enacted. In this last instance, it is the racial imagination that leads white dancers to take these movements out of the realm of dance and into the realm of minstrelsy. As Ellison's remarks echo through the cross-cultural embrace of the Lindy Hop, the minstrel, the mask, the imitation, and the question of what identity is continues to confound our understandings and enactments of what race is.

WHITEWASHING

> The white American's Manichean fascination with the symbolism of blackness and whiteness expressed in such contradictions as the conflict between the white American's Judeo-Christian morality, his democratic political ideals and his daily conduct-indeed in his general anti-tragic approach to experience. Being "highly pigmented" as the sociologists say, it was our Negro "misfortune" to be caught up associatively in the negative side of this basic dualism of the white folk mind, and to be shackled to almost everything it would repress from conscience and consciousness.
>
> *Ralph Ellison (1995a, 213–14)*

As Ellison remarks, it is the symbolism of blackness and whiteness, whether consciously or unconsciously, that shapes and influences the ways we interpret race. The conflation of blackness with negative traits and whiteness with positive traits leads to an either conscious or unconscious repression. One way this repression of blackness can occur is through the process of whitewashing. Whitewashing, the process by which cultural forms are severed from their cultural identities, is another mode of engagement that defines the white embrace of African American culture (see Fusco 1995; Lott 1995; Ziff and Rao 1997). Whereas minstrelsy is an overexaggeration and caricatured performance, whitewashing is its antithesis, defined by its underexpression and inhibition by which whites maintain their distance from blackness.[20] While these poles of engagement have nothing in common in terms of their presentation, their effects are the same, in that they serve as mechanisms to reinscribe racial essentialism and racial domination. Through whitewashing, white society is able to indulge in its desire and attraction to African American culture, while at the same time, through assimilation, it does not have to confront blackness and the consequences of its embrace. As a mode of engagement in dancing the Lindy Hop, whitewashing occurs through two forms of distancing: first, through the failure to actively acknowledge the historical origins of the dance in context, and second, through the inhibition of expression that characterizes the cultural logic of the dance. This dual process of whitewashing (historical-emotional) has nothing to do with the capacity or ability of white people to perform or excel at the Lindy Hop. It has everything to do, rather, with the consequences of white engagement with African American cultural forms and with how this engagement changes the cultural logic and aesthetic to fit the needs and tastes of white society. This assimilation, when taken to its fullest extent, removes all signs, traces, and articulations of blackness, resulting in a complete racial and cultural erasure of African Americans, as these cultural forms become normalized and canonized within white society. This whitewashing can be seen in the following anecdote reconstructed from my fieldnotes, in which I first saw the "Khakis Swing" ad by the Gap clothing company that ran during the spring and summer of 1998.

•

As horns began blowing the tune "Jump Jive and Wail," the Brian Setzer Orchestra's cover of the classic Louis Prima song, around ten couples of white twenty-something dancers, all clad in khaki pants, began dancing in front of a stark, empty white background. As the music played, they jumped, twisted, spun, and performed acrobatic lifts and tricks, all caught up in the movement and pleasure of Swing dancing. This flurry of passion lasted a brief fifteen seconds, and the Gap commercial ended with the lone words "Khakis Swing."

•

This group of attractive, fashionable people provoked a feeling of viewer participation—as if the audience could be there, too, dancing away with their friends. Yet nearly all Lindy Hoppers that I spoke with who had seen the ad were disappointed and outraged that it didn't feature "real" Lindy Hoppers like themselves who could really dance, not just "models." Most dancers felt that the commercial distorted the dance for the public because it didn't portray the dancing "like we do it" or "authentically."

What none of the Lindy Hoppers called into question in their critique was the racial politics of the images presented; all the dancers were white, set against a white background, with white musicians performing the music. The "distortion" for them had nothing to do with "race"; it was not that this was the complete erasure of any connection with African American culture, but that it did not portray "the dancing" properly. These layers of whiteness (the dancers, the music, the setting itself an empty space with whiteness as the background) overdetermined the image as a complete absence of context, which inadvertently mirrored the relationship between white society and African American culture. This stark acontextual representation becomes the epitome of the whitewashing of African American culture; without acknowledgment or recognition, African American cultural forms like the Lindy Hop have become the ahistorical backdrop for white pleasure and white consumption.

I interviewed Ryan Francois (a black British Lindy Hop master instructor, dancer, and choreographer who is considered one of the three best male Lindy Hop dancers in the world) on what he thought of the Gap ad. Ryan spoke candidly:

> What was the catalyst that actually made this a worldwide phenomenon? It was a commercial, a Gap commercial. The thing that is so powerful about that commercial is the fact that we got young, wholesome-looking, lily-white Americans, clean-cut right down to their haircuts, clean image, sweet and wholesome, acceptable to the white community. Slap! Bam! Instantly the white world is happy, we have a craze on our hands. Louis Prima and "Jump Jive and Wail" and this white guy pulls it out, Brian Setzer.... It was so clean I thought of that ad as almost being Nazi; it was not seeing it in its approach, it was so "white people are beautiful and this is a clean thing that they do" that it was scary. If that made Swing extremely successful on a world scale—I mean, they show this in London, across the world—what does that say about them and what they consider an acceptable image about what they enjoy about the planet? It says to me that in an era where we're supposed to have dealt with these problems, we are still in a period where we're more comfortable with seeing this white Nazi image of white Gap commercial dancers. If you look at the top three teachers of this dance, they're black: me, Steven [Mitchell], and Frankie [Manning].

Ryan's comments were not the only ones that I encountered that made the issue of race and representation the central issue. Another African Ameri-

can dancer and professional dance choreographer I interviewed expressed
her concern over media representation and the Lindy Hop accordingly:

> It is hard not to be disheartened, you don't want to be paranoid and think
> "Oh God, white people are taking over everything." But it seems so system-
> atic with everything going on. You look at the Gap ad, and the movies, and
> the ways that black dancers don't get any publicity or airtime. I choreo-
> graphed this commercial for Eddie Bauer that was all Lindy Hop, and I in-
> sisted that I wanted at least some black dancers in it. We put so much time
> in on that and it was barely ever shown. It had more black dancers than
> any other commercial out there that had "Swing" going on. I didn't think
> about it, really until you asked, but I mean it makes more sense to me now.

It is against these dominant representations that Lindy Hop has received
that highlights the tension between the origins of the dance and its current representation circulating in a global context. With little or no visibility, the African American influences and historical connections with the
dance become visually obscured. Whether intentional or not, this lack of
representation leads to a sense of the Lindy Hop as being exclusively a white
cultural form.
     It is not simply the media that whitewash African American culture
through their representations. The Lindy Hop is also whitewashed in its
enactment by Lindy Hop dancers themselves. The following anecdote taken
from my fieldnotes represents the performance of the dance at its height of
popularity in Chicago. This was a rare performance for the Jazz Rhythms
night at Dance Chicago, a five-week–long dance festival featuring a pan-
orama of jazz dance styles and showcasing some of its best talent.

·

As the lights faded and the audience clamor tapered off into silence, I could
feel my heart beat in my chest. My stomach churned with nausea as I waited
for the music to begin and the curtain to rise. I heard the cheers of the Swing
kids in the balcony above us as they anticipated our friend's performance.
Here in the crowd of the Athenaeum Theater at the Dance Chicago festival,
I was waiting for Big City Swing, one of Chicago's Lindy Hop performance
groups, to perform a Big Apple (various jazz steps taken from the Lindy
Hop, danced in a circle with a finale culminating in Lindy Hop partner dancing that is often undertaken at a breathtaking pace). Big Time Swing Time is
a commercial dance troupe that sold Lindy Hop performances as entertainment to weddings, corporate parties, and social events. Their troupe was

performing tonight amid some of the best jazz dancers in the city. Expectations were high for all the Lindy Hop dancers, because while most dancers would have loved to be part of this troupe, it was invitation and audition only, with only a handful of dancers asked to participate. Here was a prime opportunity for a group of white dancers to show that their engagement with the dance was not some act of minstrelsy, but rather its finest contemporary cultivation of the dance. I opened my program to the description of their performance:

> Big Time Swing Time "Saturday Night Fish Fry" by L. Jordan
> With the rediscovery of swing music and social dancing, Lindy Hoppers around the world have maintained strong ties to the dance. It was in the Savoy Ballroom in the '30s and '40s where African American dancers combined traditional African dancing and the Cake Walk of the slave era with the popular dances Ragtime and Charleston. To strut their stuff, the original Lindy Hop troupes would circle up to show off their best jazz steps in a dance called the Big Apple. This is our tribute to those great entertainers.

As Louis Jordan's "Saturday Night Fish Fry" started to play over the speakers, I watched the performance unfold in front of me. The dancers emerged in their bright candy-colored costumes and began to circle around the center of the stage, proceeding to run through a litany of dance steps from the '30s and '40s. Rather than overwhelming the crowd with dynamism and enthusiasm, their lifeless interpretation fell flat, as their tricks failed to muster any spectacle. While the choreography included many of the classic steps, their performance was sluggish and hesitant as if running at half-speed. The frenetic and reckless abandon that marks the Big Apple as a dance was missing. The dancers' steps and figures were recognizable, but their movements were staid, almost a clinical reproduction. My friend, seated next to me, turned to me and laughed, "What's next?" with an eye-rolling look of disappointment. I looked back at him, stunned. This was not a tribute that captured the spirit of the dance. Instead, it was something we wanted to forget. What made this performance any different from the mass-media treatments of the Lindy Hop, as seen in the Gap ad?

•

The underperformed and inhibited style often displayed in performance was not limited to the subculture of the Lindy Hop; it influenced national productions and live presentations of the dance itself. At its zenith, the Lindy Hop revival became such a popular dance craze that it made it onto the Broadway stage for *Swing! The Musical*. After its run on Broadway, which included Ryan Francois and his partner Jenny Thomas, the show toured without them in the cast. I reconstructed that evening from my fieldnotes:

•

Tonight we went to see the musical *Swing!* downtown at the Oriental Theater in Chicago. The show is now touring after the craze has faded and the dance has receded back to a small subculture. While this felt like the endnote of the dance, many of us in the Lindy Hop community hoped that as the Broadway show made its way across the country enthusiasm for the Lindy Hop could be drummed up again. The show was so bad, I couldn't imagine anyone being interested by it. Unfortunately for the dance, all the dancers on stage, including the two African Americans in the show, were trained ballet dancers. Classically trained dancers move like classically trained dancers, with their stiff upright posturing trying to do a street dance like the Lindy Hop. It was so stiff, so uninspired, so wrong, none of them looked like they were doing anything that even closely resembled Lindy Hop. I can't believe that with all the labor the Lindy Hoppers have put into reviving the dance and cultivating it, this is the product that comes out. This is worse than what the very beginning Lindy Hopper could do. I wonder deep down how the audience would've reacted if they'd seen real Lindy Hoppers up there, who could dance the dance with the right movement and enthusiasm—I wonder what a traveling show like that, of this magnitude, could do for the dance?

•

Afterward I called Ryan Francois to discuss how the show turned out the way it did and what happened to the role he played in it. As he commented,

> They didn't use anything but one Swing couple, i.e., ourselves. They've seen them all; they've seen the Rhythm Hot Shots [the most prestigious Lindy Hop performance group and principal revivalists from Sweden], they've seen all the dancers we've brought them, but they're not interested. They see that I'm able as a Swing dancer to choreograph swing numbers, yet in their wisdom they decided to bring in a ballet choreographer to be both director and choreographer of a show about Swing. To the point where we had a person who had to read books from the day she got the job to learn anything about Swing, even the names of swing bands and swing tunes. Even to this day she doesn't know anything about the actual dances that were created within the Lindy Hop or any other side of Swing. She wouldn't have known what a Big Apple is unless we told her—however, she represents the establishment of the Broadway community and of course she be-

came the choreographer. This concern with making Lindy Hop palatable for white audiences not only shapes the way it's presented to audiences, but it also reflects the audiences who come to see those performances. And then you remove the one Swing couple . . . and there you have it.

In another interview, Ryan commented on how this process of assimilation affected the whole of society:

Moving your hips to something that was considered to be "animal"—it was jungle things that black slave people did—any suggestion that any dance that has that in its frame structure can have anything to do with white culture is silly, but that's the way things go. What happens is that in white communities, they assimilate the culture of an ethnic group, which is the same for Broadway and the established show business areas. They assimilate a culture and then assimilate it to dancers, who are usually white and learn through a white system known as ballet. They come in and assimilate these cultures, break them down so they're much more presentable to white audiences. And pretty soon what you have is a version of the original style which is simplified to meet the needs of white audiences, who have money and culturally still go back to the idea that Glenn Miller is the king of swing. It maintains the status quo that you don't have to be truly educated as to the reality of what that is—because the reality is that you have to move over to somebody else's culture to understand it.

Assimilating African American cultural forms into white communities by altering their aesthetic and style leads to a whitewashing of the dance from its original context.

This process of whitewashing goes on not only in the performance of the dance, but in everyday social dancing as well. In an interview with Steven Mitchell, he commented,

People are not dancing together. They're going through the steps and motions but they are not dancing together. You can't find the pocket by yourself. Together you must find that pocket, that groove—just right in there. Dancing together—trying to do this so people dance together, that's what it's all about. Waltz, Salsa, Argentine Tango—it's the same thing in Swing, too. But without the connection, it looks like this wild dance. That's why black people don't like it, because there is no connection in it—there's no spirit in it—there's nothing in it now. Mind you, it's better now than it was before. But what's missing in the dance is the love, the love and—I don't know—if love is enough, it's just because love means different things to different people. What's missing is the sensuality. There's no sex in the dance—I think we are afraid of using those kinds of metaphors. Maybe we need to say those things that are missing in the dance—come on, ladies, dance with this man like you're making love to him. We say, Oh, I need this, I need that, and we're afraid to say, Can you just grind the hips more? I don't know if that's the thing to say, but it seems that those are the things that are missing. There's no sensuality in the dance at all. What's wonderful about this is that you have a man dancing with a woman, but there's nothing when you don't feel it. When I'm looking out on the floor, it's not because it's a colored thing; it's because there is no sensuality in the dance. I don't see any warmth, I don't see any color—I don't see any passion. There's no passion; it's just been sucked out of it.

This notion of the sexuality of the dance, the blackness of the dance that has been removed, is a result of the white mode of engagement that simultaneously desires the dance and yet holds out reservation in its execution. Just as the racial imagination conceptualizes blackness as more sexual, it negotiates that boundary by denying the sexuality of the dance in whites' enactment of it. When asked if this could change, Steven replied:

If you never felt the Blues then it is hard to get people to feel the blues, it is hard to mime something you never felt, part of the problem is that if you have never felt these things before, it is hard for me to convey to you and have you move to it, if you don't know what that feeling is. . . . It really is about the feeling. I'm not saying it's impossible. Why would I teach if I thought it was pointless? It just takes a long time to get people to get into expressing themselves in ways they are not used to at all. It is one of the biggest challenges, to get open up. People are just so constrained and tight. It's like people are scared to express themselves. Once you start hesitating and being self-conscious, then you lose the feeling. Sometimes it just makes you wonder why?

This sense of "feeling" linked to notions of expression is a key element in the way that the dance becomes underexpressed. As indicated above, it is not impossible for whites to feel the dance, but the unfamiliarity with this type of dance leads to a hesitancy and self-consciousness that prevents dancers from fully engaging the dance.

Since so few images of African American culture or identity accompanied the contemporary formation of the Lindy Hop, I decided to ask the few African American Lindy Hop dancers how they thought this identity shaped the ways that people engaged in the dance. Two close friends and former students of mine, David Stevens and Michelle Boyd, sensed this feeling of racial erasure. One evening after dance class they told me that sometimes they made an effort to go out and dance less for the pure enjoyment than for the political aspect of representation: "We feel like we need to go out and dance sometimes if for no other reason than just to remind people that there are black people who dance, who do it, so they don't forget that black people do it too, or that it was a black dance. I mean, if we didn't, there wouldn't be any black people out there."

The absence of African Americans from the Lindy Hop world perpetuates its alienation from African American culture and identity, to the point where most young people have no idea where the dance came from. In fact, one African American female friend who was not a Lindy Hop regular had this to say during an interview:

> I was with a few of my [African American] girlfriends at Liquid one time, just so they could check it out, and I went out on the dance floor and danced a couple of songs. When I came back, my friends looked at me stunned, like, "I can't believe you know how to do that." I told them, "Yeah, well, it's our dance, we created it." They had no idea it was a black dance. I mean, they really thought this was just something white people did. They were totally shocked when I told them.

I asked her if she felt this was a widely shared belief in the African American community. She replied that in fact it was:

> Yeah, sad to say, but most black folks just think it's a white thing. They have no idea, but then again, look at who's in the movies and on the ads, and who the clubs advertise to. White clubs, white faces. It's something that is not marketed to them or their interests.

The further the Lindy Hop is whitewashed from the African American community, the more complete the racial erasure becomes. This ends in a perverse irony: the few African American Lindy Hop dancers learn from white instructors, who are teaching them an African American social dance. When I shared this thought with an African American dancer I met at the Herräng dance camp in Sweden, she agreed that it was one of the dangerous outcomes of white engagement with African American culture. But she offered a way out: "Man, if Puff Daddy made a video and put a bunch of black dancers in it doing Lindy Hop, and he did it, too—if they saw Puff Daddy doing the Lindy Hop—this place would be overrun with black people. There would be so many of us here that you wouldn't know where to put us." If there were a visible or articulated link to African American culture, this could help prevent the dance from becoming erased from African American consciousness, as well as from the underexpression that white society is engages it through.

By examining the way that whitewashing underexpresses the dance, we can come to understand both the erasure of the African American cultural influence and history, and the mode of white engagement it fosters. As a result, we see how notions of race create ambivalence and hesitation, whether subconsciously or consciously, about the ways that race operates within the world of the Lindy Hop. Not only does it inform, whether consciously or subconsciously, the ways that people perceive and understand each other racially; it also informs the ways that dancers perceive and understand themselves and others as they engage the Lindy Hop.

COMMODIFICATION

One of the most insidious crimes occurring in this democracy is that of designating another, politically weaker, less socially acceptable, people as the receptacle for one's own self disgust, for one's own infantile rebellions, for one's own fears of, and retreats from, reality. It is the crime of reducing the humanity of others to that of a mere convenience, a counter in a banal game which involves no apparent risk to ourselves. With us Negroes it started with the appropriation of our freedom and our labor; then it was our music, our speech, our dance and the comic distortion of our image by burnt-corked, cotton gloved corn-balls yelling, "Mammy!" And while it would be futile, non-tragic, and un-Negro American to complain over the processes through which we have become who and what we are, it is perhaps permissible to say that the time for such misappropriations ran out long ago.

Ralph Ellison (1994, 171)

The third mode of engagement through which white society embraces the Lindy Hop is that of commodification. Through marketing and brokering African American cultural forms as "white" property, white society has been able to produce its version of "blackness" to entertain white audiences and sell other consumer goods. Through the commodification of blackness, whites are able to embrace blackness as a thing rather than African Americans as people. Through the process of commodification, African American cultural forms like the Lindy Hop—a once-oppositional practice formed under explicit segregation and racism—are turned into a consumer good like any other commodity in the marketplace. Because the Lindy Hop went underground for so long, it had to be brokered back into mainstream society; these cultural logics and aesthetics of translation shape the way that the Lindy Hop is presented, conceptualized, and embodied today. Not only does this dominate African Americans by turning their practices into objects in the marketplace, it also dominates whites, as they can never fully grasp culture as practice or, in Raymond Williams's (1989) terms, "as an entire way of life," and instead are prevented from fully engaging the Lindy Hop.

When the Lindy Hop dance featured in the Gap advertisement became a national sensation, other companies immediately started utilizing the dance in their own marketing. Companies such as Haggar Clothing, Buick, Kahlua, Brummell and Brown, TNT NBA Basketball, Toyota, Dockers, Disney, Burger King, Carson Pirie Scott, and even Coca-Cola sought to cash in on the latest trend-setting craze (Coke's campaign was called "It's the real Swing"). Vintage and recycled stores started running ads promoting their "vintage '40s" Swing attire; stores started selling zoot suits, fedoras, cocktail dresses, and other accoutrements for the new Swing dancer. Record stores marketed their "swing" music and videos, record companies repackaged ever-changing combinations of "classic" swing songs as theme music to the Lindy Hop, while dance accessory stores offered "swing" shoes. Broadway theater in its endless run of musicals tapped into the market with *Swing! The Musical*. The commodification of the Lindy Hop reached its zenith when it became an exercise routine. *Fitness* magazine ran an article on Swing dancing in its December 1998 issue that promoted the Lindy Hop as an alternative workout to the gym, which "will get your blood moving, heart pounding and calories smokin'." In an interview, one formerly influential Chicago instructor, Penny Huddleston, claimed that Lindy Hopping had certainly changed her life: "Swing dancing is a fabulous cardiovascular form of exercise. . . . I used to run and do aerobics religiously, but now I dance at least four nights a week. It's practically replaced all my other strength and aerobic workouts."

Commodification not only generated an outpouring of products, it created an entire "scene," with fashion norms, slang, and nightclubs, that was covered in weekly and monthly magazines as the latest trendy social scene. Swing magazines and Web sites proliferated with reviews of music, CDs, dance venues, and endless lists of dance instructors. Local weeklies began running "guides" to their respective scenes, while across the country, national magazines like *US News and World Report*, the *Smithsonian*, and *GQ* ran feature stories about the Swing revival. *Sunset* ran a story on the Lindy Hop revival and where to Swing when in Denver; even Southwest Airlines ran a lengthy feature in their in-flight magazine called "The Joint Is Jumping," with a list of contact numbers and clubs in the cities at some of its major airport hubs. The Lindy Hop exploded into national television and film: in the TV shows *Beverly Hills 90210, Everybody Loves Raymond, Ally McBeal,* and *Dharma and Greg* and movies such as *Three to Tango* and *Blast from the Past.*

Live dancing was featured on the MTV Music Awards, the Grammy Awards, the Super Bowl Halftime Show, and the Orange Bowl Halftime Show.

Not only was the Lindy Hop mediated through media spectacle and consumer goods; it also was disseminated by brokers of the dance who made it accessible through demonstrations, performances, and dance classes. As the Lindy Hop was exploding in popularity, everyone from ballroom studios and salsa dancers to country western dancers began offering Swing dance lessons. Newspapers, magazines, local and national Web sites, and advertisement fliers in bars and clubs constantly promoted venues to dance and places to take lessons. One Lindy Hop teaching group went so far as to market their lessons with the description "as seen in the Gap ad 'Khakis Swing'" in order to attract customers. Almost immediately there were Lindy Hop instructors everywhere, offering group and private lessons, classes, and workshops. As the Lindy Hop reached its peak, marketing took the dance to new realms. In an attempt to market the Lindy Hop in new ways, there were no longer simple stages of dance progression: beginner, intermediate, and advanced. Now classes were diced up into ever more specialized areas in order to sell the dance; suddenly there were classes on turns, spins, tricks, jazz movement, and other catchy titles like "swing on it" or "Lindy Hop heaven," a constant repackaging to divide the Lindy Hop into as many consumable portions as possible. Despite the proliferation of classes, this did not necessarily mean improvement in the quality of dancers or a deepening in the quality of the community. As one international instructor said,

> Oh yeah, we show up somewhere and look around, and everyone and their brother can teach you Lindy Hop. But people don't know, and that's the problem—without education, how are people supposed to understand what is real and the like? And then when you see that it's not even their culture that they are peddling, it makes it more unconscionable. Yet that's the way that certain communities make their money.

This frantic Lindy Hop commodification meant that instructors were sometimes just steps ahead of their students. Many teachers started to teach Swing dancing with only a few months of lessons, if that, while others would take a dance class on one night and teach the very same moves to other students later in the week.

After a few years, as the Swing scene started to decline in interest, the dance instruction company I was working for had an instructors-only meeting. We were invited to participate in planning the company's future, now that the Swing scene was fading in popularity. In looking for new ways of promoting the dance and piquing dancers' interests, we considered widening our scope and teaching other dances related to the Lindy Hop. Unfortunately, since so few people had any dance training outside of the Lindy Hop, this led to a frantic search for information in order to keep the machinery of Lindy Hop dance classes going:

•

All the Lindy Hop Inc. instructors had gathered that evening in order to brainstorm new ideas for the Lindy Hop community, focusing specifically on how we could increase the number of students and thereby sustain our level of pay, as the scene was starting to fade. One instructor commented that it would be nice if we could offer other types of classes in addition to Swing, if we could be more of a general social dance group. Another instructor suggested that we start offering classes in shag, an upright dance done to swing music that had been popular in the bobby-soxer white community. But no one in our group knew how to do that dance, let alone teach it. A third teacher suggested that the group "should fly me to Washington D.C. for a one-day intensive and I'll come back and teach it." Embarrassingly enough, one of the original Swing revivalists who had been dancing the Lindy Hop for fifteen years, one of the founding members of the great Swedish performance troupe the Rhythm Hot Shots, was in town for a visit and had attended the meeting. Upon hearing the third teacher's suggestion, he slowly leaned over and whispered in my ear, "I think it's a little bit more complicated than one day of lessons to acquire enough knowledge to teach those steps. That's just my opinion."

•

Two years into my dance education, I started to notice a new form of commodification develop.

•

One afternoon, I went to Best Buy looking for a CD. I walked down one of the aisles and a Swing dance video caught my eye. I immediately turned and examined it: a two-video set called *Swing Craze* that claimed to offer a history of the Swing revival and the basic steps. I noticed that it was just one of almost a dozen videos on the shelf, all promoting themselves as instructionals for Swing dancing. This one in particular offered "2 Swinging Tapes" that would enable me to "Learn the walk, the talk, and the basic steps plus a few swank moves. It's killer-diller!" Having attended several international camps by this time and started my research on the Lindy Hop, I was amused to see that none of these tapes featured any of the master teachers I'd met or even heard of over the past two years.

•

As I was writing this chapter, I performed a search on Amazon.com to see what I could find under "Swing dancing" and "Lindy Hop." The search pulled up fifty videos on Swing instruction, with titles like *Let's Swing Dance, Lindy Hop: The Basics, Swing Craze, Everybody Dances Swing!, Let's Dance Swing, Learn To Dance and Swing , Romance of Dance—Swing,* and *Bring Back the Romance of Dance.* Even dance franchise chains like Fred Astaire offered videos on Swing. One especially interesting video described its instructor as the author of the Lindy Hop syllabus for the Arthur Murray Franchise. While instructional videos are helpful for students learning the dance, small-time local instructors from Chicago, Minnesota, Washington, DC, and Paris, among others, hosted all but one or two. Not all instructors feel that this is the best thing for advancing the dance. Two world-champion Lindy Hop dancers, Kenneth and Helena Norbelie, from Sweden, told me:

> It seems like the typical American approach, to try and make money off of something, make videotapes of yourself, promotional tapes or instructional tapes or whatever you want to call them. We're hesitant because sometimes we don't think we're worthy of doing it, I think it is a big decision, one we're not ready to make. It's like teachers. Some people come to us and they take two hours of privates and then they go home and they think they can teach. It really takes more work to master a dance than most people think. There are more issues to think about before people think they can just put out a teaching video of themselves. And it is terrible for the dancing because you have dancers who don't know what they are doing trying to learn from the videos of people who don't know what they are doing.

While commodification has taken the Lindy Hop to its most accessible form—DVDs enjoyed in your own home—at the same time the dance has been ripped from its cultural form to be sold at the nearest video store, translated by instructors who are not recognized as "masters" of the dance by the international community.

This rush to commodify the dance does not stop at the moves and steps; commodification overtakes the dancers and innovators of the dance. The story of buying and selling the Lindy Hop is an old story, according to international instructor and principal revivalist Ryan Francois. From the beginning, he claims,

they [the New York Swing community, who were some of the first to promote the revival in the United States] brought in people like Frankie, thinking that he was going to be treated better. But no, the thing they did best
with people like Frankie and Pepsi was to have their pictures taken next to
them to validate anything that they did: "This is accepted by Frankie Manning, that great black person, and look at all of us standing next to him."

In fact, he later told me that this was the context in which he met another
future principal revivalist, Steven Mitchell:

> A group of us were sitting in this person's basement, and they had invited
> Frankie and Norma, and at that time Lindy Hop was really up for grabs.
> They knew Frankie and Norma had something special, but they also knew
> they had to get something out of them. Now I was in the Jiving Lindy Hop-
> pers [an English performance troupe] at the time, and Steven was just Ste-
> ven with Erin. So there was the Jiving Lindy Hoppers, a troupe made up
> of all white people, barring myself, and Sylvia and Jonathan and a whole
> bunch of white people, and Frankie and Norma. Now what made Steven
> and I connect with each other, actually, was that I saw Frankie for the first
> time, a black man from a certain era. But I also saw a black man across
> the room, another black guy. And just as I saw him, he saw me. We both
> had that same look on our faces—that look of support you give someone
> when they're an outsider to that system. The thing is that all these people
> were picking like little pigeons at Frankie and Norma, being friendly with
> them because they wanted something, they wanted to get their ideas;
> they wanted Frankie and Norma to see them as wonderful people so they
> could get something from them. We were the only two people in this
> orgy of white people not firing compliments at them and doing anything
> they needed to get what they wanted from these black people, to be great
> Lindy Hoppers themselves, to create their own power structures in order
> to move on with it. I looked across the room, and then I realized that the
> only people who were giving Frankie and Norma any space were the only
> other two black people in the room—and we didn't even know each other.

Steven Mitchell comments on how this commodification of himself still
plagues and disturbs him today. His response to my question was simply,
"Man, they will bleed you. They will bleed you dry of your knowledge of the
dance, of your gift." This sense of ownership, of controlling the Lindy Hop
like a consumer good, continues to run though the dance.
   The ultimate act of commodification came one evening when I arrived

late to Club Liquid. The following anecdote is a reconstruction taken from my fieldnotes that documents that experience.

•

One Thursday evening in the summer of 2000, I arrived at Club Liquid around 10:30. As I approached the building I saw a few friends standing outside the door. Leaving the club and walking past me were a number of young African Americans. They were all very well dressed in suits and ties; a few were even wearing tuxedos. I did a double take—was I at the right club? Was this the right night? Why were all these young African Americans here? What was going on? I went inside and saw about a dozen African Americans having drinks at the back tables of the club—more African Americans than had ever been there on the Swing night. They seemed to be checking out the scene. None of them was dancing. There was swing music playing, African American artists playing swing, and some Swing kids dancing out there on the floor. I thought to myself, What an ironic situation—black people watching white people dancing to African American music and doing an African American dance. I wondered what they thought. I asked the bartender and some of the wait staff; it turned out that a black charity event had been held that night before the club changed over to its swing theme. Not long after I arrived, the Swing kids started pouring into the club. The racial mix was quickly dissolved as the club became almost all white. As a result, the remaining African Americans quickly left; they either were uninterested or felt uninvited. It was a strange, almost surreal scene.

•

Later that night I checked my phone messages. A friend who had attended the charity event had left me a message, telling me to call her. We discussed what we had each seen that night:

B, it was crazy. You should have been there; it was insane. We had this fundraiser at Liquid and the crowd was pretty high profile, some really nice people turned out for this event. There was a comedian and then the DJ played, some hip hop and some R&B, really chill, it was a real good time. And when the event was over, they announced that there was a Swing night next and we should stay and check it out. Then the music changed over. Right there, no mixing it in, no progression, just boom, that's it, on to Swing. Which was okay. But you could see it like the changing of the guard. When it was still hip hop and R&B, when there were still people hanging out, they had opened the doors and the Swing kids were coming in. They were all lining up around the dance floor. I felt like we were being surrounded. Then when the music changed, it was literally like the Swing kids came on and pushed us off the dance floor. I have never, ever in my life seen black people leave a dance floor; it was so bizarre. And there was no mixing—I mean, the music ended and then the blacks got off and the whites got on. And it wasn't like we felt like we were welcome; I mean, we were literally pushed off the dance floor.

This seminal anecdote illuminates the great irony of the Lindy Hop in contemporary society. Here at this club, whites were excluding African Americans from the dance floor while they danced African American dances to African American music. The changing of places in a social space, the whites moving onto the dance floor and then excluding African Americans, suggests that this happened for a reason. The white dancers wanted to take over the space and perform their African American dances and listen to African American music without any interference, especially not from actual African Americans. The entitlement that they felt suggested their deep belief that this was their space, their time, their dance.

This mode of engagement with the Lindy Hop as cultural property enables a selective engagement with African American culture: the ability to sever African American culture from African American people for white consumption and pleasure. This is not cultivating interracial participation or multiculturalism; this is the entitlement of white society to exercise their control over black culture while defending their segregated use of it. However, there were several strong opinions against this view when I spoke with a few of the teachers and workshop organizers of the Lindy Hop:

It is a business. This is what I do; I'm a professional. Why do you think some of us don't want to be filmed? This is my property, these are my ideas. This is my livelihood, this is how I make a living. When someone else steals what I'm doing, that's taking food out of my mouth in a sense. I love to teach, but I don't do it for free.

Another responded to my question of the buying and selling of culture question:

You act like people haven't gotten paid for this. Why do you think people perform? Whitey's Lindy Hoppers got into the movies, they got paid for it. People pay for lessons, they pay for workshops, people pay to go to the clubs, to dances, since when was this not about money?

This sense of payment and the exchange of money as justification for current practices, while true, misrecognizes the larger social issues that emerge from the unintended

One African American dancer in the Chicago scene told me she was interested in trying to get more African Americans involved in the scene and that she hoped there could be more marketing to African Americans. She emailed the most important Lindy Hop dance instructor who owned the dominant teaching company on the Lindy Hop scene in Chicago and asked him about marketing classes on the South Side of the city, which is predominantly African American. In a phone conversation I had with her later in the week, she told me,

> He wrote back and basically said that he didn't know there was any interest for it, but if I wanted to set it up he would be happy to teach classes. Yeah, so I do all the work so he doesn't actually have to extend himself to the black community, and that's gonna fly? I don't think so. Whatever.
> Sometimes I feel like saying "this is our dance." Because we are responsible and sometimes I fall back to black pride and say white people will never be able to dance this like black people will and that's just ludicrous, but I do think some it is a race thing with some of the dance troupes will ever be as hardcore, maybe it is a race thing because other people see some of these groups as good as Whitey's Lindy Hoppers, some people see them equally, but I see it differently. It comes from our culture, from African Americans, it's ours.

White people use African American culture for their own economic gain. They package it, produce it, and rewrite history to justify the ways commodification maintains racial domination. When examining who is making money, who is buying, selling, and utilizing the dance as a resource in the marketplace, the racial identity of whites comes to bear prominently. There are so few African Americans involved, either through choice or through systematic neglect, that we must stop and question how this form has been severed from its original historical context. Commodification as a mode of engagement also serves as a mechanism of racial domination by decontextualizing African American history; it turns the Lindy Hop into just another commodity in the marketplace. This acontextual market logic serves as a timeless responsibility-free vacuum within which racial domination does not appear; by using the logic of the market, commodification appears as a normal and natural outcome of what people do with culture in American society. While commodification as a process may circulate through all cultural forms, the consequences that this has on African Americans—that racial domination and economic exploitation go hand in hand—go to the very heart of the way that white racial domination has organized society in relation to African Americans.

Some may see people dancing, having fun, socializing, and blowing off steam at clubs, while others may see racial domination occurring through the particular modes of engagement by which the dance is inculcated and enacted. By examining these modes of engagement and the way that race is conceptualized and enacted, we gain insight into how racial essentialism and racial domination are reinscribed in society. By examining these modes of engagement as negotiations between blackness and whiteness, we can see how the contradictory desire for and disdain of African American culture and people generates these particular modes of engagement. As the sociopolitical climate has changed in the post–civil rights era of colorblindness and multiculturalism, so have the mechanisms of domination. Considering the long and complicated history that frames and structures white interaction with African American culture in America, we can understand that the symbolic politics of these current representations are linked to much larger historical trajectories and that people are caught up in and participate in cultural struggles not of their own making. As these processes of the racial imagination, minstrelsy, whitewashing, and commodification operate, the structural gap between "playing" black in white society and being black in white society creates the context and conditions of race, culture, and identity by which African American cultural forms are negotiated. By examining this contradiction of attraction and repulsion through the enthusiasms, self-consciousness, and reticence that define engagement, whites never have to confront or understand the African American experience or the historical ways that whites have dominated African Americans and exploited their cultural forms, because nothing is at stake in their mastery of African American cultural forms other than their own self-interest and pleasure.

By examining this cross-cultural dynamic of whites appropriating and practicing the Lindy Hop, we can see how the racial imagination naturalizes racial difference through bodily difference. This leads to an ironic end of the investigation; while the mechanisms of white racial domination usually operate positively by normalizing white interests as natural, in this case whiteness is working negatively to make sure that African Americans, racialized as rhythmic and innate dancers, do not turn into history and reveal the labor and cultivation that African Americans undertook to create their art forms (Bourdieu 2000a). The irony here is so powerful because it is white people who are so invested in the labor of learning African American dances like the Lindy Hop (the years, effort, money, and dedication that the white community has invested to cultivate the dance), and yet none of this leads to any curiosity or need for greater cultural understanding. This allows whites to engage African American cultural forms without having to value and respect African American people as cultural laborers and contributors. Allowing nature to turn into history, allowing the arduous labor necessary to develop and cultivate African American cultural forms like the Lindy Hop to go unrecognized, would undermine the myths of racial difference between whiteness and blackness. As the racial imagination through which we conceptualize and enact our understandings of race and racial difference in the world continues unexamined, our modes of enactment reinforce racial domination. Even though white Lindy Hoppers may not perceive their actions as perpetuating racial domination, by examining their modes of engagement with the dance, we can see that their bodies are caught in the act.

While for most of the Lindy Hoppers the issues of race goes predominately misrecognized, their actions have repercussions beyond the context of the dance subculture. By locating our engagements with popular culture, how we come to embody those forms within which we participate, we can locate the body within larger contexts of ideological representations beyond the realm of dance alone to see how the racial imagination is enacted and produced through the body. Since cultural forms are not autonomous and our understandings of social life are not compartmentalized, the engagement with cultural forms of any type shapes the social interaction and social relations in everyday life. Cultural forms offer the symbols and sites where we negotiate the Ellisonian contradictions and conflicts over our notions of who and what we are. While it may be argued that there is a break between the past and the present, between our segregated past and the multiculturalism of present-day life, the notions of blackness and whiteness of the past and present remain intertwined. Just because caricatures are social constructions does not mean they are any less real in the effect they have on social life. As Ellison reminds us, whether consciously or unconsciously our racial imagination is overdetermined. Our participation in everyday life constantly socializes us into the social roles we go out and perform. And somewhere between our true self and the world out there, between fact and fiction, are the racial masks we use to act out these roles and construct the identities we believe to be our own.

3 PUT A LITTLE COLOR ON THAT!

> This unwillingness to resolve the conflict in keeping with his democratic ide-
> als has compelled the white American, figuratively, to force the Negro down
> into the deeper level of his consciousness, into the inner world, where reason
> and madness mingle with hope and memory and endlessly give birth to
> nightmare and to dream; down into the province of the psychiatrist and the
> artist, from whence spring the lunatic's fancy and his work of art.
>
> *Ralph Ellison (1995b, 99)*

Having been through a grueling day of dance lessons on Catalina Island, I
settled down for a glass of iced tea and a conversation with Lennart Westerlund. Lennart was one of the primary Lindy Hop revivalists from Sweden,
and was also the ringleader of the most spectacular performance troupe
in world—the Rhythm Hot Shots. Lennart and I had spoken many times
before, but this was my first chance to actually sit down and interview him.
As we settled into the living room, I asked Lennart what he thought about
the issue of race in relationship to the dance, and how, if in any way, he saw
it playing out in the ways that people danced.

> I think that the main problem is that jazz, Afro-American dance, is not our
> [whites'] culture. It is Afro-American culture. I think most of us, when we
> grew up, I think we grew up during other circumstances than people did
> in the '20s and '30s. And the Afro-American culture was probably very
> different during that time from, should I say, an ordinary white kind of
> culture. So I think the main problem is we have never been living with an
> Afro-American culture close to us.

As usual, Lennart's comments were thoughtful and suggestive. I asked him
to expand on the idea of "our" culture and how this made a difference. After
pausing for a long moment, Lennart went on:

> I think this dance, it is their dance. We can never change that. It is their
> dance, and I don't think we can get all the pieces. It doesn't matter how
> much we try because we never grew up with it. And it must be inside you
> from the very beginning if you should get it 100 percent. And that's the

main problem we are facing, I think. It's Afro-American dancing, and we are not Afro-Americans.

Lennart's comments blurred the boundaries between history, culture, and race. While he was pointing out the historical context of the time that the Lindy Hop emerged on the one hand, on the other he was signaling the innate capacity of African Americans to dance in a particular way. This linkage of nature and nurture was one that I would come to encounter time and time again. In discussing the same issue with Kenneth and Helena Norbelie, two world-class Lindy Hop dancers also from Sweden and heads of an up-and-coming performance troupe Shout 'n' Feel It—they responded with a different take on the issue:

Kenneth: I think the question you ask is a difficult one for us as Swedes. We really don't think about these issues of race.

Helena: We don't have your race problems, so when people talk about black and white in the States, it took some time for us to understand these politics.

Kenneth: I agree with Helena. When we were in New York for the first time, we wanted to go to Harlem and see the place where the Savoy Ballroom used to be. When we got back to the hotel and told some of the Americans, they thought we were crazy. The said, "You shouldn't go walking around there by yourselves. Are you nuts?" They said it wasn't safe and that we would get mugged or something.

Helena: They asked if people starred at us. I didn't understand why people would stare at us at first until they explained that white people didn't walk around Harlem like that.

Kenneth: We thought it was kind of funny, actually, that they would say that.

Helena: Like I said, we don't have your race problems so we didn't think about where we can or cannot go. I remember thinking why would they stare at us? Being Swedish, it just doesn't occur to us. As for the dancing, I think we as Swedes all know it is a black American dance.

Kenneth: I think that is one of the reasons we got so into it, because it is so different from the kind of dancing normally in Sweden.

As Kenneth and Helena pointed out in their comments, the issues of race are not obvious to everyone. Certainly in the case of Lennart, Kenneth, and

Helena, the cultural and geographic distance gave them a unique perspective on the issue. It was their distance from the issue that provoked my curiosity about how American dancers thought about the issues of race, culture, and identity.

Ralph Ellison's discussion of the problem of language in American society is a call to analyze the contexts and circumstances by which language mediates the "truth about processes and relationships between people in this country" (1994, 457). Ellison aims to explore the taken-for-granted assumptions of our language, to interpret its meaning, which is never transparent. In order to understand both our past and our present, we must come to terms with how this language was not ours, rather something we inherited and adapted to new circumstances and contexts in a new world. For Ellison, the issue of language is an issue of interpretation; the meanings that inform our language form the understandings we have of society. In this sense, language is constitutive of our social life and therefore always a matter of interpretation.

In order to take up Ellison's call, we must consider the context within which we consider issues of race, culture and identity in today's society. Among others, two dominant themes structure our outlook in contemporary American society: colorblindness and multiculturalism. Colorblindness is defined by the belief that we are all equal under the law. As a result, people feel that race no longer—or should no longer—matter, in any way. Based on this, people often claim that we live in a society that openly accepts and promotes the tolerance of multiple cultures. Multiculturalism defines society as one of cultural pluralism where groups are able to express their cultural views and expressions without prejudice or hostility because there are no longer racial or ethnic biases against groups. These two dominant themes form an interconnected web of meanings, each supporting and reinforcing the other, that create the dominant American ideology that often goes unchallenged in society. These themes are not something imposed on us from above, nor are they added onto our already existing ways of thinking about the world; instead, they form the basis through which we have been socialized and conceptualize the world as commonsense.

On the surface, the Lindy Hop revival is a story about a creative subculture deriving pleasure from and constructing identities out of the cultural resources of everyday life.[1] Given that most dancers have been raised within this cultural context, most dancers have a difficult time recognizing or accepting the racial dimensions of their actions or understanding the history of racial oppression that makes the issue of white consumption and participation in African American culture so contentious. The very mention of "race" draws immediate rejection and incredulity that they are involved in something that may have to do with race. While this narrative could focus on the various ways that dancers find joy and excitement in their engagement with the dance, this chapter uses the Lindy Hop as a window into the racial dynamics of society. Having taught the Lindy Hop to hundreds of students and having had hundreds of conversations with dancers, teachers, and performers over the years, I have noticed the emergence of a dominant theme: people are adamant that, despite how it may appear, the Lindy Hop has nothing to do with race.

Although it is an integral part of African American history and culture, little if any discussion has been made of the racial identity of this cultural form. Whether taught by local dance teachers, discussed on Internet sites, represented in television commercials, or written about in popular press articles, depictions and descriptions of the Lindy Hop are always framed as the "American dance" or the "national dance." While some have acknowledged that the dance originated in Harlem, and some have even made specific reference to its purported birthplace at the Savoy Ballroom, nothing has been said about the culture or the people that cultivated this particular form (DeFrantz 2002; Emery 1988; Gottschild 2002; Malone 1996). This racial absence leads many to mistake this as the revival of the Jitterbug, the white name for the dance that emerged when whites first embraced the Lindy Hop in the 1930s and '40s. Even the issues of the dance's name leads to a further deepening of the issue of trying to identify a pure identity or "origin" by which one could measure out exactly how history "really" unfolded. Those who are familiar with the dance or have attempted to learn about it may have some vague understanding of its link to African American culture through old video clips of dancers, magazine photos, or the very few living original African American dancers who still teach the dance. However, to the casual observer or dancer, the consistent representation of the Lindy Hop encountered in everyday forms of mass-mediated culture, as well as in the teaching, performing, and promoting of the dance, is one that is exclusively white. Without knowing any better, one would naturally assume that the Lindy Hop is a white dance and an integral part of white identity. Although the historical emergence of the Lindy Hop as an African American cultural form cannot be denied, it is not articulated or acknowledged in its contemporary context. This absence of the African American identity of the Lindy Hop raises serious questions about how race, identity, and culture operate in American society.

In the pages that follow, I reconstruct the Lindy Hop points of view through the discourses that dancers use to articulate, express, and explain to themselves and to others their engagement with the Lindy Hop.[2] In doing so, I reject the notion that there is one single point of view and instead insist that we must look at multiple and competing points of view to understand the dominant logic at work within this world (Auyero 2001; Wacquant 1995a). In this reconstruction, I extend Bourdieu's notions of symbolic power, symbolic violence, and misrecognition to situate the discourses of the Lindy Hop within the larger framework of racial domination in American society. Doing so exposes how racial domination is produced and perpetuated through everyday cultural practices in the ways that dancers think and feel about their engagement with the dance. These discourses are not specific to the Lindy Hop; they are drawn from and emerge from larger racial frameworks of understanding that circulate throughout society as a whole.[3] In presenting this particular overview of the Lindy Hop, I offer a way to understand how racial domination is perpetuated without strategic rationalization or manipulation. Rather it is a form of misrecognition of how racial domination works through everyday cultural practices without collapsing discourses, structures, or the participants under investigation into a one-dimensional analysis that obscures the different modalities and mechanisms of racial domination.[4]

Analytically separating these components of language becomes of paramount importance when trying to contextualize people's ideas within the wider discourses that circulate in American society about issues of race, culture, and politics.

•

On one occasion I was chatting with a pair of highly regarded instructors from San Francisco who were teaching a workshop in Chicago. We were discussing a recent documentary on the Bravo television network that chronicled the swing revival and its significance in contemporary American society. I thought the documentary embodied the discourse of having fun, as it celebrated the enthusiasm and passion of the revival's participants but failed to ground the dance in any cultural or historical context, leading casual viewers to believe that African Americans were marginal contributors to or participants in the Lindy Hop. One of the instructors and I had this exchange:

BH: Well, I was disappointed. It was ahistorical and didn't develop any relationship between the dance and African American culture. From the documentary, you really had no idea that this was a significant dance in the African American community; the whole thing was just white dancers, white neo-swing bands, and a celebration of white people having fun.

Sharon: Don't you think you're overanalyzing this? I mean, it's just some documentary that somebody was given a deadline for, that someone who knew nothing about Swing had to slap together. They just took whoever was available to get it done. Besides, it's great for the dance—the publicity, getting people aware of it, showing the excitement and how much fun it is to be part of this community. I really don't think people think about it like you do; I think you might be reading into this too much. But then again, you probably hang out with smart people who talk about this kind of stuff, whereas me and my friends sit around in cafés and talk about what new restaurant just opened—so us regular people don't think like you do about things like this.

                                                •

What struck me about this exchange was both her acceptance of the documentary makers' innocence and her belief that the positive images of the dance overrode any concerns about the presentation of the dance. Here I was being criticized for overanalyzing the dance, or rather for putting issues of race into situations where it is perceived not to belong. Taking the dance as an object of academic study, rather than experiencing it as recreational or a pleasurable pastime, seemed to violate the commonsense "logic" of the Lindy Hop community—something that they had defined outside of discussion at a preconscious level. It is here in at the level of the preconscious that our racial imagination forms our ideological conceptualizations of differences about body types, cultures, races, and identities.[5]

WHAT WE TALK ABOUT WHEN WE TALK ABOUT RACE

Whereas previous eras of white racial domination have been explicit either physically or symbolically, in the post–civil rights period of colorblindness and multiculturalism white racial domination works "without racists" in an implicit and often invisible form.[6] This position is one where many race scholars have argued that white racism continues to structure American society in racial inequality, only it is shrouded in "colorblindness" and "multiculturalism" that serves to conceal or disguise the real institutional arrangements of white supremacy.[7] The colorblind ideology position holds that inequality is perpetuated without ever going noticed as mentions of race become significations of reverse racism or barriers to equality and inclusivity.

In order to understand race in American society we need to understand not only the effects of racism, but the logic and ways we conceptualize and articulate race, consciously or unconsciously, in the concepts, narratives, and discourses that structure our racial imagination. It is through the racial imagination that we conceptualize, interpret, and attribute meanings and connections among the categories of culture, race, bodies, and identity. In order to do so, it is necessary to explore the ways that language itself frames and shapes the ways that we express our beliefs and understandings about the world around us.[8] We don't think before we speak; we just use the language we have, the shared social language into which we are born. As a result, the socialized ways that we have come to think and speak about the world that reflect us as both individual and social beings. More often than not, when we speak we do not think the words through before speaking, then speak; we simply utter what we are thinking. Of course, there always exists the possibility for conscious manipulation or for deliberate conscious reflection on what they we say, but normally people just respond through language without thinking about the words they use.

In thinking about language in this way, we can come to understand that what we say and what we mean can oftentimes be at odds without us even recognizing it. When this happens, it opens up an opportunity to examine what is meant by what a speaker says and the social conventions or normative ways of talking that frame those comments. Much of academic discourse on colorblind ideology seeks to expose the conspiratorial moves on the parts of whites to say the "right" thing when they really would rather say something else, or hide their real thoughts or motivations in "acceptable" language when in the presence of nonwhites. These studies look for the meanings underneath the meanings when whites speak, searching for the real "truth" hidden within their statements of their real racist sentiments.

Rather than assume conspiratorial positions, by which people avoid, rationalize, or manipulate their remarks before they utter them, this chapter will proceed by exploring the tension between what people say and what they mean. In doing so, it will highlight how and when people unthinkingly engage in cultural practices and misrecognize the symbolic and material consequences of their actions.[9] As a result, the dominant social order gets reproduced not through coercion or manipulation, but through the complicity of people unaware that they are even participating in or perpetuating the very mechanisms that dominate them (Bourdieu 1991b, 180). In this way, the theoretical framework that informs this course of study is borrowed from the work of Pierre Bourdieu, who provides the tools through which we can understand that racial domination is not the cultivation of a false consciousness, or the strategic manipulations or covert strategies of whites to disguise their racism, but a racialized commonsense embedded in our dispositions and everyday practices.

As the study progressed and more and more dancers found out about the project, not all were as open to discussing issues of race as were my friends from Sweden. Even though I had not fully worked out the whole project, specifically how I was going to address talking about race myself, I was confronted occasionally by dancers who thought I posed some sort of threat in pursuing "issues of race." One particularly memorable exchange I had with a veteran dancer and friend captured this:

Tom: You keep asking about race and the Lindy Hop. I've heard other people talking about it. So why haven't you asked me? Are you asking everyone their opinion or is it just special people? What are you trying to get at anyway? What's the whole race thing about, is this for school? Are you trying to make some big sociological point?

BH: Actually Tom, I'm not trying to make a point, I'm trying to understand how race works in society. The Lindy Hop is just an example. Don't you think it's kind of strange that so many people have traveled here from different states to come to this dance camp? In this heat? This isn't just summer vacation for everyone, people have jobs and . . .

Tom: And?

BH: And what?

Tom: So why are you making this about race? Our grandparents danced it. It is everyone's dance. I don't see any reason why black people should get more credit for the Lindy Hop than whites. In fact whites maybe should get more because they revived it. Almost everybody here is white.

BH: I'm not saying that white people can't do it, or shouldn't be here or [cut off] . . .

Tom: What I've heard is you going around and asking the instructors, I heard you been following a couple of people around in particular, what about our views? If you don't talk about what white people think, that's reverse racism. Don't you think? How many white people have you interviewed? If you make it a racial issue that's just reverse racism; why don't you just have fun like the rest of us? It's a dance camp, not your dissertation. Everything isn't about racism.

The notion that talk of race would immediately lead others to think about "reverse racism" or "reverse discrimination" brought me to realize how often whites are unaware that race is a problem until it affects them directly. Raising the issue of race within the Lindy Hop community generated an immediate sense of unjust persecution against white people, or for whites to feel that they must defend their actions against perceptions of racism.[10]

In turning to examine the particular discourses that Lindy Hop dancers use to articulate and express their world, it is necessary to consider how these discourses are not separate or autonomous frames of thinking, but are wrapped up in much larger symbolic systems. In contemporary American society, the discourses that dominate the discussion of the Lindy Hop are not specific to discussions of the dance alone; rather, they are embedded in our everyday racial commonsense. By thinking relationally, we can see that discussion of the Lindy Hop, through discourses of colorblindness and multiculturalism, links to larger discussions of race and power in American society. Through this relational analysis, we can see that these discourses, despite the intentions or interests of their participants, uphold and perpetuate white racial domination by conceptualizing their engagements with the Lindy Hop through the same misrecognition that reproduces white racial domination on a national level. In addition, these processes in turn dominate whites as well by preventing them from reaching a complete understanding of the Lindy Hop and from achieving full cross-cultural participation, because all human potentiality remains circumscribed by racial essentialism rooted in the racial imagination.

These discourses of the Lindy Hop serve as mechanisms that enable whites to embrace and enjoy African American culture, while simultaneously engaging in a dehistoricizing and decontextualizing of these forms from their racial and cultural contexts. Second, by doing so, the goal is to develop a way of theorizing the perpetuation of racial inequality that moves past the "logic of the trial" of convicting racists and exonerating antiracists. Instead this chapter offers a way to understand how racial domination is perpetuated without strategic rationalization or manipulation but rather operates through "the complicity of those who do not want to know that they are subject to it or even that they themselves exercise it" (Bourdieu 1991b, 164; 2000b, 180). In this way, we can come to understand how racial domination works without collapsing discourses, structures, or the participants under investigation into a one-dimensional analysis that obscures the different modalities and mechanisms of racial domination.[11]

One set discourse illustrates engagement with the Lindy Hop; I examine a variety of overlapping and interlocking ways that people express and articulate their positions. These are the discourses of marking whiteness, blaming the victim, talking around race, and talk of having fun. By turning to an analysis of the way that dancers articulate and express their engagements with the dance, we can begin to see how these schemas of thought serve to perpetuate white racial domination. All this maintains the hegemony of the dominant racial imagination: history doesn't matter, race issues are over, and there is no connection between what people do in everyday life and the perpetuation of racial domination.

Only by unmasking and revealing the discourses through which people conceptualize and articulate their worlds can we begin to reconceptualize and reorient our understanding not just of the Lindy Hop but of the need for a critical politics of race. This is not just a matter of changing people's minds, but changing the very logic through which they conceptualize and articulate the world. What goes misrecognized here is the domination of African Americans in terms of the instrumental use of African American culture without credit and the severing of cultural forms from their social contexts. Ultimately, this perpetuates the white domination and African American marginalization, while simultaneously coming to dominate whites in their own practices. Just as African Americans are dominated, whites are kept ignorant of history. The intended or, more often than not, unintended consequences of their actions prevent them from having a full understanding of the dance. In turn, this keeps whites locked into essentialist notions inhibiting what people can become by circumscribing blackness and whiteness in essentialized terms and by simultaneously denying that race is a factor in the way the world operates.

MARKING WHITENESS

Ironically, one central discourse for understanding and articulating the Lindy Hop is that of marking one's own white racial body. White racial domination as a system of social organization need not always deny that white identity exists as a category of racial classification; in fact, part of its very strength and power lies in its flexibility, in its ability to acknowledge that white racial identity exists while minimizing the privilege that racial identity has. The discourses in the Lindy Hop scene that function to minimize white racial domination come in two forms: (1) the celebration of certain African American natural "talents" such as rhythm, grace, or expressiveness in counter distinction to implicitly marked white identity; and (2) the use of expressions that denigrate white identity by magnifying white deficiencies or disadvantages in dancing ability. Both serve as mechanisms for symbolic violence in that they impose an understanding of race neutrality around the Lindy Hop. The symbolic violence of marking white identity causes dancers to misrecognize the structural relations of racial domination by leaving them to see all races as equal and racism as an individual pattern of attitudes and beliefs, rather than as something woven into social organization. The making of white identity comes through a gamut of forms ranging from praise to self-mockery to frustration and trepidation.

In one of my very first interviews, I asked a veteran Lindy Hop dancer an open-ended question about how race might play a role in the revival of the Lindy Hop. The dancer responded matter-of-factly that

They are just better dancers. Black people can just dance better than white people. I mean, look at Ryan and Steven. They are the best dancers and they're both black. I'm not being racist—they do it better than whites. That's not a bad thing; that's something they should be proud of.

Yeah, well, look at the best basketball players and football players, they are all black. So I mean it's no different. The best jazz musicians are black so it makes sense. When was the last time you had an awesome white basketball player? There's no white MJ [Michael Jordan].

This acknowledgment of black superiority in the ability to dance, within the larger context of multiculturalism, appears to be a flattering comment. But such flattery masks an alternative understanding that is echoed in an anecdote reconstructed from my fieldnotes.

•

One late afternoon, a group of us assembled at a dancer's apartment to watch videos of Lindy Hop dancers and try to pick up some steps from the tapes. These video sessions were common occurrences early in the Lindy Hop revival, as people were ravenous to learn as much as they could as quickly as possible. As if it were scripted, when viewing video footage of the famous African American dance troupes from the 1930s and '40s, one of the dancers would always make a general comment, as if speaking for everyone present, about the obviousness of racial difference and dancing, which would lead into discussion that usually went along lines like this one: "Oh my God, if I could look like that it would be awesome. I mean, they look great doing it. Black people look so natural dancing; white people look so stiff." "Yeah, true. It's so true. Just look at them" "They are so awesome, how come we can't dance like that." "I know, it's like we look dorky and clumsy. Everything they do is so smooth and graceful." These comments of racial difference were accepted without reservation or question and seemed to be implicitly shared among most of the dancers I encountered.

•

One interviewee rejected the idea that racism played any role in society at all; he thought that the idea that there were any "racial issues" with whites dancing the Lindy Hop was preposterous: "Look at the top dancers, the top athletes, the top musicians: they're all black. Since we [the Lindy Hop community] appreciate that and admire that, how can we be racist?"

After teaching classes with one dance partner for several weeks, I attempted to confide in her my initial thoughts on the racial dynamics of the Lindy Hop scene. Incredulous at my comments, she foretold the way that

I would come to understand how most Lindy Hop dancers conceptualize their engagement with the dance:

> Don't you think you're overreacting? All this fancy talk about race all the time. I work around plenty of black people, and they're always talking about going dancing. I told them we do Swing dancing, and they said, "Girl, we've been doing that for years," like they could care less that people like their culture. You make it sound like white people are to blame for everything—and that's what a lot of them at work say. They say all sorts of things about how racist white people are sometimes when they think I'm not listening. But I treat both black kids and white kids the same; I don't see their color. I mean, how can we be racist if this is from Harlem, and we've learned all that stuff you say about their history and culture in our [dance] class, and we still want to dance it all the time?

Beneath this veneer of colorblindness is the way that race implicitly operates in the minds of Lindy Hop dancers. Because the dominant racial logic of colorblindness shapes their understanding of racism as being simply prejudice and discrimination grounded in individual thoughts and actions, not present on a social or systematic level, this perpetuates the symbolic violence that white interest in African American culture has no relation to white racial domination.

Marking white identity also takes the form of explicitly denigrating or making fun of one's whiteness. As both a student and an instructor, during Lindy Hop classes I would often hear white students, when frustrated by trying to learn a move or step, exclaim in embarrassment—when not in earshot of the occasional African American students—"Oh my God, I feel so white." I would see dancers look for empathy in another dancer: "This really makes you feel white, huh?" Occasionally, out of pure frustration, a dancer at a workshop or dance class would become so upset with themselves they would blurt out, usually to know but themselves, "I can't get this! I'm so white!" These discourses of white deficiency, exhibited through the admission of lack of natural talent and rhythm, dramatize the essentialism of racial differences grounded in the racial body. While these discourses of self-denigration may appear to be flippant and self-mocking, they reinscribe the racial essentialism and traditional pejorative status of the naturalness of the African American body.[12] When out dancing in a club, female dancers have said to me either in prefacing our dance or when making a mistake while dancing: "You'll have to forgive me; I'm dancing so white tonight." Other times, when watching another more skilled dancer, people might say, "Doesn't he make you feel white?" Once while teaching a Lindy Hop class with a top Chicago instructor, my partner made a dramatic error when demonstrating a particular step and tripped over herself in front of a crowded room. As she regained her balance and got back on her feet, she turned to the students and, in an obviously embarrassed moment, raised her arm and said, "white girl here!" as if this whole episode were racially self-explanatory. A few dancers I encountered expressed frustration, not so much in the sense of not being able to dance, but feeling that their white identity made them inherently inferior as a dance in relation to one particular world famous Lindy Hop instructor:

> I know he's one of the best. No doubt about it. He's awesome, but he never makes you feel like you can get it. It's always like he's looking at you because you're white. I don't know if it is true or not but that's the way I feel sometimes. It's like he makes fun of us, like when he does all those exaggerations of how he thinks we look. It's like dude, just chill with the whole damn Frankenstein routine. Get over yourself, like I'm white, I get it. Enough.

Another dancer/workshop organizer expressed a similar sentiment and that he would no longer be bringing this instructor to town.

> Yeah he's a great dancer, everyone knows that. But he makes you feel like you can't do it. It's just the way he talks about things, the way he teaches, it's always so snide. I think that it is really negative. Steven [who is also black] doesn't make you feel that way. That's why I don't want to bring him in to Chicago. I think people get the wrong idea.

Marking white identity, implicitly or explicitly, while simultaneously minimizing the importance of that identity reinscribes the centrality of thinking of culture in terms of race. An anecdote reconstructed from my fieldnotes serves as the ultimate expression of how white identity can be marked all the while dismissing the importance of race.

•

During the summer of 1999, the Lindy Hop dance instruction group that I worked for and the Joel Hall Dance Company, which was not in the upper tiers of Chicago's dance talent, shared dance studio space right next to each other. This proximity to another dance company often caused great duress for the white Lindy Hop instructors, not only because this was a professional dance company holding jazz classes next to amateur Lindy Hoppers, but more important because Joel Hall was almost exclusively African

American. This racial difference created an unspoken anxiety: whites were claiming to be authorities on the "jazz" dance of the Lindy Hop, and yet they were shying away from any interaction with professional jazz dancers. For instance, one of the Lindy Hop instructors claimed to have many years of "professional" dance training, which she promoted in order to justify her position and portray herself as the top instructor. Yet when confronted with the African American dancers, she immediately downplayed her dance skills. One evening, we students had an hour to kill before our class started, so we decided to watch one of the Joel Hall Company's basic jazz classes. Since it was an open class, the instructor invited us to participate in a gesture of friendship. I suggested to the Lindy Hop instructor that we take the class. "I don't want to go in there—I'll be so white," she replied. I countered, "Yeah, but you teach Lindy Hop, which has all sorts of jazz steps. Why is this a big deal?" She answered, "Because I'll look like a dork, this white girl in there trying to dance." Only when confronted with a perceived threat, that her white body would look arrhythmic or awkward compared to the black dancers in the class, did she downplay her dance knowledge and expertise. Her comments suggest that it was not her skill as a dancer that was called into question, her claimed "training," but the aesthetic of her body—her white body that would be juxtaposed with black bodies. Without even attempting the class, she confirmed a predetermined outcome of the white body as deficient and the black body affirmed as natural. Later that evening, as she led our class by directing students and correcting their movements, I couldn't help but notice that this episode did not seem to dislodge in her any feelings of entitlement to teach and perform African American dances to a room full of only whites.

•

By looking at these discourses through Bourdieu's categories, we can see that the dominant group is just as dominated through their own categories of thought as is the group that is less privileged (Bourdieu 2000a). Symbolic violence creates a misrecognition that prevents whites from understanding how white racial domination works against them in their understanding of the natural distinctions and capacities of different racial groups.

BLAMING THE VICTIM

Another discourse that dominates the discussion of the Lindy Hop is that of blaming the victim. This discourse manifests itself through an abstract liberalism and racial pluralism that conceptualizes society as racially neutral, as well as through explanations of the absence of African Americans in the Lindy Hop scene as a result of choice and disinterest. By blaming the victim, dancers fail to understand how the white embrace of the Lindy Hop may not be the result of a lack of African American interest in the dance, but symbolic of the structural dynamics that define racial relations in contemporary American society. During an interview that I conducted with a popular white international instructor from the United States (one whose dress, musical tastes, and language were heavily influenced by African American culture), I asked how he felt about whites embracing the Lindy Hop and if he thought that this was "appropriating" African American culture in any way. He responded,

> Why do you think that this is just a black dance, or that this is racist, or that white people are wrong for doing the dance? If African Americans want it back, then they can go work for it. I mean, black people dropped the ball on this, and white people picked it up. Is it the fault of whites that blacks dropped the ball and whites picked it up? Black people didn't revive this, white people did. So why are whites to blame? Why are you blaming white people for this? They didn't do anything. In fact, they did something great: when black people didn't want anything to do with the Lindy Hop, they revived it and brought it back. White people brought this back when black people didn't want anything to do with it.

Another dancer added,

> You can't say it's because of racism that blacks aren't doing the dance. Blacks don't care about it. If they did, they would dance it. There is no segregation anymore. All the clubs are open to the public; no one is telling them not to come. People can get on the Internet and find out where to go. It's not like it's a secret. I think it just has more to do with the fact that black people keep to themselves, and there aren't a lot of black Swing dancers because it just isn't popular with them. I mean, they avoid white people too. Racism isn't just white on black.

In framing his response in terms of a "game," in which blacks dropped the ball and whites picked it up, this instructor illuminates a much deeper logic of the way that race operates in American society. Whether or not these thoughts and actions are taken for granted or instrumental, the metaphor of the game resonates with the logic of abstract liberalism whereby race is viewed as an individual problem and not the fault of one group having more power, money, or resources in influencing the way that society is con-structed. All racial groups have equal opportunity to compete in society and should be held responsible for the choices and decisions they make (Bonilla-Silva 2003). This logic of equal competition in the marketplace generates a symbolic violence whereby the belief that all racial groups have the same power in American society obscures the historical trajectory of white en-gagement and cultivation of African American culture. It is this historical trajectory, one structured under racial dominance, which enables whites to consume African American cultural forms in a way that reinforces racial domination.

Because white racial domination is foundational to the structure of so-ciety, this inequality enables whites to consume African American culture instrumentally as a resource with greater or lesser degrees of impact than other groups. Since whites are a majority of the population, and control more resources than other groups, their tastes and trends often become legitimated and taken for granted without self-reflexivity. In this way the white appropriation of African American culture can become an inten-tional or unintentional consequence, specifically when racial identity, cultural forms, and their historical emergence, development, and refine-ment are separated. In the simplest terms: if the cliché that the winners write the history books holds true, then more than one version of a story has been left out. By contrast, the African American consumption of white cultural forms does not generate enough symbolic power to unsettle white cultural practices, since African Americans are not in a position of struc-tural dominance. For example, if African Americans were to suddenly take up country-western line dancing, and denied its cultural-racial historical development, this would yield little in the way of undermining or dimin-ishing white identity. Since white identity is so embedded in American so-ciety, African American aesthetics and preferences are unable to achieve the same level of legitimation and institutionalization by which to make their views dominant. In this sense "power" or "control" has everything to do with institutionalization, not with participation, preferences, tastes, or appreciation.[13]

By misrecognizing these structural dynamics, whites conceptualize the current state of the Lindy Hop as an issue not of white racial domination but of African American neglect or lack of interest. This sense of "dropping the ball" resonated with many of the dancers I spoke with over the years. Two of the more prominent Lindy Hop instructors with whom I taught, one my regular teaching partner and the other my girlfriend at the time, offered up what they thought would be a good topic for my dissertation. One evening, between teaching classes, the two approached me, my girlfriend speaking for both of them:

> Kristen and I have been thinking about your dissertation, and we think you should write about why there aren't any black people doing Lindy Hop. Why don't they want to do it today? I mean, there are almost no black people who do it. How come? That's a race thing, if they don't have any interest in it. Why don't you write about that?

This attitude of framing the lack of African American involvement in the Lindy Hop in terms of African American "disinterest" could be seen as a way of "blaming the victim," whereby all the responsibility falls on the shoulders of African Americans and has nothing to do with white engagement (Bonilla-Silva 2003; Bonilla-Silva and Doane 2003). This is not to question the sincerity of the speaker or equate her remarks with racial prejudice; rather it requires a bracketing of those value judgments in order to see comments like this, which could be considered anywhere from naïve to insightful, as keys to larger issues that circulate in the contemporary collective consciousness. These notions of disinterest and blaming the victim resonate with the much larger ways that society has conceptualized the relationship between African Americans and white society (Mead 1986; West 1993; Wilson 1987, 1997). Instead of asking about "disinterest" in the politically tame world of the Lindy Hop, we can pose this same question in the realm of education: Why is it that African Americans have no interest in higher education, given their low representation in that arena? Now the political nature of explaining racial group interest in terms of choice becomes more palpable and explicit. In the case of the Lindy Hop, this discourse of African American neglect or lack of interest generates a symbolic violence through the notion that African Americans would dance if they wanted to, so since they do not dance, this must reflect the simple fact of their lack of interest in the Lindy Hop.

I once talked with one of the best dancers in the Lindy Hop scene, who is white but heavily influenced by hip hop and hip hop dancing, about what parallels could be drawn between these two African American cultural forms: Lindy Hop from the past and hip hop from the present. He commented,

> Black people don't care about this stuff. They've already moved on to something else now. They're into hip hop. They're only interested in that now, not some old dance. They're only interested in something new. They

don't care anything about Swing dancing and Lindy Hop; that's what white people are doing. Black people just create stuff, they do it, then they toss it away and move on to something else. They don't give a shit about the Lindy Hop.

Another dancer I interviewed put it even more succinctly:

It's not our fault if black people don't want to do [the Lindy Hop]. I mean, they should have taken more pride in their culture. Why is that our fault?

And yet another international instructor remarked,

But it seems also like white people have a tendency to, shall I say, dig into the history and recreate things. Black people, when it comes to dance and music, are inventing new things, and they very seldom go back, it seems, to the roots that their parents or grandparents had. But white people have more of a tendency to restore or recreate things. So it's too bad, I think, that we don't have so many African Americans doing this dance. I think it is very much something that interests white people, cataloguing and classifying and documenting, especially when it comes to African American culture. I am not sure what it is, but it seems that many more white people are interested in this than black people are in their own culture. History in a way seems like something that white people do, whereas black people just keep making culture and really don't spend a lot of time analyzing it. Even the book you're writing, I think, may be part of that.

By articulating the dance using expressions that project motives or thoughts into the heads of absent African Americans, dancers generate a symbolic violence of assuming that all racial interaction is equal and that African Americans have no interest or even pride in their culture.

Presenting and articulating the world as racially neutral or as a place in which groups have equal opportunity obscures the exploitation of African American culture that has historically occurred and the ways that the actors of one racial group shape the actions and reactions of others. This lack of African American interest could stem from numerous factors: the lack of marketing by Lindy Hop groups to African American communities; the lack of images of the Lindy Hop featuring African Americans in contemporary circulation; in Chicago, the fact that it is danced on the segregated white North Side of the city in white venues; and the fact that many African Americans interested in social dancing are socialized to go Steppin', a popular social dance in Chicago's African American communities. Articulating the dance in the context of what African Americans have or have not done misrecognizes the very racial dynamics that inform the structure of American society. By exploring these racial dynamics at play in the discourses that circulate through society, there is no "groupthink" that is being appealed to, rather it is the common consensus of ideas and opinions that form the background of our thinking. In no way should it be construed that the analytical categories used here, "white/whites/whiteness" or "black/blacks/blackness," are in any way stand-ins for the complex and contradictory sentiments and opinions that circulate within any one racial group, let alone the diversity we encounter once we factor in other aspects of division such as class, age, gender, and so on.[14]

Since there is no correlation with one's racial category and the way one thinks, it is always necessary to problematize any relationship between thought and social category. However, the issue here is more one of how despite our constructed racial differences, and even prejudices and mythologies that go along with them, like mass media, we are all part of a larger social picture through which we come to construct our particular and general outlooks on the world. It is this simultaneous individualism/socialness that makes the issue of thinking through the connection between race and culture so precarious. As a result, it is important to keep in mind that these views of race neutrality, equal opportunity, and African American interest are not the exclusive beliefs of whites. In a telling interview, the black British instructor Ryan Francois commented:

> If black people aren't dancing the dance now, they've allowed white people to appropriate it. In some ways this is history repeating itself. I get very upset when there is no mention made or no reference to Lindy Hop as a black dance. In many ways it's about education; they don't do it on purpose. If you are a white person from a white neighborhood, you are probably not aware, so when you teach you can't blame or attack or alienate white people. I can't blame white kids for learning what they've learned, but I can blame them for not being critical. Ignorance is no excuse; if you learn something, really learn about it. My responsibility as a teacher is to open doors to other avenues, but students also need to take some of that responsibility. I don't like when people don't respect the roots of the dance. But black people gave away this dance, so they shouldn't feel too bad.

Another African American dancer told me:

> I was out with some of my girlfriends one night at a club, and people were Lindy Hopping. Several guys were asking me to dance, and after a few

dances, when I came back to the table, they were like "Where did you learn how to do that?" (As in, that white dance that all those white people are doing.) I was like, this is not a white thing, we created this dance. They had no idea; not one of them—and there were five of us—had any idea that the Lindy Hop came from black culture. It's so ironic in a way. Black people are always complaining about white people stealing everything, and yet when she said this, I thought, you know, that's such a problem with black folks. So many of us don't know anything about our history. So it's not like whites have to steal it—we don't even know what we've created, we don't know what's ours to be taken away to begin with.

The tension expressed in this view highlights how strong the dominant racial logic is; even members of the dominated group utilize the same discourses as do the dominant when they frame and express their views on the dance.

Considering the dance through these different discourses led me to share with my then-girlfriend some thoughts on how I was going to execute my research project. Because she was a central member of the Lindy Hop scene in Chicago, her sentiments shaped the ways that hundreds of students came to understand the dance. One afternoon we were sitting in a café talking, and she explained that she was dumbfounded as to why I would be thinking about the Lindy Hop in terms of race. She said,

I know we've had a few black students in our classes; I've seen some. I mean, Riley comes out, and Kim. Look at Riley—he doesn't have any problems with it, so I think it's kind of unfair to say this is a race thing. And besides, look at Steven, he's black, and so is Ryan. They're both black, and they don't have a problem with it; in fact, they dance with white women. I mean, aren't you missing the point that it isn't race? It's not our fault if they don't want to do it.

The discourse of blaming the victim, as expressed through racial pluralism and cultural choice, also serves to frame the participation of African Americans in the Lindy Hop scene as proof that we live in a race-free world. By their very presence, the few African Americans who participate become spokespeople for the race, and as a result they reinforce the commonsense thinking that there are no racial consequences to the white embrace of the Lindy Hop.

In returning to the issue of individual/social, the interviews that highlight the particular sentiments of those African American dancers should not appear to form an unquestionable unified view. Since not all African

Americans danced the Lindy Hop in the past, nor would all African Americans identify with the Lindy Hop in any of its historical formations, the argument made here for the discourse that circulates as "blaming the victim" is one that operates as an essentializing expression of cultural ownership. The issue of "ownership" is not if it belongs to one person, or one group; in fact, ownership distorts what the real base of the issue is: how do cultural forms remain or become erased from our collective memory?[15] In doing so it first conflates race and culture as one being the incarnation of the other (racial groups participate in their cultural forms because their cultural forms belong to those racial groups) and, second, it holds a strict separation between race and culture (such that if you knew that the Lindy Hop was an African American dance and decided not to pursue it, then you disowned your culture, and if you didn't know it was African American, then you didn't care enough about your own culture in the first place). The discourse of blaming the victim obscures the underlying institutionalized racial dynamics at play by contradictorily both fusing race and culture on the one hand, and maintaining its strict separation on the other. As result it prevents whites from understanding the consequences of their actions or why racial divisions remain so deep in contemporary American society.

TALKING AROUND RACE

Another discourse of the Lindy Hop concerns naming or not naming the dance. This particular discourse of naming takes on many forms in the ways that dancers discuss and conceptualize their engagement with the dance. The Lindy Hop is described as the "real" Swing dance and it is considered "authentic," and yet at the same time this real and authentic dance is never racially marked or discussed in terms of its African American identity. Others use the discourse of naming to not racially mark the dance. This nonracial marking generates a symbolic violence by which the dance is decontextualized and deracialized.

When the Lindy Hop craze hit in the late 1990s, it seemed as if everyone was promoting the teaching of "Swing dancing" instead of referring to the dance by the name of Lindy Hop.[16] In fact, the dance's soaring popularity necessitated that the Lindy Hoppers distinguish their particular style of dancing from the other "Swing" dances being taught all over the city. Not long after I started dancing, I overheard people talking about the dance in terms of the "real style" or the "authentic style" that they had seen in *Swingers* or in the Gap ad "Khakis Swing." One amused Lindy Hop instructor commented to me that during the boom, he was getting around twenty calls a day asking if this was the dance group offering "real" Swing dance lessons.

This only made the dance harder to conceptualize in some ways: What is Lindy Hop, Jitterbug, Swing? And which one was real? Which one was authentic? How did I know what I was really dancing after all?

At one of my first dance classes, a pair of students approached our teacher and asked if he would teach us the "Pretzel" (a move in which the leader and follower continuously twist around each other, forming a pretzel-looking shape that is often seen in rockabilly or rock-'n'-roll dancing). The students proceeded to demonstrate their rough estimation of the step for him. Disgusted, the instructor replied in a loud tone, so the entire class could hear, "We don't teach that—that's street Swing."

At the same time there was also a conscious effort to distinguish the Lindy Hop from the more formal version of Swing dancing also known as "Jive," which is performed in ballroom competitions that ballroom dance teachers were promoting at their studios around town. As the Lindy Hop scene distinguished itself from the street Swing and Ballroom styles, veterans and dancers in the know were no longer referring to it as Swing dancing: it was now "the Lindy Hop" or even "Savoy style Lindy Hop" (Stearns and Stearns 1994). But while the dance's proper name—the Lindy Hop—was reemerging, the dance's racial and cultural identity remained in a vacuum.

When I first started giving private lessons, one couple called me on the phone:

> We got your name from a Ballroom teacher that we've been taking lessons from, and he recommended that we call you. We want some Swing lessons. We know the basics, but we're interested in getting the style down. We have several moves now, but we want to get the style—we just want to look like you guys look. You know, like the real thing, the real style—not like Ballroom Swing dancers, not the way we dance.

The notion here is that there is a real way to dance the dance, one that is certainly different from the aesthetic of the ballroom world. But this aesthetic remains unnamed in the common discussion of the dance. In fact, the notion that this real and authentic dance has any connection to any specific racial or cultural identity remains silent. The following anecdote, reconstructed from my fieldnotes, illustrates this issue.

•

During my first summer of fieldwork, a few dancers discovered that I was working on a dissertation about the Lindy Hop. A group of us were on Catalina Island, just off the coast of Los Angeles, for the annual Catalina Swing dance camp. Several of the world's best instructors teach classes for several days during the first week in June. Each night of the camp a dance is held in the ballroom on the island. One evening before going to the dance, I stopped by the house that several Chicago dancers had rented for a pre-dance party. As we all sat around talking, the conversation turned to how people had seen me interviewing the camp instructors. They were all curious about what I was doing and what kinds of things I was asking, since some of them knew that I was also a graduate student in sociology. One dancer finally confronted me:

> Hey, I hear you're writing on Lindy Hop and race or something like that, 'cause I hear you're interviewing all the instructors. So what kinds of questions are you asking them? I mean, what kinds of things about "race" are you asking? I'm just curious: how are you connecting race and Lindy Hop anyway—what have they got to do with each other?

Later, as I walked from the house down toward the ballroom, I wondered to myself, Is it me or are people just oblivious? Why don't they see any of this?

•

While taking a dance workshop, we broke off from our respective partners and formed rows of dancers so that we could work on our individual movement. This exercise has dancers engage in movements they do not normally do or forces them into movements that get them out of their comfort zone. This not only helps dancers become more fluid in their general dancing, it also helps them become more familiar with the ways their body can move. During one jazz routine that Steven Mitchell taught us, he stopped the music and said:

> Focus on the rhythm. It is not up here [up here in the body], it is down here, get the grove in the spring, otherwise you can get in the pocket of the music. Put a little color on that! Take it across the water back to Africa on that. Wait. Wait. I've got to keep you honest on that, I've got to keep you honest. It don't matter. It don't matter, we were Swinging back in the '30s and we've never been there so come on.

I finally asked Steven his thoughts concerning the avoidance of identifying the Lindy Hop as African American. What did this say, I asked him, about the climate of the dance and possible future consequences for it? Reflecting on the previous day's workshop he replied:

> I must have been thinking about what you said the other day, because I
> was in class and I slipped and said, "Put a little color on that" [referring to
> a particular dance step that he was trying to teach], and I thought, Oh shit,
> I'm losing it. But People don't want to go there. I mean, we have to go all
> the way there and talk about all the African in the dance, and people just
> don't want to go there. Look at the originality and where it comes from.
> It's African movement—that's what's missing; that's what it boils down to.
> This is where I don't go. I mean, can we get serious and talk about where
> this comes from? Can we really talk where it comes from? All these hip
> things? The shimmies? The stomps? I don't make a big deal about this, but
> I want to sometimes.

The constraint of discussing the dance within such narrow deracialized parameters, even among African Americans, was something that would serve
to ignite my interest in pursuing research on the dance and fuel my own racial politics. As I became more and more involved in the Lindy Hop community and as my dancing became the focus of my research, this racial reflexivity started to change the way I thought about the dance and informed the
way I would go on to teach it. As I brought my academic and political agenda
into my project of dancing and teaching the Lindy Hop, I began to vocalize
some of my concerns to students, both inside and outside class, about the
lack of attention paid to the history and significance of African American
culture, as well as to the "politics" of the cross-cultural consumption going
on in the contemporary Lindy Hop community. The following anecdote reconstructed from my fieldnotes illuminates the reception that this received.

•

I was teaching an introduction-level Swing class for the most influential
Lindy Hop group in the city, at a private gym in a trendy neighborhood on
the North Side of Chicago. While I was instructing, several students kept
dancing and talking without paying any attention to me or my partner.
This disrespect finally became so distracting that it disturbed the class and
drowned out the voice of my partner, who was then unable to communicate
with the rest of the students. After the disruptive students ignored several
polite suggestions to curb their behavior, I lost my temper and gave them
an ultimatum:

> Look people, this isn't some minstrel show. We are not up here for your
> amusement. We are trying to teach you an African American dance, and
> as white people doing this, there are some serious politics involved that we
> need to be concerned with. Now I can't do anything about what you do with

the dance when you've left this room, because you're gonna do whatever you do, and I have no control over that. But as long as you are in here, you are going to respect the dance; otherwise you need to find another class.

This direct confrontation with the politics of the white consumption of African American culture, as well as my explicit censure of students, was bound to cause some trouble. Sure enough, two days later the owner of the company I was teaching for called me to discuss the incident. He offered me his own ultimatum:

> I have a problem with you portraying it as a black dance. Why do you in-sist on telling people it's a black dance? It may have started in a minority community, but in its heyday many more whites were doing it than blacks, even before the Swing renaissance. This is a predominantly white country, and since so many more whites danced it than blacks, you can't say it is a black dance. It may have started in the black community, but it moved out into the white community. You can't say that just because it was danced in the white community it's less authentic, even if they didn't have the same social dance background. What we have today is highly influenced or pre-dominantly influenced by the white dance community. Let me put this in perspective. I just got a $3,000 insurance bill. I think what we should focus on is trying to get people out there to have a good time. If some pursue the history of it later, they will. Otherwise, I think you need to tone it down or not mention it. I think people can only take about five minutes of some-thing they may not want to hear before they get turned off. You need to focus on showing people the steps, especially in Swing I [the introductory Swing dance course], and for those who go on, let them find out about the history if they want to. But I don't think you should force something on them that they may not want. Our job is to teach people how to dance, not to give them a history lesson. The point is to get as many people as possible interested and into the Swing I classes, and hopefully those who go on will learn more about it. I don't think our competition says anything about the [dance's] history. I don't mean here in Chicago, but nationally. None of the instructors talk about it, so I don't know why we should. We need to come to some sort of an agreement here: you can tell them that blacks were among the original dancers, but you cannot say that this is a black dance. If you can do that we can work together; if not, then we can't.

•

By framing the dance as racially unmarked, in effect as unnamed or "color-blind," the constant reiteration of this understanding severs the African

American identity from the dance. By separating the dance from its historical and cultural context, by arguing that the dance cannot "belong" to African Americans because there are more whites dancing it, eviscerates the significance of African American culture, influence, creativity, and expression of the dance.[17] Whether knowingly or unknowingly with the best of intentions, the ways that dancers think about the dance leads to an acontextual outcome:

> What's the point of trying to figure out whose dance this is? You ask this question about blacks and whites as if it really mattered. Everyone dances the Lindy Hop. Just look at the scene. You have some black people, some Asian people; you have all kinds so that to say it "belongs" to someone just raises more issues and make it divisive rather than bringing people together. Isn't that just making race an issue out of something that is not.

While racially neutral in approach, the rejection of race leads the white embrace of African American forms to generate racial domination through white people's simultaneous rejection of the identity of those forms.

Teaching and cultivating the dance without explicit reference to African American culture denies the very stylistic distinctions and dynamics that define the cultural form itself. This colorblindness is tantamount to cultural erasure; by naming or failing to name the dance in the context of African American identity, only certain particular racialized views of history, racial identities, and cultural struggles are acknowledged and institutionalized. The fear that bringing up race, by marking the dance as having a racial identity, will negatively impact the dance scene precludes the opportunity for the dancers to deepen their understanding—not only of the dance itself, but of the history and trajectory of the very dance form they are actively cultivating.

This censure from the owner of the company was not the only resistance I encountered in cultivating my vision of the dance. The owner of the performance company for whom I often worked also made it clear that my employment depended on a more toned-down racial perspective. The following incident recounted from my fieldnotes captures this specific exchange.

•

After a performance gig that we did for a private company party (in which we entertained by first doing a dance demonstration and then teaching the guests a basic Swing lesson), the owner spoke with me about her concerns about discussing the dance as part of African American culture. She commented in a way that demonstrated her understanding of my position while emphasizing her objective as a business owner: "I know you have strong feelings about the dance, and I think it's a good thing to promote the history and let people know that it comes from African Americans, but I think it's best if we downplay that to get the business."

•

This concern about what I might say in dance classes lingered for the entire time I taught. In fact, I discovered that the owner of the teaching company I was working for had asked one of my teaching partners to monitor me and report on my actions and comments in the classroom. One evening she confided in me that he had asked her to do this and said she felt guilty for complying with his request. I asked her what she was waiting for me to do. What was it that she was looking for me to say that she could report back? She responded,

> [The owner of the company] asked me, "Does he make racial comments? Does he talk about black people in classes? Why does he care so much? What's with that? Why is it so important for him to talk about black history? It will scare customers away; it's just a bad idea. Nobody else does it. Even Steven's favorite partner is white. What does that say about how much race matters?"

She then offered her own explanation about the whole situation:

> I'm just telling you what he was asking. I mean, he's not mad, but he just wonders what you do, so he's checking on you. I really played it off, but that's because I don't see it as a race thing anyway. But I know you do.

What was it about knowing that this dance was part of African American culture that would scare customers away? Why would this jeopardize the business of teaching people how to dance? If people discovered the true racial identity of the Lindy Hop, would this make it less pleasurable to dance? If confronted with the racial identity of the dance, would this force them to confront their desire for and pleasure taken in African American culture? What makes this discourse of naming or not naming the Lindy Hop so powerful is that keeping it racially unmarked enables the white embrace of the dance to go unexamined. By calling the dance anything but African American, white culture maintains its distance from African American culture and at the same time embraces it in consumption. Here, perversely, the persistence of racial inequality is grounded not in white racism, but on the very invocation of race itself.

As I continued to merge my scholarship and my dancing, my racial politics grew more vocal and more problems ensued as I continued to violate the logic of the dominant discourses surrounding the dance. Instructors grew nervous to teach with me, and I often thought about giving up teaching completely; I could not continue to work for that company and be complicit in the cultural erasure of something that I was so invested in academically and personally. A year later, I traveled to Sweden for the summer to continue my fieldwork and dance training by attending the Herräng dance camp and working privately with two former world champion Lindy Hop dancers and performers. Having developed into a well-respected instructor and having found a new dance partner, Julie, the best female dancer in Chicago and someone who shared my sentiments, I told the owner of the company that from now on I would teach only with her. I told myself that this was the only way I could continue to improve as a dancer and stay true to the dance, offering my students the very best of my knowledge and abilities. I felt that this period of intensive training in Sweden with some of the world's best Lindy Hoppers would influence the way that the company owner viewed my commitment and my desire to master the dance. But his concern ultimately had nothing to do with my skill as a dancer or educator. During my stay in Sweden I was sent this e-mail:

> Hey, I haven't heard from you about teaching—I need to know if you will only teach with little Julie. I'm going to ask you not to make any more references to race in the class, except to say that blacks were among the original dancers. Can you teach within those constraints?

I quit working for the company when I returned from Sweden. The dominant discourses through which the dance was articulated offered no alternatives. Abiding by their logic would not only compromise my teaching and dancing, but it would also affect my relationships with African American friends and colleagues, as well as my academic and personal racial politics. If white people were afraid of the dance because of its African American origins, if this was something that would "scare" customers away, then I wanted no part of that world. If white people in today's society were not able to face the fact that they were taking pleasure in African American art and culture, and anything that challenged these discourses violated the norms of the community, then I had nothing to offer this milieu.

While the possibility of cultivating the dance in more reflexive directions grew more difficult as public enthusiasm for Swing dancing waned in later years, I tried to assess just how much ground had been gained over the last few years of its cultivation. At one of the last Lindy Hop workshops

I attended as a dancer, held in Cleveland, one of the central teachers in the Lindy Hop scene confided to me during the lunch break about his sadness over the decline in the dance's reflexivity:

> I think it's gotten worse. I mean, back then [at the height of its popularity, 1997–2001] people at least called it Lindy Hop. People don't even call it Lindy Hop anymore. It's gotten that bad. If we walked back into that room [the dance hall where the workshop was being held] and asked all those people what dance they were doing, I bet all of them would say Swing. Not one would say Lindy Hop. It saddens me that it's come to this. We could be close to losing it, not just the dance but the history—the history that's so rich and connects us to something so much larger in American history. If we lose it, it could be gone forever.

These words continued to echo in my mind as I wrote this dissertation, as I looked back at the trajectory of the dance and the precarious state in which it exists—simultaneously a wealth of history and culture and an unmarked cultural form that could easily vanish once again from public awareness.

Keeping the dance unmarked and never discussing its African American history decontextualizes and deracializes the dance. Just as African American culture is appropriated and exploited without acknowledgment, whites are also dominated through this logic: it prevents them from understanding the rich cultural history of African American dance and from participating in a full cross-cultural understanding, as their understanding of the Lindy Hop necessarily remains impoverished and incomplete.

HAVING FUN

Another dominant discourse that circulates throughout the Lindy Hop community is that of "having fun." Despite the apparent innocence of this expression, this discourse takes on a different connotation when examined within the historical context and the contemporary racial dynamics of white interaction with African American culture. When African American cultural forms such as the Lindy Hop are practiced in insulated and autonomous white spaces, "having fun" leads to historical erasure or racial amnesia of the context and culture within which the form was cultivated. The issue is not about whites taking pleasure in dancing, but how the discourse of having fun belies the racial politics and racial context of the dance. Since the days of minstrelsy whites have taken pleasure in African American cultural forms, but this pleasure has usually come at the expense of African American people, who have often been degraded in the process.[18] Whether having fun intentionally mocks people as in the form of minstrelsy, or the pleasure is taken without intentional degradation, this discourse of having fun ultimately serves to sever African American culture from its racial context and prevents whites from fully participating in the Lindy Hop experience, because they are not fully aware of the historical context of their cultural engagement. Thus the discourse of having fun generates a racial obliviousness and historical amnesia, sealing off the possibility for whites to cultivate a true multiculturalism built around reflexive cultural participation.

When I questioned Lindy Hoppers informally about what drew them to the dance, common responses were based around pleasure. One dancer told me, "Why do I dance? Because it's so much fun. Why else? I mean, it's so much fun to get out there; you can just let yourself go." Another dancer echoed those feelings: "My day job is pretty boring, so when I get to dance I can just totally forget about work. That's what's so great about Lindy—it's so expressive and fun to do."

When discussing the pleasure of dancing the Lindy Hop, I would always ask whether the dance's African American identity was a significant factor in dancers' attraction to the art form or in their sensation of pleasure when dancing. While this question was intentionally aimed at gauging the cultural and historical awareness of the dancers, it was always misinterpreted as accusatory, provoking the same defensive reaction: race had nothing to do with the dance. In fact, most dancers I spoke with held firmly to the dominant belief that discussing race—the African American identity of the dance—would somehow undermine the dance's enjoyment. This sentiment was expressed in numerous ways: "People dance it just to have fun. It's fun to go out and dance. It's nothing more than that." "We're just dancing— what's the big deal?" Most dancers seemed to feel defensive and would immediately ask why I was "bringing race into this." Some thought that I was "bringing up something that's not there" or "making it into something that it's not." They were perplexed by my interest in the Lindy Hop's connection with issues of race. "Why does it [the dance] have to be so serious?" they'd ask. "Why does it have to be about race?" One veteran dancer and instructor, who considered my question a bit more, said:

> I don't think people ever really think about stuff like that. I don't. And I can't really say in the time I've been doing this that anyone has ever really talked about race. I mean, Norma Miller has definitely brought up issues of race. She even accused this one white woman of stealing the Lindy Hop at a panel that was hosted at one of the dance camps, where some of the old-timers were telling stories about what the dance was like back in the day. But that's why she is so marginalized; nobody wants to hear that stuff.

That's why she doesn't get invited to any of the events anymore. She's just way too intense and really puts people off. They just don't want to hear that stuff at dance events. They're just there to dance.

Another dancer I interviewed put his response in these terms:

Why do you have to bring race into this? This isn't about race. Why does it have to be black? Why is that so important? Why can't white people just happen to like a dance that just happens to be black? And these people just happen to be white? Why is there a race issue at all? Race doesn't really have anything to do with it. We're just having fun; we're just dancing. Why does this have to be an issue?

While having fun and taking pleasure in the dance remain the focus of the dancers' comments, their juxtaposition of having fun with issues of race makes the historical and cultural context of the dance and its racial identity appear as if they were in opposition, or as if cultivating this knowledge would somehow dissipate the pleasure of dancing.

My sociological immersion in the Lindy Hop paralleled my immersion in the dance as an instructor. As I continued to teach the Lindy Hop, I increased my discussion of the cultural and racial context within which we were all cultivating the Lindy Hop. As a white teacher instructing white students in the practice of an African American dance, I made it part of my pedagogy to impress upon the students the dance's history and the politics of cross-cultural consumption, especially those within which whites have engaged African Americans, as necessities for maintaining the vitality of the dance as an art form and sustaining a thriving dance community. Part of what made me so sensitive to the inculcation of the dance was my own attempt to make the socialization of the body a reflexive and self-conscious process of critically examining the practice of dance as we learned it in the classroom, rather than just mindlessly drilling dance steps to music.

As a result of my explicit endeavors to bring these racial issues and politics to light, I was reprimanded by the owner of the dance company where I was teaching. One morning about a week after the last class I taught for the session, I received the following e-mail from the owner:

As you know, we are doing a survey about classes for next session. I received the following comment from the survey—the only specific comment I received about a current class, and I am passing it on to you. In general ... you have scored well in the "which teacher would you like to have" category. But I urge you to take this comment seriously if you are teaching this class differently than you have taught it before. It is important that we keep the beginning students coming back.

The following is an excerpt from the evaluation:

I am very disappointed with my current Swing class taught by Black Hawk and his partner (don't know her name). I am currently taking Latin dance on Sundays at Dance Connection and am having a wonderful time. Alex is very encouraging and makes class fun from the very beginning. Swing I, on the other hand, is decidedly not fun. Perhaps salsa dancing is vastly easier than Swing dancing, but I felt like during the first night of salsa class I was dancing and having fun. Black Hawk and his partner are far too serious and critical—this is *dancing* and it's supposed to be fun, not stressful. So far I have not had fun at all, and question whether I am learning to dance at all. I will not take another class from these instructors. They might be good for more advanced classes, but for beginners they are too negative and intense.

The idea that information about the racial identity and cultural history of the dance must necessarily be separated from the pleasure of learning the dance was disturbing, but this sentiment was even more worrisome because it had become an impediment to the cultivation of the dance (and, more important, to the economic profit for a select few gained by keeping students enrolled in dance classes). Why would raising the issue of African American identity turn students away from the dance? The discourse of having fun seemed necessarily to exclude discussion of race or historical context as somehow antithetical and incongruous to cultivating the dance as something that one could just enjoy for the fun of it.

The dominant conviction that race is irrelevant to the dance belies the deep anxiety through which whites have to subconsciously negotiate their attraction to African American culture. The following exchange occurred during one of my first interviews with some of the top Lindy Hop instructors in the world, who were teaching at a prestigious weeklong dance camp just outside of Boston. This interview was a seminal event in my research. It started as a private conversation with three master Lindy Hop instructors— Ivan, a Swede who left shortly after the conversation began; Ryan Francois, a black British man; and Steven Mitchell, an African American—which turned into a rather heated conversation when a white male dance camp student joined in without invitation. What makes this exchange so important is that the random camper who intruded upon the conversation served as a touchstone for the way people think about the dance. The following is the entirety of that conversation, which captures the dynamic within which these issues unfolded:

(Random camper enters the conversation uninvited.)

Random camper: I think that the Lindy Hop era of the '20s, whenever it started, was subversive, down and dirty, back then.

Ryan: Down and dirty to white people?

Random camper: Yes. I don't know, I wasn't there, but like hip hop or rock-'n'-roll at the time, like many things in black American culture, white people homogenized it, took what they wanted. And I think the resurgence has nothing to do with that. I think the resurgence has to do with the Gap commercial because it looked like fun—people realized, Wow, that looks like fun, why aren't we doing that?

BH: But the consequences of white people doing nice good clean fun at—

Ryan: At the expense of—

BH: At the expense of black people.

Random camper: How does this hurt black people?

BH: How does minstrelsy hurt black people?

Ryan: Yeah, that's what we're looking at.

Random camper: What? What are you talking about? This is about dancing; this is about having fun!

BH: Minstrelsy used to be good clean fun, and at the time no one thought anything about what that did to the people being imitated, so . . .

Ryan: Yeah, Jump Jim Crow.

BH: You could consider this a form of that.

Ryan: I think it's a wider reaching structure than what you see. You know, in some ways whether you know it or not you actually represent something, because you don't know it, because you don't get it, you represent something that hopefully, when this is done, might actually open some doors to help you get it. Because the problem with racist prejudiced structures is that we don't see them anymore; you don't see the problem because you don't think. You see it as all innocent and harmless stuff.

You think that because it doesn't harm you directly, you don't see it, and I think ... you're doing it right now ... what you are doing right now is in a strange way what white people do.... I can see it ticking around in your head, thinking this is all too deep for me, and you'll walk away from this.

Random camper [laughing nervously]: No ... I can tell you now, I've heard all this before, I don't have to ... I don't have to prove myself to you.

Ryan: But we are not asking you to.

Random camper: I'm here to have fun. This is *fun,* and if you guys want to teach, and you're willing to teach it, that's great. I assume someone is paying you, I paid a certain amount and that's great.

Ryan: Yeah, but you know what?

Random camper: And I'm grateful.

Ryan: Yeah ... I'm not saying that. You actually came in on a conversation that was not involving you and you felt you had to say something about it.

Random camper: I wanted to contribute.

Ryan: All right then, contribute, but right now I'm not saying stuff you want to hear, and so you're now going, "I've just come here to have fun. I don't want to have to deal with this."

Random camper: I thought what you were talking about had to do with where the resurgence or the resurge in interest in Lindy Hop begin. I thought you were talking about the Gap ad, and I came in and was fascinated to hear that Ivan hadn't even seen the Gap ad, and he's been dancing for so long.

Ryan: No, not everyone has seen the Gap ad. But Ivan was doing this fifteen years ago like me; we've been doing it for fifteen years. But suddenly the resurgence happens when this Gap ad came out ... and I think that is something particularly telling about the way that society works. It was a commercial of all young white people jumping around dancing and having a blast, and there is no mention, not even a hint, that this has anything to do with black people ... that's what we're talking about.

Random camper: We don't know each other. I'm grateful to do this and I think the Gap ad is similar to the *Ed Sullivan Show* for the Beatles. It just—

Ryan: Ed Sullivan was another place black culture was destroyed, because they had an agenda for what showed and didn't and who they stole from and who they gave credit to. I don't see the *Ed Sullivan Show* as being anything other than another Gap ad, and if you quote Ed Sullivan to me that's no point.

BH: They shot Elvis Presley from the waist up on *Ed Sullivan*.

Ryan: That's right.

Random camper: What did that have to do with black people?

BH: That had everything to do with black people. What do you think the hip shaking represented?

Steven: You see, it's something that you just don't see. We're not blaming you for it. We're not saying it's your fault; we're trying to get you to see that this whole issue of race is more complicated than just someone not serving you in a restaurant or looking at you differently. But these are things that you don't see because you don't have to. You can go through life in this country without ever even having to consider the fact that you can take it all for granted and . . .

Ryan: And that's what we're looking at . . .

Random camper: No!

(Random camper immediately gets up and walks away, shaking his head.)

What makes this exchange so important is the failure of the participants to sustain an open dialogue about the issues of race surrounding the dance. Rather than accusing white people in general of being racist, Ryan and Steven made what could be considered structural arguments about the way that race shapes how people perceive the world—an important moment for capturing the defensiveness of the discourse of having fun. That the "outside" white dance student's response demonstrated such visceral defensiveness to any suggestion that race played a factor in the dance signaled that there was obviously more at stake than simply having fun.

The discourse of having fun is used by whites to articulate the dance as if African Americans (or all black people) by fact of biology were reflexive about the dance. But in fact, African American dancers in the Lindy Hop scene share and deploy the same dominant discourses. This indiscriminate use of the discourse of having fun is illustrated in the following anecdote reconstructed from my fieldnotes.

•

I walked up to the only African American woman in the dance club. I had seen her before, yet I had never danced with her; she appeared to be new to the Chicago scene. As we proceeded to dance, I started up a conversation about where she was from and how she got involved with the Lindy Hop. I asked if her parents danced it or taught it to her. She said no, she'd learned it in classes, and she wanted to know why I was so interested in how she learned to dance. I explained that I was writing a dissertation about the Lindy Hop and that I was looking at how the Lindy Hop revival had taken the dance from a predominantly African American setting to all-white clubs and an almost exclusively white dance community. She found that interesting and wanted to know what I thought about it as a white person. I said that I was interested in the fact that when whites appropriate African American culture, it usually doesn't lead to an appreciation or inclusion of African American people. My dance partner suddenly became aggravated and defensive. She told me to look around the club and notice that there were people of all races there that night. At this point we stopped dancing and focused on our conversation. I scanned the room and saw one or two Asian Americans and one Puerto Rican, all of whom were longtime regulars on the Chicago scene. "No," I said, "except for a few folks, it looks like almost everybody here is white." After conceding that most of the dancers in the community were white, she asked what difference I thought this made. I then asked her if she thought any of these folks knew this was an African American dance or understood its significance as an art form within the African American community. Did she think that they were aware of what they were participating in? She replied that most of them probably were not.

At this point, I made a comparison to hip hop, stating that it was another contemporary example of an African American cultural form that could be considered under siege from white appropriation, especially with the rise of Eminem as arguably the world's most popular rapper. But, I added, hip hop had retained its African American identity and was struggling vehemently to prevent the same type of white appropriation that had happened to other African American cultural forms such as jazz, rock-'n'-roll, and the blues. I noted that hip hop had become quite multicultural and yet retained its African American–dominated identity, that hip hop was an example of multiculturalism that people in the Lindy Hop world should model themselves after. My dance partner just looked at me, incredulous. She then tried to change the subject, saying that when she attended Lindy Hop events with her African American friends, it was clear that they were much better dancers than everyone else. I asked her why she thought that, especially since I considered her new to the scene and had never seen her and her friends at any Lindy Hop events. She looked at me with a matter-of-fact expression and said that it was simply their "cultural ties" to the dance and then proceeded to laugh and say she was just joking and that I was "taking this all way to seriously" and should "just lighten up." She thought most of the dancers in the Lindy Hop scene gave respect to the original dancers of Lindy Hop, but actually they did not need to, because this was not about race: "People do this to have fun and because they love to dance, that's all."

·

While the investment in maintaining a colorblind or race-free community is again couched in terms of the discourse of having fun, the outcome of racial domination can be seen not simply as a strategy of white rationalization; it is found among African American dancers as well. By following this discourse across racial lines, as one shared by blacks and whites, we can see the extent of its influence in the ways that dancers conceptualize and articulate the world of the Lindy Hop. A variation on this theme can be seen in the discussion of the Broadway musical *Swing!*, which was nominated for six Tony Awards. The *New York Times* billed the show as what "Neo-Swing style is about: Swing dancing from a modern perspective." This show became the "Riverdance" production of the Lindy Hop with nonstop advertisement and promotion. Lynne Taylor-Corbett, the director and overall choreographer, is quoted in the *New York Times* saying:

> But it's more than a revue. . . . There's no Talmudic dissertation or socio-logical material, but there is a message about Swing dancing, which is that you can't do it alone. What we know about Swing dance, which was especially popular between the '20s and the 1940s and is enjoying a comeback now, is that it never went away. It underlies rock-and-roll, and it keeps morphing. No one wrote something out and said, "Let's put this up," but in the course of developing the show, we began to group the dances and musical numbers. Some of the groupings are shorter anecdotes, and some are in longer form. . . . I also knew what would make the show exciting was to be as inclusive of as many styles of Swing as I could find, and to find as many championship couples to do it as I could. We have Lindy Hopping, jive, Western, hip-hop. I'm putting them together as a kind of privileged curator and theatricalizing the arcs of these different dances. (Aloff 1999, 26)

The notion that there is no message, that this is just fun and exciting entertainment is once again apparent. The framing of this as a great melting pot of Swing styles obscures the different socio-historical-political contexts within which these different dances emerged and their cultural significance. While celebrating inclusiveness, in claiming a generic universalism in "everyone's dance," the African American history that is constitutive of the dance gets eviscerated. That the discourse of having fun is always used to counter or is juxtaposed to any discussion of race in relation to the dance, as if knowledge of the dance or the acknowledgement of its African American identity were somehow antithetical to having fun, suggests that the discourse belies much deeper sentiments about the negotiation of white desire in relation to African American culture. The discourse of having fun misrecognizes the material and symbolic consequences of the white appropriation of African American culture by suppressing the need to acquire any information about the cultural form other than what is needed for whites to draw pleasure from. In a multicultural world where cross-racial interaction could be cultivated through the explicit and reflexive participation in shared cultural forms, the discourse of having fun seals off this possibility, generating an amnesia or vacuum around the dance. As a result, it is not just African Americans who are dominated through the severing of the form from its historical and cultural context, but also whites, in their inability fully to comprehend the cultural forms in which they are participating, prevents them from the possibility that taking pleasure in African American culture could also lead to a greater understanding of African American people as well.

Since discourses are never truly autonomous, the notion of having fun can be spoken about at the same time that one articulates other discourses about race as well. The following, taken from my fieldnotes, expresses how multiple discourses can operate concurrently.

•

Norma Miller, one of the great original Lindy Hop dancers, came through tonight. Norma, a slender eighty-year-old African American woman, was once part of the famous Whitey's Lindy Hoppers dance troupe that is considered to be the greatest group of Lindy Hop dancers ever seen. I was so excited; I had my notepad, my digital recorder, my questions, just in case. I thought, this would be my great chance to interview her. Perfect. The buildup was frantic. I got to the club two hours early just to get a table for me and a couple of friends right in front of the dance floor to position myself for an introduction when she came through the door. I had read about her, watched video interviews with her, heard tales of her from older dancers talking about how vocal she was, episodes they had heard or heard about where she vocalized her opinions, about how proud she was of this being an African American dance. She was at the point of being shut out by a certain section of the Lindy Hop community because of her "strong" opinions on issues of race. Preparing to go to the club that night, I was ready to cut right to the heart and get my questions about race out there. She came in with a group of dancers who had surrounded her. Once things settled down, and she was introduced to the crowd. I would have to wait until after the event to get my chance to speak with her. She walked out to the middle of the dance floor and spoke to the crowd:

It's the most fun dance, nobody realizes, what, you see, you're beginning to realize what we knew; we had a hell of a lot of fun. You never saw anybody walk off the dance floor after they got finished Swinging that wasn't smiling. You know what I mean? It brought joy, it brings people together. I mean this is the greatest dance that ever happened. Like I say: if you don't dig Swing, baby, you don't dig fried chicken. Fried chicken is basic. You know when you realize this country exported the greatest two commodities in the world, we did more with swinging jazz and fried chicken than all the diplomats in the world, I'm telling you. You can go to any part of the, any pocket of the world today and get some fried chicken; you can go to any pocket of the world today and you can hear some swinging jazz. So you see jazz and Swing are American. It was the only dance we created in this country. And it belonged to all the people. When I come along, like you see we had as many white dancers on the floor as we had black dancers. Everybody was swung back in those days. We had white dancers that tried to kick our ass all the time; we couldn't allow that, of course, but it made great competition, it made great camaraderie; see, we didn't know there was a difference in people at the Savoy. It took many years later that I knew this other bullshit was going on, but in the Savoy we had a way of life that was unusual, people from all walks of life, if they came to New York, the first thing they did was get in a taxicab and headed straight up to Harlem. Why? Because Harlem was the entertainment capital of the world and in Harlem came the great bands, the great singers, right there in Harlem. I met Ella Fitzgerald, Chick Webb, Duke Ellington, Billie Holiday, Count Basie, we were all on a first-name basis. All of it came to this place where you guys are sitting like that. We used to sit on the bandstand and there was the great Chock Webb with the drums and who was out on the floor singing? Ella Fitzgerald. When she got finished singing, she'd dance with us just like you dance with us so it was a way of life that was extraordinary and that you are beginning to feel part of this new resurgence of this new feel of Swing because you are real Americans because in America we are united.

I introduced Swing dancing here in the Chicago area in 1937 at the Chicago theater. I was with the great Ethel Waters and you know she used to come to the Savoy Ballroom to learn how to Swing dance or Lindy as they called it then, because in those days, everybody did the Lindy, so everybody did the Lindy then. Ethel Waters was a big star and she wanted to put the Lindy in her show. She would come to the Savoy ballroom and the only person she would dance with was Frankie Manning. I would dance with her escort, Archie Savage. I would dance with him. If any of you have seen the photographs in *National Geographic*, that male dancer was Archie Savage. I taught him to dance. And you see we boldly brought Swing across the country and we came here and it was through Ethel Waters that we went all the way out to California, resulting in us making that movie called *A Day at the Races* with the Marx Brothers, and then Frankie's group took Swing dancing over to Australia physically in 1938.

You see we were the ambassadors, the people who went across the country doing this dance, showing this dance around the world and that's how Lindy got across the country, we took it out physically. Out to California and you know, when I went to Australia in 1956, you wouldn't believe this, I introduced fried chicken to Australia. That's right. And you know, we had a big party for the media and we invited all the people from the television and the reporters and what not, and you know what was on the menu? Fried chicken and potato salad—that's as basic as you can get—and they loved it. But it's this type of thing—and it's this type of communication that we did around the way we did around the world—that results in the Lindy being here today.

I was taken completely by surprise; I wasn't certain what to expect, but this was nothing that I had anticipated. This was certainly not what I thought would have been said. Sitting at our table, my friends and I launched immediately into conversation sorting out what she had said and why. Both friends, whom I had talked extensively with about the project I was working on, were also shocked. We all looked at each other in a haze of confusion as if each one wasn't sure the other had heard what they had. Each of us started talking at once:" Did you hear her say . . . ?" "Wait, wait, wait a second . . ." "What the hell was . . . ?" all talking past each other at once. What exactly was this speech supposed to mean? Was this to "make up" or apologize for past instances where she spoke her mind about racial politics and the ensuing alienation that occurred? We all turned collectively toward each other, lowering our heads below the bellow of applause so as to hear each other's comments. One friend asked first, "Was this a way to make the white audience feel included in the history of Lindy?" I asked, "Was this because she was in front of an almost completely white audience?" My other friend looked at both of us and said, "Was fried chicken a euphemism or a metaphor for black culture? If so . . . I'm not sure I feel comfortable with that." I responded, "Didn't she say that this was everyone's dance and that race didn't matter, but also that whites tried to be better dancers than blacks and that she and her friends wouldn't allow it?"

Each of us kept spilling questions out of our mouths, trying to find the words that could interpret what she said, as if reading between the lines of what was happening and figuring out what she "really" meant was just a matter of time. To hear her speak of blackness and whiteness, of all that "bullshit" happening in society in the '30s (overt segregation and racism) and yet how race didn't matter inside the Savoy, that this was taking place in Harlem and yet there were just as many white dancers as there were black, left each of us puzzled. Which one was it? Did race matter or not? Was she claiming this to be an African American dance or everybody's dance? Who exactly was she referring to in the "we" of "we" gave the world Lindy Hop and fried chicken?

•

This event troubled me long after it had passed, but it brought to light many of the complexities that gave rise to the multiples ways the Lindy Hop was being discussed: it was about whiteness and blackness, it was blaming the victim and blaming the victimizer, it was talking about race and talking about race directly, and finally it was about the significance of African American culture and having fun all at the same time. What came to fruition long after I came to terms with that night was the multiple, criss-crossing, and even contradictory ways that each of us, all of us articulate our thoughts that may be about race and not about race at all at the same time.

CONCLUSION

Taking up Ellison's call to interrogate our own language and by using Bourdieu's concepts of symbolic power, symbolic violence, and misrecognition with ethnographic analysis allows us to move beyond the racist/antiracist rhetoric that frames much of the work on white interaction with African American culture and the outcomes of that interaction, using what Wacquant (1997) refers to as the "logic of the trial": parceling out guilt or innocence to participants in attempts to convict or vindicate whites of racism.

Instead, the alternative theorization presented here, grounded in Wacquant's analytic of racial domination, illuminates the ways in which these discourses serve as mechanisms of racial domination by decontextualizing and dehistoricizing the Lindy Hop from its African American cultural and historical context (Wacquant 1997, 226). By shifting the focus of investigation away from individual expressions and psychological guesswork over the "real" intentions or motivations of any particular individual, the focus was to illuminate the "in the moment" interactions by which historical conditions are erased, not through manipulation or deception, rather through people's ahistorical immersions into a cultural form that they decided to participate and cultivate for numerous reasons. In this way, we can see how the immediacy of our interests highlight those aspects most important to us in the moment, that necessarily blur larger contextual issues that reside in the background from our attention.

In order to excavate this background that more often than not is out of the realm of our conscious awareness, the focus of this analysis was to understand the logic at work in and behind the discourses of their expressions. In doing so, I expose how these multiple viewpoints on the Lindy Hop are articulations of larger racial ideologies that are not separate from but rather embedded in the very ways that people conceptualize and articulate everyday cultural practices. This analysis reveals how the seemingly innocuous ways we conceptualize our everyday worlds are never neutral but always the product of invested power relations; even in what people believe to be race-free settings like the Lindy Hop. The racial domination that is a product of these expressions may be contrary to the intentions and desires, both conscious and unconscious, of those who participate in them. As a result, we can understand how a society organized in racial domination does not consist simply of whites dominating African Americans through the severing of cultural forms from their social contexts or distorting the role that race plays in structuring everyday life. Rather, these relations of power dominate whites themselves, as they are prevented from full participation in the very practice they are trying to cultivate and denied the opportunity for forging a cross-racial multiculturalism built around common investments in shared cultural practices.

Only by revealing the mechanisms through which symbolic power/ violence operate can we begin to dismantle a system of social organization structured in racial domination. This is a matter of changing not just people's minds but rather the very logic through which people conceptualize and articulate the world. Through this new form of conceptual schemata, based on a different racial logic, we can transcend the liberal myths of multiculturalism based on cultural appreciation and begin to forge an alternative multiculturalism based on cultural participation.

4 STEPPIN' OUT OF WHITENESS

> You got to understand, stepping is not just a dance, it is a culture, it is the way
> we live; it is what we eat, think, and breathe, you understand me. See, you out
> there on that dance floor and you're with your partner and you're all holding
> hands and you're all swinging, and swaying, and you turning 'em, twisting
> 'em, and dipping 'em, and it is such an exciting feeling you get, you know
> what I mean.
>
> *R. Kelly*

> For even as his life toughens the Negro, even as it brutalizes him, sensitizes
> him . . . it *conditions* him to deal with life and with himself. . . . He must live it
> and try consciously to grasp its complexity until he can change it; must live
> it *as* he changes it. He is no mere product of his sociological predicament. He
> is a product of the interaction between his racial predicament, his individual
> will and the broader American cultural freedom in which he finds his am-
> biguous existence.
>
> *Ralph Ellison (1995b, 112–13)*

•

One night at the end of August, Julie and I finally decided to go out Steppin'. After some searching on the Internet, we decided on a place. It was a
warm humid Saturday evening as we drove down to Mr. G's, a well-known
banquet hall on Chicago's South Side. After a relatively short drive down
the Dan Ryan interstate, we hopped off at the exit and parked on the main
street a block away from the club. A massive painted brick building stood
half a block in from the corner. Several African American men, dressed in
bright-colored suits and hats, mostly shades of red, were milling around
outside the club's entrance. Some were leaning against the wall, a few were
smoking, and all were engaged in spirited conversation.

We maneuvered through the crowd and made our way into the lobby
of the building. The narrow entryway led straight ahead with a coat-check
to my left, where a woman chatted away with one of the patrons. The music was loud and pulsing. I could feel the bass lightly vibrating through the
floor. At the end of the lobby, a long banquet table was positioned in front of

A version of this chapter was originally published under the same title in *Ethnography*
6(4) (December 2005): 427–62.

two curtained French doors. The table was draped in a white tablecloth with only a small cash box on top. Behind it stood two men, each dressed in red suits, black raw silk shirts, and lightly patterned ties that coordinated the look. Both had bright pocket squares and felt derby hats. They were freshly shaven with tight haircuts as if they had just arrived from the barbershop. We approached the table and I said, "Hey, what's going on?" Looking a little puzzled, one of them asked, "What party are you here for?" Thinking that this was open to the public, and not a private event, I was a little confused. Maybe he thought we were lost. I asked the man at the door, "Do you have Steppin' going on here?" "Sure. You're here for Steppin'?" he asked incredulously. "Yeah, that's what we're here for." Amused, he said, "Well, all right then, it's ten dollars apiece. Come on in." We entered through the double doors into the cavernous banquet room.

The room was awash in the color red. From head to toe, from hat to heel, every conceivable shade of red was represented, creating a kaleidoscope of patterns against the cool cream-colored walls of the room. (Only later were we to learn that many of the parties have a color-coded theme, and that night it was obviously red.) The dance floor was visible, not because we could see it, rather because of the undulating waves of people swaying to the music in the middle of the room contrasted with the rather placid tables of people chatting, relaxing, and socializing. Large rectangular tables formed rows, each slightly separated from each other, with every seat seemingly occupied. The tables were scattered with advertisements, or "pluggers," for future events promoted by various groups. Although many Steppers' events are called "parties" we were to learn that they were sponsored by a single or several Steppin' groups. They're open to the public and other promoters are allowed to pass out pluggers for their events. There was a table of CDs to my right, selling what I imagined must be mixes of Steppers' music. I turned to Julie, "Let's try to get a table in the back; it looks really crowded up here." We made our way through the packed room, zig-zagging between tables and around an enormous parquet dance floor that stretched from one side of the room almost all the way to the other side. Other than the greeters, no one paid us any attention; I wasn't sure if this wasn't private after all.[1] We made our way back to one of the few unoccupied tables almost at the back of the room and slid our chairs around to face the dance floor.

The lights were low, and despite the size of the room the music was loud enough for dancing, yet soft enough that people could be heard having conversations. The music was smooth and steady, a string of mid-tempo songs blurred together keeping a buoyant feeling throughout the club. The dance floor was crowded, yet all the dancers seemed to have enough space as they all navigated the dance floor. The men in their overly wide-legged trousers and alligator shoes shuffled and slid past their female partners dressed in tight-fitting pantsuits or long flowing dresses. Whereas the Lindy Hop can be highly syncopated at times, making it appear chaotic, here partners were floating past each almost effortlessly in motion. Whereas Lindy Hop has a certain bounce in the syncopated rhythm, here in the R&B-influenced dance the bounce was taken out for a calm almost skating approach to moving on the floor. Several couples were doing the classic "sugar push" move where the woman is pulled into the man and then pushed back out giving the appearance that she was on wheels as she appears to glide in and glide back out.

As we sat there watching the different couples on the dance floor, we quickly starting pointing out to each other stylistic differences or footwork patterns that differed from the Lindy Hop: The shuffling of the feet for both men and women, the women doing less swiveling, and more dipping of the hips as they moved. Whereas in the Lindy Hop, partners are constantly switching places, Steppers would sometimes dance in place connected by their arms paralleling their partner's movement side to side. Other dancers of all skill levels were executing various turns and spins with their partners, all of which looked familiar in form if not content to what we knew from our dance experience. The music may have been slightly different and the dance modified to reflect that rhythm and feel, but this seemed so close to but not exactly the Lindy Hop. With slight variation, this was like a modified Lindy, done to contemporary music. After spending several songs picking up as much choreography as we could, we decided to give it a try and made our way to the dance floor. Tonight we were no longer Lindy Hopping; we were Steppin'.

•

On the other side of town, far from the white Swing dance world, is the contemporary manifestation of the Lindy Hop—a dance known as Steppin'.[2] Because hip hop dominates the popular conception of African American culture, the Steppin' scene exists mostly beneath the radar of mass-mediated popular culture. People mistakenly think that before the Lindy Hop revival in the late 1990s, Swing dancing had been dead all these years, whereas in fact it never left the African American community. In the 1950s Swing moved off the popular radar and went underground; the dance then transformed and mutated into the form we see today in Steppin'.[3] Steppin' has been a part of the African American community in Chicago since the death of the big bands. Not to be confused with the African American fraternity and sorority step shows featured in Spike Lee's *School Daze,* in which men and women perform choreographed moves in a line, Steppin' is a slower and smoother version of Swing dancing (Fine 2003). With the rise of bebop music, the Lindy Hop could no longer be the social dance of the day; the faster tempos and extensive solos necessitated a different mode of dancing. Dancers who listened to bebop remained connected to their partners yet executed their steps in half-time to the music, which smoothed out their style and made it less syncopated. By the 1970s, Steppers danced to pop and R&B in order to stay current with contemporary music, but the dance remained smooth and cool. More recently, the success of Steppin' as a cultural form led to a weekly TV show called *Steppin' at Club 7*, which aired on Friday nights from 1995 to 1997. This nationally televised show, coupled with migration, has cultivated vibrant African American partner dance scenes in many cities around the country, including not only Chicago but also Minneapolis, Milwaukee, and Detroit, where the dance is known as the Hustle; in Washington, DC, where it is called Hand dancing; and in Atlanta and Houston, where it is known as Boppin'.[4] While many other cities have taken an interest in Steppin', however, any Chicago Stepper will boast that Steppin' is a Chicago thing. The Chicago style is also known for being smoother, slower, and more bluesy than the styles practiced in other cities.

Since Steppin' has been around for decades, those who participate in the dance are African Americans who range in age from their mid-twenties to their seventies. In Chicago, Steppin' can be seen in clubs on the West Side, South Side, and near the south end of the Loop. Despite the Lindy Hop revival, and even despite *Steppin' at Club 7* the Steppin' scene has remained largely underground in relation to the white mass media. It made its sole big-screen appearance in the 1997 film *Love Jones*, made by local Columbia College Chicago graduate Theodore Witcher and starring Lorenz Tate and Nia Long. Herb Kent, a legendary Steppin' DJ and personality on radio station V103, says that Steppin' did not explode with Swing because "it is just too Black" (Rhino Records 2001). The African American cultural forms that tend to be appropriated by the white communities either are extreme examples of culture, like "gangsta rap," that are marked as transgressive to white society, or else cultural forms that easily lend themselves to becoming whitewashed by their accessibility, like rock-'n'-roll or Swing. Steppin' is too mainstream within the African American community and too subtle to fit the binary of either an explicit renegade African American identity or fully assimilated cultural form. As one writer described it, "Steppin' is right in the rhythm of the African American lifestyle, with the grit and the polish all in one solid package" (Fountain 2001). Because of its aesthetic and because it is practiced almost exclusively within African American neighborhoods and social circles, Steppin' exists apart from the larger white society and has remained mostly insular to the segments of the African American community where it is practiced. This is due in a larger part to the extreme historical segregation of Chicago, as well as the bifurcating socioeconomic dynamics that have kept these geographical and cultural spaces apart with little or no interaction on an everyday interactional level.[5]

Without cross-promotion or cross-marketing into the media, there has been no youth movement or identification with this African American cultural form like that seen in hip hop. Similar to what Robin Kelley has argued with other forms, Steppin' is a cultural practice that validates the African American community and provides expressions of "a distinctive sense of African American humanity in cultural spaces separated and differentiated from the dominant culture, spaces in which the dominant culture's scorn, devaluation, and rejection are replaced by affirmative expressions of self" (Kelley 1996, 33). Steppin', in its autonomy from white society and mass-mediated trends, sustains an alternative African American world, one seldom frequented or even noticed by whites.

IMMERSION

The effectiveness of Negro music and dance is first recorded in the journals and letters of travelers but it is important to remember that they saw and understood only that which they were prepared to accept. Thus a Negro dancing a courtly dance appeared comic from the outside simply because the dancer was a slave. But to the Negro dancing it—and there is ample evidence he danced it well—burlesque or satire might have been the point, which might have been difficult for a white observer to even imagine.

Ralph Ellison (1995a, 255–56)

As Ralph Ellison remarked years ago, African American cultural practices, especially those of music and dance, are not always what they appear. Since many of these practices were created in the oppressive conditions of slavery, their function as entertainment for white audiences may have been readily accepted. What white audiences missed was the dual function of these forms, which also provided a medium for social critique. Long after slavery, as these practices became engrained in African American society their performative aspects were no longer forced upon them. This is not to say these cultural expressions were simple reactions to slavery or that they were autonomous and have persisted unchanged throughout time. For Ellison, it is the notion of folk expression itself that still retains that social criticism, albeit a commentary of which African Americans themselves may no longer be conscious of even if performing. It is this aspect of African American cultural forms that remains elusive to the casual observer.

My first exposure to Steppin' happened while I was a Lindy Hop instructor. I helped run a Swing night on Wednesday nights, during which we had a band and a dance lesson beforehand. The event was held at Green Dolphin Street, a popular jazz club located on the Near North Side of the city which had live music six nights a week. Since the venue was a regular jazz club, it attracted a different audience than the other Swing events. Green Dolphin was the only Swing venue on the North Side that had any regular African American clientele. Often on Wednesdays, a few African American men in their forties and fifties would hang out at the bar and listen to the music. Sometimes, I would strike up conversations with them about dancing or jazz for both academic and personal interests. Given that this was the only mixed racial space where the Lindy Hop was danced, I wanted to see what they thought of the Lindy Hop scene. Several different men on separate occasions mentioned that the Lindy Hop or Swing dance was similar to what they did today—a dance they called "Steppin'." One evening, a pair of men whom I had chatted with before at the Green Dolphin suggested that I check out the Steppin' scene at some point. Although the Steppin' scene is not covert and information about events is readily available if you are looking for it, I had no knowledge of where to go until I met these two men. In Chicago one of the most popular African American radio stations, R&B station V103, has Steppers' music sets on Saturday nights and advertises the World's Largest Steppers' Contest and other Steppin' parties on the radio. In addition, Steppin' groups have Web sites on which they list their upcoming events.

My interest in pursuing Steppin' came long after my knowledge of its existence. At that time, I was so invested in the Lindy Hop scene personally and professionally that I was completely submerged in that world. I had now stopped teaching and quit working for any of the performing Swing dance groups. I felt that I needed to pursue some other avenue, not for the dissertation but for pleasure, to keep dancing alive for me. As the fad of the Lindy Hop passed and the community returned to a small subculture, I felt I needed a new creative outlet, one that captured the vibrancy and aesthetic and ethic that the Lindy Hop scene now lacked. I did not get into Steppin' earlier because my dissertation focus was on the Lindy Hop, and I felt that I needed to be there to continue my research. I was writing about the Lindy Hop, not about Steppin'. This was purely a personal interest, whereas the Lindy Hop remained my academic focal point.

As I became more immersed in the world of Steppin', it became clear that this was also something that mandated discussion in and of itself: not only because I was enchanted by it, but also because it was such a wonderful world for investigation. In the end, only by pursuing personal interests could I have expanded this intellectual project. This was not a calculated field site; it was what I discovered while pursuing my own passions and letting them work reflexively back onto my intellectual academic work. Steppin' was a new outlet and an ideal opportunity.

The great irony of my dissertation project was staring me in the face. I started out studying an African American dance with an interest in African American culture, and I ended up doing a study of white society and the appropriation of the Lindy Hop by whites. During the Lindy Hop revival, I could easily enter the scene, since it was overwhelmingly white and primarily on the North Side of Chicago. There was no "racial" problem of immersion or entrance. In the case of Steppin', however, this all–African American dance culture was far removed from the white Lindy Hop's North Side venues. The social dance world of Steppin' was not unfamiliar to me—even the dance was not too different from the Lindy Hop. Although the dance was close enough to the Lindy Hop that we could "pass" as Steppers, the aesthetics and practices of the Steppin' scene were very different from the white North Side norms. Here I could study the issues of race from my own marginalization, as I myself was an outsider marked by my skin in almost every situation. This brought interesting surprises and afforded me the opportunity to undertake a "practical inquiry" into the object of study— African American dance forms—by testing the usefulness of my ideas in practice (Bourdieu and Wacquant 1992).

My involvement and immersion in the Steppin' community came after having spent four years of intensive dance training in the Lindy Hop, taking dance classes, practicing, social dancing three to five nights a week, and traveling the country to participate in intensive dance workshops. In addition, as I progressed as a dancer in the Lindy Hop world, I went on to teach and perform the dance professionally. My dance partner, Julie, was a professionally trained ballet, jazz, and modern dancer. She had been Lindy Hop dancing for several years at the time and we had also been teaching and performing the dance professionally together for the last two years. In addition, we also studied other forms of dance such as ballroom, hip hop, and Argentine tango. Our expertise in the Lindy Hop, and our social dance skills more generally, provided us with the skills and bodily knowledge to adapt our bodies to different styles of dance and music that enabled us to make the transition into the Steppin' community with relative ease.

Through word of mouth with African American friends not involved in the Lindy Hop community and through African American newspapers and

Web sites, I started doing research on the Steppin' scene. We started going out to Steppin' clubs, parties, and dances all over the South and West sides in the city of Chicago. After learning where the best dancers, DJs, and clubs were, as well as the best nights of the week to go out, we were eventually out dancing regularly from three to five nights a week.

Like any subculture, the Steppin' scene has its own styles and codes. The Steppin' style—with its Ragtime 2000 look—was an aesthetic that immediately drew me in (Rhino 2001). As our investment in the Steppin' scene grew, we started going to African American shopping centers on the South Side and looking for styles that were popular in the clubs we were frequenting. The style of clothing and the dance itself were different modes of distinction and helped us assimilate into this world. I bought trousers, alligator shoes, silk shirts, in bright colors and patterns, while Julie purchased strappy high heels, bold printed blouses, and long flowing skirts that were fashionable among the women. This change in our dress style signified more than an acquaintance with fashion; it was something we needed to master, like the dance, in order to fully assimilate into and demonstrate a complete grasp of the world in which we were now involved. In this new environment, we had to learn the codes and norms by listening and watching to establish trust and respect. Being outsiders made respect much harder to come by and made us that much more attentive. We often felt that we had to prove we were good dancers so that people would recognize us as something other than mere "spectators" or appropriators of African American culture.

The ability to adapt to the world of Steppin' was not difficult for a trained dancer. The competence and skills necessary to adapt one's dancing to the style of Steppin' are those possessed by a number of expert Lindy Hop dancers. As much by chance as by desire to learn Steppin' and explore other dance worlds, we were the first from the Lindy Hop community in Chicago to immerse ourselves as regulars in this world. It was not our dancing abilities alone that made us unique in this community. It was also our willingness as outsiders to participate according to the normative orientations and rules of this dance community, and our willingness to break the dominant patterns of segregation by traveling to all–African American neighborhoods that made us stand out in this community. The result of being the only white people in an all-black space generated a number of responses to the incongruity the community perceived that we were simultaneously marked as racial outsiders, and yet through our dancing marked us as insiders within the world of Steppin'. As I tried to come to terms with this new social world, it became clearer and clearer that this was not about us; rather, it was a question of identity in general when we started to explore the hazy terrain where race and culture collide.

A QUESTION OF IDENTITY

The exploration of Steppin' provided an entry into examining the Ellisonian question of identity by looking at the ways that we violated the everyday racialized commonsense of race, culture, and identity. First, through our extensive Lindy Hop dance training we were violating the norms because we could dance in ways that were unexpected—here our physical skills in relation to our racially marked bodies were out of place. Second, our willingness to adapt our aesthetics in terms of dance and dress style to meet the norms of the community violated the idea that whites rarely desire or adapt to non-white norms or codes. Third, our desire to participate and travel to the clubs and parties in the Steppin' community violated the assumption that whites fear black neighborhoods and need to feel secure in their own environment. These violations of racial commonsense generated responses that are worth investigating to understand how the racial imagination works not just in white society, but in African American communities as well.

Steppin' is learned like all other cultural forms of dance, not only socially through friends and family, but through structured dance classes and workshops held on a regular basis in African American communities. This infrastructure within the Steppin' community offsets stereotypical racial ideas that whites have to learn to dance in classrooms, whereas dancing just comes naturally to African Americans. Given the receptions and responses to our dancing—with the assumption going into any Steppin' event that not only should we not have the ability to dance, but also we could not learn if we tried—this dominant racial mythology about these distinctions played out just as powerfully in the minds of African Americans as it did in mainstream white society. This analysis enables us to understand that African Americans subscribe to the same ideologies of race, culture, and identity as the dominant white society that reinscribe and uphold societies structured in racial dominance (Hall 1996).

When entering the Steppin' scene as a white person, the question of race is inevitable. We quickly learned what it was like to be the only white persons in a room. The tables were turned: white people almost never feel like a minority. My experience going to the Steppers' clubs was similar to what Du Bois called "double consciousness." But my situation was Du Bois' idea reversed; here were white people (my dance partner and I) who were self-conscious of feeling racially marked as a minority and out of place in an African American world. Since we were the only white people in the club, it was obvious that people noticed us. The significance, symbolically or literally, of being white in African American parts of town, doing an African American dance, in an all–African American club, surrounded by all African Americans, must be looked at through this prism of race and reflexivity, especially in the context of whiteness that dominates the racial organization of American society.[6] One male dancer, who I came to know rather well, stated this incongruity bluntly: "I have to tell you this, and you probably already know this, but you stick out—it's not the pants or the hat or the shoes—but you definitely stick out—and it's certainly not the way you dance, but you stick out—I'll tell you that."[7] While some of the dancers I met told me that other whites had come to Steppers' events before, in the course of two years spent Steppin' we encountered only four other white people, and only one of them was dancing.

The marked visibility of white people in this environment created an ideal, ironic opportunity to examine whiteness outside of its usual invisible racial status.[8] In most cases racial identity is transparent to whites, because they never have to leave the white-dominated world (Hartigan 1999). Whereas whiteness may serve to explain macrolevels of structural domination, here in the world of Steppin' it is not whiteness that is hegemonic; rather, blackness is dominant.[9] Here African American fashion, language, style, and norms of social interaction define the local landscape. This is not to say that whiteness is irrelevant; rather, here it is displaced from its centrality of power and marked as visible and nonnormative. Here in these specific spaces where African American codes are dominant, whiteness and white people are marginalized as the racial other.

Our entrance into the Steppin' scene was by choice. This double consciousness of identity occurs only by choice for whites in the United States because they are rarely, if ever, in situations where they are the racial minority. Because white people are a rarity in the Steppin' scene, we were met with immediate apprehension and suspicion. The case of whites going to an all–African American club by choice made us an oddity; since whites never *have* to feel all eyes on them as the only white people in the room, why would they come there? Our entrance into this world was visibly obvious and socially precarious. Not knowing anyone or anything about the social norms of these clubs, we were unsure of what to expect. We self-consciously chose to be reflexive about our situation: we reflected on our own nervousness, hesitation, and intimidation and determined how this changed the formation of our thinking and our racial practices. This reflexivity reveals a great deal about the structural relations between racial groups because whites as the dominant group have the luxury and privilege of never having to be racially self-conscious. It is no surprise that most whites do not consider race to be an issue. Or, if they do consider it an issue, it is often a minority problem that minorities have to deal with and overcome, or for others a problem that should be downplayed so it will go away.

THE WORLD OF STEPPIN'

Classic blues were both entertainment *and* a form of folklore. When they were sung in theaters they were entertainment; when danced to in the form of recordings or used as a means of transmitting the traditional verses and their wisdom, they were folklore.... Bessie Smith might have been a "blues queen" to the society at large, but within the tighter Negro community where the blues were part of a total way of life, and a major expression of an attitude toward life, she was a priestess, a celebrant who affirmed the values of the group and man's ability to deal with chaos.

Ralph Ellison (1994, 286–87)

Ellison's discussion of the dual function of the blues as both entertainment and part of "a total way of life" resonates with the cultural traditions of using artistic mediums as dispositions towards everyday life. In Ellison's case, the blues, like Steppin', is an expressive cultural practice. This is crucial to understanding African American communities because they were often forced to cultivate their social worlds within the constraints imposed upon them by the dominant white society. Social spaces and embodied expressive cultural practices are intertwined. These spaces are places apart from, and designed to be free from, the dominant white society, which marginalized and oppressed African Americans.[10] These situations provided a counter-space to exercise cultural freedoms and expressions that affirmed commonality and solidarity in the face of adversity. In these spaces, a sense of community is constructed through an alternative set of values and social relationships than those of white society. These social spaces created sites where the exploited working body was reclaimed for self and for community. These were spaces for constructing alternative identities from backbreaking wage work, low income, and pervasive racism, to take back one's body for more authentic freedoms that can be enjoyed only on nonwork time.

The black body is celebrated here as an instrument of pleasure rather than an instrument of labor, by using these practices as a form of recovery and recuperation (Kelley 1996). By understanding the material context within which cultural practices are cultivated, we can understand how identity and practice are linked to material conditions of existence. Stuart Hall echoes Kelly's sentiments in his discussion of the black Diaspora. "Think of how these cultures have used the body—as if it was, and it often was, the only cultural capital we had. We have worked on ourselves as the canvases of representation" (Hall 2000, 470). African American reliance on the body as a means of expression has a long history tied to racism and economic impoverishment. As a result of the dearth of resources afforded them, African Americans developed culture out of what was available; they utilized the body in place of the deprivation of other resources as a way to eke out pleasure and identity. As a result, African Americans developed rich physical manifestations of cultural identity in bodily activities such as dance and sport for the creation and sustenance of individual and group identities against domination and social erasure (see Hall 1996b). This strategy gives African Americans a voice and allows them to represent themselves and their community in a much different way from the dominant white society. Dances such as the Lindy Hop and Steppin' became forms of counterpolitics against segregation and exploitation, by redefining the African American body as desirable, beautiful, dynamic, and creative (see Gilroy 1993, Gottschild 2003, and Kelley 1996).

Recognizing the importance of the body as a medium of expression in African American social dance is key to understanding the significance of embodied cultural practices for defining African American identity in America. Therefore, it is necessary to map out the dynamics of the world of Steppin' in terms of its style of dance, attitude toward the dance, venues for the dance, music, and style of dress to understand the crucial role they play in defining the meaning of this world for its participants.[11] In addition it was imperative for us to understand these dynamics, not just from the outside, but by undertaking the cultural labor of learning, understanding, and abiding by the norms and codes of this world, so that we were able to earn the trust, respect, and membership of this community. I will now turn to map out these dynamics in detail to fully understand the process of our acceptance.

Steppin' is a fluid style of Swing dancing. This dance form has an easy grace—dancers glide across the floor and their steps seem effortless, as opposed to the strenuous athleticism of the Lindy Hop. The Steppers' dance moves are less intricate and more streamlined than those done in the Lindy Hop. In addition, the Lindy Hop is often syncopated and asymmetrical, whereas Steppin' is fluid and symmetrical. Steppin' is less fast-paced than the Lindy Hop, and it is not as rigorous on the body. Compared to the controlled chaotic aesthetic of the Lindy Hop, Steppin' is cool, contained, and never out of control. While Steppin' is certainly influenced by Swing, tap, and hip hop, it is done within the musical framework of the R&B, soul, and smooth-contemporary hip-hop genres that accompany it. The Steppin' footwork is structured like the basic six-count traditional Swing dances (East Coast Swing and Jitterbug), in which there is a rock step, triple step, triple step format. However, Steppers have replaced the initial rock step with two restrained shuffle steps. Steppers also break apart from their partners more and walk around each other while keeping the rhythm. Despite being African American and social, it is still structured and learned like all other cultural forms. Just as many African Americans learn the dance through classes and formal instruction as they do socially by growing up in the culture. Despite the myth of natural rhythm, there is an elaborate network of Steppers' dance classes and schools of Steppin' taught around the city, just like other cultivated dance forms.[12]

"Let's go to work" is a phrase often overheard at the clubs, used by the DJ or by someone walking around the dance floor talking to the dancers. This statement relays encouragement, approval, and group solidarity to inspire the dancers to work harder and be more creative. This self-conscious statement of "labor" initiates a call-and-response with the audience and furthers a collective expressive behavior.[13] It is ironic that Steppers use the word "work," which evokes the idea of labor, when everything about the Steppin' scene is supposed to appear effortless and far removed from the labor of the workday. Often clubs will have "After Work Sets" beginning at 5 p.m., when people can come to escape and unwind right after they get off work. The distinction between this sophisticated aesthetic and everyday labor is supported by the fact that Steppers are not even supposed to show signs of sweat, no matter how hard they dance. The men carry handkerchiefs in their back pockets to promptly wipe their brow should they begin to perspire. On the sidelines, men and women often use fans or wave pluggers to cool themselves off. Urging people to "go to work" also encourages individual expression, to do your own thing and strive for individualism within the group—not apart from the group, but to contribute one's own labor to the community.

Steppin', like other subcultures, has an inner crowd that travels to certain clubs on certain nights. This ensures both a certain level of dancing and a certain type of person in their community. Because Steppers are working- and middle-class people and are anti-thug and anti-"gangsta," their weekend events are almost always private parties held at rental halls. This is not to say that there is no possibility for crossover, but Steppers' events attempt to prohibit gang activity through strictly enforced dress codes and normative orientations. Like other subcultures, Steppers differentiate their own aesthetics, values, and orientations, and here we can see a differentiation through class-connotated aesthetics. In this way we can simultaneously see not only how class aesthetics work, we can see how internally "appearing" homogenous groups, by racial category or geography, cultivate their own boundaries and symbolic markers as one subculture differentiates itself from other subcultures while sharing the same racial identification. By viewing the Steppin' community in this way, we can see how race as a set of homogeneous categories imposed on people from the outside clashes with the heterogeneous reality of life within those categories. In the case of Steppin' subculture, African American racial identity is intersected by a myriad of other modes of identity, such as culture, style, and social disposition, which defy any monolithic understanding.

Steppin' music is dance music. It's the *groove* that Steppers want, and that overrides the racial identity of the artist: if it's a good tune for dancing, it's played. Usually the music is by African American artists, although occasionally a white artist, such as Phil Collins, will make the cut with what many consider a "classic" Steppers' song, "In the Air Tonight." Steppers' DJs have also played Hall and Oates and other artists from England's blue-eyed soul movement. Most often the music is divided into contemporary artists such as Dave Hollister, Aaliyah, Angie Stone, Mary J. Blige, and older R&B "dusties," as they're referred to because they're songs so old they collect dust, such as the Whispers, and Harold Melvin and the Blue Notes. Occasionally, DJs also play pop tunes and mellow hip hop such as Dr. Dre and Snoop Dogg. The key is that you cannot dance to everything, and much like Swing ("If it doesn't swing you can't dance to it"), in Steppin' if it does not have the right groove it just does not step. Herb Kent commented on the music tradition of Steppin': "Chicago is such a jazz town. The roots of Steppin' really are in jazz and all that bebop, which was just settling in the '40s here in the city of Chicago. So it just naturally took off from there."[14] As a result, it is not hard to see and hear the parallels as we move from the Lindy Hop world to the Steppers' world and back again.

Steppers have their own style of dress, known in the community as "Steppers' sharp." Historically, fashion in the African American community has been a way of shedding the degradation of work and collapsing the status distinction between themselves and their oppressors; dressing up offered a medium to construct a collective identity based on something other than wage work, presenting a public challenge to the dominant stereotypes of the black body and reinforcing a sense of dignity that was perpetually being assaulted (Kelley 1996, Gilroy 1993, and White and White 1999). In Steppin' the men's long suit coats, baggy trousers, hats, and ties in splashy colors echo the refined and polished style of the Roaring Twenties, but with a contemporary African American twist (Rhino Records 2001). A woman's Steppin' attire consists of at least two-inch heels to accentuate her legs and a dress in a color to match her partner's outfit, fitted around the hips and with just the right amount of length and flare to add dazzle to her turns. Leopard-skin patterns, silks, pencil heels, and hip-high slits all accentuate her body. Some couples wear matching or color-combined outfits. The women never wear hats, but their hair is styled to complement the Steppin' attire and attitude. On big event nights, it's easy to see that the majority of the women have spent time in beauty salons earlier in the day. This aesthetic is reinforced on all advertising pluggers: "No gym shoes, no athletic gear, no jeans, and no denim." The strict dress code reflects a desire to keep the crowd more upscale and maintain a rigorous set of norms. This aesthetic distinction belied a much deeper sentiment about African American social life. An excerpt from my fieldnotes illuminates this sentiment.

•

It was about midnight at the best Friday night spot to go Steppin', the popular African American partner dance that thrives on Chicago's South and West sides. People were dancing, drinking, standing around chatting, just having a great time. The DJ started playing popular hip-hop artist Snoop Dogg's cover of the James Brown classic tune "Revenge." He announced that Snoop Dogg was in town and might stop by that night. There was a buzz throughout the club as people wondered if the famous hip-hop star would show. I found our friend Larry and asked if this hype about Snoop Dogg was true. Larry said it was likely, since tomorrow night was the annual "Players' Ball," to be held that year in Chicago, where the infamous "Pimp of the Year" award would be handed out to mark honors in that subculture.

After a few dances, my partner and I returned to our table and started talking to the people next to us. Suddenly, the song changed midstream back to Snoop's tune. The DJ, Sam, broke over the song and announced, "We would like to welcome Snoop Dogg. Snoop Dogg in the house!" He turned up the music even louder to mark the dramatic entrance of Snoop and his entourage. I turned to look over my left shoulder, and there was this lanky 6'4" figure walking in through the back of the club, towering over the massive group of bodyguards and thugs that surrounded him. Rather than the denim suits and basketball jerseys I had seen him wear in magazines and videos, Snoop was dressed in a lime-green suit trimmed with sequins. He was sporting a matching green sombrero as big as an umbrella and large white oval glasses that covered half of his face—he was a vision of excess. Next to Snoop was the infamous pimp Bishop Don Magic Juan. Don Juan was also cloaked in green and gold; as he has explained in the HBO documentary *Pimps Up, Ho's Down*, "Green is for the money and gold is for the honeys." The whole thing was like a surreal dream; two urban superstars from different eras together at once, standing only a few feet away from me.

I grew up listening to Snoop's music and am familiar with Don Juan from *Pimps Up, Ho's Down*, from the Hughes Brothers' film *American Pimp*, and from hearing his name in numerous hip-hop songs. Seeing Don Magic Juan and Snoop together, dressed up like this, made me feel like I was watching a music video, if not in one. Never in my wildest dreams had I thought that learning the Lindy Hop would put me in the same room as these legends. Other pimps, players, and hustlers followed them. These men were dressed in floor-length fur coats of all colors of the rainbow, many with matching fur hats, as well as thick gold rope chains, opulent rings, and jewelry. Ice cream–colored bowler hats bobbed in their circle, and some carried canes and scepters, while others carried "pimp cups"—large goblets with their names encrusted on them in faux jewels and rhinestones. Here was the ultimate manifestation of what we usually think of as the mythic pimp world and aesthetic. The guy in the candy-apple red hat and suit, Scorpio, had been covered in the documentary as last year's winner of the Pimp of the Year award, and Lex, the sole female pimp from the documentary, was also there. Surrounding these underworld celebrities were their enormous bodyguards and clinging to them were numerous scantily clad female prostitutes (several of whom I recognized from the documentaries), forming a large entourage.

Almost immediately, a divide occurred between the dancers and the pimps and prostitutes. Here were two radically different scenes colliding in one space. Each group was paying little attention to the other; the dancers kept Steppin', but they gave the pimps plenty of space by keeping to their side of the club.

The woman in front of us turned around and asked if we knew the identity of the man in the green sombrero. I replied, "Yeah, sure." "Wild, huh?" she said. We shared a half-amused, half-incredulous look. For some time, my dance partner and then girlfriend, Julie, had been talking to Monique, the woman next to her. I turned to them to see if I could gain more insight into why these guys were here. I asked Monique what she thought about it, and if this had any connection to the Players' Ball. Monique could tell that I was more than a little curious about the whole affair. She shook her head, rolled her eyes, and leaned in close so I could hear. "Don't go to the ball. Whatever you do, definitely do not go to the ball tomorrow night. That's not something you want to get involved in. Believe me." We continued talking, but that was her last word about the Players' Ball. While the documentary had shown the Players' Ball as quite a party, the fact that it was intersecting with the world of Steppin' made me want to learn more about it. But it was clear from the gulf between the parties at the club, as well as from Monique's stern words, that the ball was not going to be a Steppers' event.

A casual observer could never tell the deep class and cultural differences that exist in this African American community underneath this club scene. While this story may appear to be about the extraordinary spectacle of Snoop and his posse, the real insight is the self-defining complexity and multilayered character of the African American community (see, e.g., Jackson 2001, Pattillo-McCoy 2000, and Tate 2002). As soon as Snoop's entourage started to fill up a sizable space and a growing shroud of marijuana smoke encircled them, many of the Steppers began exiting the club. As we left, I could not stop thinking about how crazy it was that I was patronizing clubs with pimps and famous rap artists. This was something I never could have envisioned when I took on the Lindy Hop as my dissertation project.

•

The Steppers' disposition is a self-conscious one that sets them apart from the aspects of hip-hop culture that dramatize the social pathology of African Americans and the glorification of the culture of deprivation. This racial essentializing is manifested in a staunch refusal to let those symbols, and in this case those people who profit and exploit such degrading stereotypes, from encroaching on their spaces of socializing.

During my time in the Steppin' scene, *Vibe* magazine, a mainstream hip-hop magazine founded by Quincy Jones, ran an entire feature article on the dance tradition of Steppin' in Chicago, entitled "Here Come the Hot Steppers" (Fab Five Freddy 2003). Written by old-school hip-hop personality Fab Five Freddy, this article depicted the Steppin' scene, with an account of the pimps and their entourage that were in attendance for the biggest Steppers' event, "The World's Largest Steppers' Contest." Rather than document the scene's actual dynamism, Freddy and the photographer captured only the spectacle of the pimps by writing about and photographing their excessiveness, ostentatious dress, and infamous personas. By cashing in on the popularity of Don Juan and the resurgence of the pimp aesthetic that has made a comeback in the hip-hop community, this depiction of Steppin' was constructed to fit a much more hip-hop–oriented audience. This portrayal was done by someone who was not a Stepper and had obviously spent little time in the Steppin' community besides attending this event. While there are some of these elements in the Steppin' scene, they are fringe elements. Filtered through the pimp aesthetic, this refraction of the Steppin' culture parallels the way that mass media often depicts the ghetto, as a romanticized place of excitement, authenticity, and excess in "ghetto fabulousness" in the hip-hop world. Freddy's depiction could not be further from the truth; he had focused on an element that is in fact unpopular and unwanted by the majority of the Chicago Stepper community.

Captivated as I was after my one encounter with this pimp aesthetic, I had asked around to find out how the Steppers really felt about it. When I recounted my experience, people reacted sternly; one person confided, "Sure, you get a couple of people like that. But Steppers are not into that at all. That is not part of the Steppin' scene." Another person remarked, "We want nothing to do with that," while yet another put it most succinctly: "Hell no! Steppers don't go in for that shit. That's not what we're about." Disappointed and frustrated to see this distortion of a community in which I had recently become involved, I watched the magazine to see if anyone felt as upset as I did about the depiction. Two months after the article ran, this reader response was printed in the August issue:

> I'm a Chicago native, and I'm very disappointed with the article "Here Come the Hot Steppers" (by Fab Five Freddy, June 2003). First, the pictures show wanna-be pimps/players. This is not the style of Chicago. No one dresses like that at Step shows or around town. There was also a statement about West Side and South Side women's views of each other. This is all so old. I just want people to know that Chicago is more than characters dressing like clowns and neighborhood quarrels. Step shows can be classy. There are some Steppers who are still stuck in the '70s, but that need not have been the focus of the article. (Ross 2003)

Just as in my own experiences and those of others I talked to, this woman's comments go to the heart of the Steppers' sentiment. Ironically, the very critiques that African American scholars have charged against whites depicting African American culture—pathology, sensationalizing, and deviance—were all on display in the way that this African American journalist portrayed this social scene. I hope that this chapter, while it will not be read by an audience like that of *Vibe* magazine, can do some justice to a sophisticated and complex world of partner dancing that has been either historically neglected or, more recently, distorted in the public's consciousness.

SOCIAL PRACTICE, DANCE, AND THE BODY

•

Despite being good social dancers, we're always a little nervous. We have not really technically trained in this style and are learning the choreography and style as we dance. We're always a little reserved—going out on the floor is always daunting at first. As a rule, in trying to follow the cultural norms of the Steppin' community, we do not perform any traditional Lindy

Hop moves like the Swing Out, Circle, or Charleston variations that would be conspicuously different from the Steppers' style. Instead, we try to adapt our Lindy Hop skills into the Steppin' framework, which is almost identical. One way we ease the tension—which has more to do with our own self-consciousness than anything anyone ever does or says—is to play guessing games about what people are thinking about us before we head to the dance floor. That night, Julie said self-mockingly, "'Okay, the white folks have had a few drinks, now what are they going to do?'" And when we moved to the dance floor, we imagined the comments: "Okay, here comes white folks; let's see how foolish they look or let's see some minstrelsy on their part. They're going to come up in here in an African American club and try and dance our dance in front of us?" Finally, gathering courage, I took Julie's hand to escort her to the floor since we had come there to dance, not just people-watch.

At first, our anxiety overrode everything else, and our movements were hesitant and inhibited. We struggled to make it through the song; we could not quite seem to click. Before the next song started, we were unsure if we should attempt another or quit while we were ahead, but we loved dancing together and this was a great dance floor. "Should we sit down?" Julie asked. "No, we just got out here; we have to keep going," I said. "Just one more, okay?" We continued to dance and tried to relax, to get the groove we saw around us. Suddenly, I noticed the DJ pointing at me and smiling. I leaned into Julie's ear. "Hey, the DJ just smiled and pointed at me. I guess it's cool." This sign of recognition eased us, and we started to unwind and get into the flow. When the song ended, Julie asked, "Okay, should we sit down now?" I replied, "We may never get up the nerve to come back onto the dance floor, so let's just keep going. Just one more." The next song was a good one, with more of a hip-hop beat, and we both got into it. I looked over my shoulder at some of the other men and tried to mimic them. I tried a spin, then a move I saw another guy do. Julie did her best to follow me even though I was not doing a great job. I was too busy trying to copy someone else, which made me slightly late in my leading. However, we were beginning to find the right groove, and it was starting to feel really good as we began to relax and fall into the flow of the music.

We saw the couple dancing next to us looking over. They were probably in their late fifties. She was dressed in all red with a few black accents, and he was decked out in a black suit with a red shirt. They smiled, and she leaned over and said, "Y'all look good. Keep on dancing!" With this encouragement, we loosened up even more. We no longer felt self-conscious of what we were doing and just got into the groove of the music. Whether this acknowledgment was about making us feel comfortable in the club or was a statement about the quality of our dancing was not clear. This newfound feeling of acceptance inspired us to return.

•

In order to fully appreciate the practice of African American social dance requires that we move away from analyses that have focused on pathological or functional explanations and instead focus on "expressive practices," which are the culture of everyday life.[15] By looking at dance as an expressive practice of the body, we can understand the dynamism and creativity of the cultural forms that generate rich narratives, pleasures, and aesthetics. Expressive practices such as dance are a crucial and integral part of African American culture and identity because they emerge as responses to everyday life in the forms of resistance, evasion, and survival within the hegemonic whiteness of society (see Rose 1994, Kelley 1996, and Gilroy 1993). These practices serve as forms of identification and generate a sense of community through a common vernacular that links the community together and gives voice to certain ideas, beliefs, and aspirations.

Because dance is an embodied practice, the body is central to cultural meaning, not only because it serves as the medium of enactment but because the body is the locus and embodiment of those very practices. It is here in and through the body that social classifications and values are inscribed in the body. As these arbitrary socially constructed distinctions become normalized and institutionalized and turned into a permanent disposition, they become misrecognized as inherent in those bodies. As racialized bodies become fused with the cultural practices that they enact, this reinforces our commonsense beliefs that these classifications are grounded in reality and are natural products of those natural differences. These classifications and values mark and inculcate the body in specific contexts through their enactment in practice. The embodiment and reproduction of these practices reproduces the system of classification through which those bodies are classified. Therefore, through their normalization in specific localized situations, bodies and the practices that they enact appear as if they were "natural" or innate rather than social constructions; for both observers and practitioners of those practices, what is socially learned is "internalized as second nature and so forgotten as history" (Bourdieu 1990a, 56, 71).

Since the body in practice mediates race and identity, when a "mismatch" between the body and the practices it enacts occurs, the naturalness and inherentness of racial identity is disrupted and broken. This mismatch shatters our expectations and breaks our commonsense anticipation of normal behavior for that racial group. When the physical body, in this case the white body, does not agree with the cultural practices, in this case African American practices, an incongruity forms between the visible body and the enacted practice. This mismatch makes explicit the way that racial identity is not established a priori, but rather is relationally defined in practiced everyday life. This exposure is symbolically powerful, because it illuminates the stability and the investment of the commonsense racial order and the circular racial logic in the inherent and naturalized grounding of race in the physiological differentiated body enacting those cultural practices that inherently define it (Bourdieu 2000a, 181). The entrenchment of the dominant racial order is perpetuated and reproduced because legitimation of the established racial order occurs almost automatically in the everyday reality of the social world. The practice of racial identity does not lose sight of the power of race to define us or its basis in racial domination, nor does it make race an optional identity or something open to immediate transcendence. Viewing the practice of identity through cultural forms, not as natural or essential practice, opens up the possibility for a new understanding of race.[16] Because of the visceral grounded nature of culture in the body, dance is a seminal place to investigate the connection among the body, culture, and racial identity.

Since the body is malleable raw material cultivated and formed through practices, it is open to being "retooled" as it is socialized and cultivated into new practices. This bodily retooling requires what Wacquant calls "body work," which is not a matter of conscious choice or obtaining intellectual information passed on through logical reasoning, but arduously acquired through inculcation, bodily labor, and training (Wacquant 1995b, 72). Viewing dance as an inculcated and embodied practical knowledge acquired through training and labor offers a situation in which we can denaturalize the body and illuminate its socially constructed and socially classified identity. When bodies engage in cross-cultural or cross-racial practices, the way they are performed and the racial ideologies, aesthetics, and knowledges that define those cultural forms are manifested through the body in their enactment. In the case of dance, what we are concerned with is not, after all, a representation as a symbolic text to be read, but embedded and embodied knowledge in practice exhibited in particular social contexts.

RETURNING TO DANCE

•

One night at a club called East of the Ryan, we attracted obvious stares, as we made our way down one of the aisles to the dance floor. Being the only white folks in the entire club, we naturally drew attention. Since this was our first time at this club, our self-consciousness made us feel as if everyone could not wait for us to make fools of ourselves in front of them. Either that, or we figured that everyone was waiting for either some act of overdramatized minstrelsy or some whitewashed version of Steppin' by whites who could not dance. As obvious outsiders, we were self-conscious and made an effort to stay out of the regulars' space on the dance floor as we made our way to the right side toward the front of the room. The music was an up-tempo contemporary hip-hop song; we started dancing and really getting into it.

Our dancing felt good that night. We were moving well together, moving in the music, interpreting and working off each other, feeling as if we were right in the pocket of the music. But suddenly I heard a woman yelling behind us. At first we were a little worried; we were not sure if the voice was directed at us, but it was loud and emotional. We turned slightly to see a woman in her early forties several tables back from the dance floor, standing up, clapping, and yelling over the music, "You go on!" This exclamation, much in the call-and-response ethic of the phrase "Let's go to work," was a call of encouragement for dancers to dance their best. As she kept clapping, we suddenly realized that she was gesturing to us; she was acknowledging us as participants in the community rather than as exceptions to it.

This acknowledgment and encouragement boosted our confidence and spurred us to dance harder and execute some of the most complex and intricate moves we knew. As I turned Julie around me, I noticed now that we were the center of attention and the entire corner of the room was now watching us dance. As we kept dancing, we heard more shouts of encouragement: "Get down" and "Yeah! That's right."[17] Later, as we turned to leave the dance floor, there was a whole crowd of people looking at us, smiling and clapping—some looked half-amazed and some half-incredulous, as if they had never seen white people dance before, or at least certainly not Steppin' the way we were dancing. Obviously we were not demonstrating the expected social behavior of whites that dominates our racial categories when we think of white people dancing.

As we passed through the aisle on the way back to our seats, the once seemingly indifferent crowd was now gregarious. People were looking us in the face and smiling. One woman put her hand up for a high five, while several men gave me reassuring head nods. When we finally reached our seats, the people around us, who before did not seem to notice us, immediately turned and started talking to Julie and me. I wondered, Why the change? Why the applause? What did they think about us? Almost instantly, in the mere minutes of dancing to several songs, we seemed to have gone from total outsiders to people who were welcomed and respected as regulars. I had come to realize one simple point: they were not responding to the novelty of our skin color; they were responding to us as dancers.

•

RESPONSES

The sight of my partner and me Steppin' in all–African American clubs destabilizes some African Americans' commonsense notions of black and white identity. Everyone sometimes misrecognizes the connection among cultural practices, the body, and racial identity. Just as the black body has been construed as naturally rhythmic and musical, the white body is seen as its opposite, devoid of rhythm and soul. In this situation, what they expected to see from whites dancing and what they actually saw was radically different. When we are Steppin', we do it in a way that is not normally associated with white racial identity or the way white people are traditionally supposed to perform this African American dance. The incongruity between the racialized body and the performance does not make sense for most people. When these do not match up, dissonance is created. We are doing something that whites normally do not do or do not know how to do. When we do not "perform" our race correctly, explanations must be given to make sense of these transgressions. Because the physical body is always seen as the underlying basis of racial identity, any deviation or ambiguity concerning the body must be quickly resolved and explained away.

Our presence on the scene both as white people and as skilled dancers with a specific bodily knowledge created a tension regarding our identity.[18] This tension concerned what to make of us as white people, as outsiders to this all–African American community violating social norms of segregation, style, and bodily knowledge. Our dancing led to one of two responses: first, by viewing us strictly through our skin color—by understanding race through the dominant social categories—and second, by viewing us through our dancing—by understanding us through our practice.[19] In the former view the other dancers used the common racial categories to describe us, whereas in the latter view these categories no longer mattered, as they defined us through our ability to dance. Here I emphasize not what we thought or felt about what we were doing, but how people responded to us. While both of these are sociologically significant for analyzing and understanding racial identity, in order to understand this alternative way that racial identity can be transformed through cultural practices, we need to look specifically at the various ways that people responded to the apparent incongruity of us dancing.

RACE AS A CATEGORY OF ANALYSIS

What I'm trying to say is that racial identity does not dominate individual culture so absolutely as you would seem to believe. Nor does it override the individual will in the aesthetic realm as certain sociology-minded critics and black militant theorists would have us believe. Accidents of birth, geography, personal contacts, the availability of models, cultural examples, individual psychic dimensions and the cultural climate in which the individual comes to consciousness can, and often do, play a more important role than racial identity—when that individual begins to function as an artist.

Ralph Ellison (1999, 42)

As Ellison remarks, categorizing individuals based on their racial category overrides the cultural, aesthetic and psychological dimensions of who and what people are. In fact, these characteristics play a more important role than race does when we begin to assess the notion of identity. In order to make sense of the incongruity that confronted them, in terms of how white bodies should move, behave, and so on, three dominant explanations emerged: First, they marked us as a different type of white people. Second, they believed that we must have African American heritage, and third, they acknowledged us as racially different yet accepted us as regulars.[20] The first type of response was that we were not "regular white folks" or we were a "different kind of white people." This became a general theme in many conversations I had. As one of the first persons I ever encountered at a Steppin' club put it,

> Man, you got balls to come up in here. How did y'all hear about this place? Seriously man, you got some nerve. I mean coming up in here, what were you thinking? You must be all right. My name is Thomas. I wanted to introduce myself. I figure if you've got the nerve to come in here, you must be somebody with something going on. You are definitely not regular white folks if you just decided to show up here.

Yet another acquaintance said:

> You two [my dance partner and I] are definitely not regular white folks. For you two to come in here and just start dancing with everybody like it's no big thing, that takes some serious nerve. You don't seem nervous at all—you must be some real down-ass white folks. That is all I can say.

This sense of violating Chicago's codes of segregation and subjecting ourselves to being the only whites in the club challenged their normative orientations of what white people traditionally did. As a result, they needed to augment the traditional racial categories, in this case "different" or "not regular" whites.

Others remarked that coming to all–African American clubs means that we must have "been around." This expression seemed to refer to our comfort at being around large numbers of African Americans or our ease in being the only whites in an all-black club. This was stated by one acquaintance I knew on the scene, who one evening told me, "You've got a little bit of gangsta in you to come here. There isn't anybody who is going to mess with you up in here. I can tell that. You're not regular white folks, I tell you that." When I asked several regulars if other whites had ever come to any Steppin' events, they mentioned "tourists that would just come to watch us dance, but never danced themselves." Because we violated these patterns of segregation and did not appear intimidated by our marginalized status, they were forced to augment their category of white identity to explain our presence and actions. In this way they could keep the dominant social category of white to explain what we looked like, but change the definition to include nontraditionally white characteristics.

A second more extreme version of this use of social categories of race is that some people took us out of one category and placed us in another. In many instances our white identity was simply rejected. After seeing us frequently and getting to know us as regulars, people at the Steppin' events began to reracialize us. As one regular acquaintance said, "Okay. Now level with me; you got black in you, don't you?" I replied that as far as I knew, I was just white. His response was a firm refusal that there was no "black" in me: "No, hell no. You've got black in you. That's a fact. Because you're definitely not white; you got black in you, the way you dance. You may look white, but you're definitely not white!" This process of reracialization, redefining us from white to black, reinscribes the traditional social categories of race— only now places us in a different category.

Another acquaintance confided one time, "I don't understand it, but you're white, because white people don't dance like that. They just don't. I don't mean to sound racist, but you know white people just—I mean, they just don't have the soul." Yet another couple one evening turned around from the table in front of us and said, "We've been watching you two dance all night. You're some down-ass white folks. So where did you learn to dance like that? You dance better than most everybody out there and those are black folks. I can't explain it, but man you two can dance." Most notable in this process of reracialization was a conversation with one dancer, Thomas, with whom we became good friends. One evening Thomas invited us to join him at his table:

Thomas: You're my nigga. That's my nigga there [speaking to his group of friends and pointing to me].

BH: Hey, uh, Thomas, let's not go there.

Thomas: But it is not like that. When I call you my nigga, that means that we're tight, that we're friends. It doesn't mean the same thing as when white people say it. So I can say it because you're straight, man. You are definitely not white. You're my nigga now. You're one of us now.

Here, race as a category of understanding is still central. In this case, the need to explain this tension between physical appearance and bodily knowledge cannot be done easily with the dominant social categories of race. Because the dominant social categories of race have such a deep hold over the way we conceptualize racial identity, these examples of reracialization show the constraints within which people must categorize. Because our presence and dance ability was problematic for the Steppin' community, they needed to reracialize us as black to make sense of our dancing and accept us into their world.

A third way that people responded to us through social categories of race was to acknowledge our racial difference, but at the same time downplay it in order to make us feel more comfortable in the Steppin' environment. One evening we were at a Steppin' party where we saw our friend Larry, who was a promoter and general social conduit on the scene. He approached our table to say hello. Larry said that he would like to introduce us to Sam, the house DJ and a local radio personality, and walked us up to the DJ stand. Sam welcomed us to the club. As we walked back to our table, Larry put his arm around me, saying:

You're family now. Ain't nobody going mess with you up in here—now you're family—remember that. You know me and now you know Sam. You don't have to worry about any problems. You feel free to come here any time we have a set. No need to feel uncomfortable or anything like that, okay?

On another evening, a promoter who was passing out pluggers to an upcoming event stopped by our table and said: "Hi. I just wanted to let you know that you two are welcome at any of the events we have. I've seen you at a couple of other events. So please don't hesitate in coming to ours as well; you two are always welcome." People wanted to reassure us that while we might feel awkward as the only white people in these contexts, we did not need to feel this way. Through these reassurances we were recognized as regular participants on the scene. This dual marking was at the same time an acceptance into the community and yet a reminder that reinscribed our racial difference through traditional social categories of race.

Since our looks did not match our actions, this created tension and confusion. Since African Americans feel that most whites never undertake this kind of behavior, the rarity of white bodies venturing out alone into all–African American communities and practicing African American culture destabilizes traditional social notions of white racial identity and forces them to make sense of our presence and our dancing in some way. Some did so by expanding their definition of what it meant to be white; others re-racialized us, while still others acknowledged our racial difference yet also welcomed us as regulars within the community. All of these responses used race as a social category to define us and treated race as static, inherent, and essentialized differences that are absolute and definitive.

RACE AS A CATEGORY OF PRACTICE

This reminds me of something that happened out at a northwestern university. A young white professor said to me, "Mr. Ellison, how does it feel to be able to go to places where most Negroes can't go?" Before I could think to be polite I answered, "What you mean is: 'How does it feel to be able to go places where most *white* men can't go'" He was shocked and turned red, and I was embarrassed; nevertheless, it was a teaching situation so I told him the truth. I wanted him to understand that individuality is still operative beyond the racial structuring of American society. And that, conversely, there are many areas of black society that are closed to *me* while open to certain whites. Friendship and shared interests make the difference.

Ralph Ellison (1994, 803)

What we see in this exchange is the racialized commonsense of the interlocutor, remarking that Ellison, due to his prestige and status, is afforded the privilege of moving through realms of white society that other African Americans cannot due to their racial category. Ellison is the "exception" to the rule. Here Ellison turns the tables and points out that he has access to realms of society that whites don't based on his racial category. As Ellison indicates, the lesson he was trying to teach was not about the racial category that one is categorized through, rather it is the cultural aspects of friendship and shared interests that allow one access to different arenas of society that override race. Pointing out these contradictions, Ellison draws our attention not to race as a category of analysis, but rather to the ways that social life is navigated through practice.

To master an embodied expressive practice like Steppin' requires a significant amount of bodily labor and years of training that are neither easy nor arbitrary. Steppin' is more than just dance knowledge and skill; it involves aesthetics, cultural values, and tastes. As Bourdieu would point out, our comportment was not demonstrated through conversation or what was spoken, but was revealed in practice by bodily knowledges and dispositions beyond the reach of language's self-censorship or political correctness. This was not just about knowing the dance Steppin'; participating as regulars in the community, adopting the aesthetic and normative codes, and crossing racially segregated spaces all contributed to the ways that people responded to us. When the stereotypical expectations of the white body are violated—where the race as a social category is transgressed through bodily knowledge—a different type of response also occurred. We were met with responses of confusion, recognition, and community acceptance. This practice became more important than our racial category in defining our identity.[21]

When I spoke to people at Steppin' events, the first question that they would straightforwardly ask—usually with a hint of suspicion—was what were we doing there in the first place? One acquaintance candidly told me, "You know, folks, I'm sure folks are wondering why you are here. I mean, white folks don't just show up out of nowhere to dance." Or as one eventual acquaintance put it, "I bet most people probably think you're a cop. Why else would some white dude be here? Look around, how many white folks do you see in here? When a white guy comes in, it's usually for some other reason and not for fun. I'm sure lots of folks here think that. But folks figure it out once they see you dance. They definitely don't think you're a cop then; they know why you're here." While at first people responded to us in terms of our racial category, once they saw us through the practice of dance, their responses became based on this practice.

Upon seeing us dance, the first and most immediate reaction people had is one of shock. The sight of white people dancing this way disturbs their normal conceptualization of white as a racial category; more shocking to them than the sight of whites at their clubs is the competence that we display dancing. My partner and I were always met with the questions of "Where did you two learn to dance like that?" "Who taught you?" "Where did you get those moves?" As Bourdieu emphasized through his theorization of the body, here the body is communicating something more important than a racially marked surface: a competence of cultural practice that cannot be faked. Because embodied knowledges cannot be explicitly articulated, they reveal more than can be controlled consciously. While whites may be out of place in this milieu, what is even more surprising is their ability to perform this African American cultural form, and it is through this practice of dance that our identity was defined.

After the initial shock wears off, a second, more important distinction is made that forms our identity—that of competence. One of the first times we were dancing in a certain club, a promoter approached us on the dance floor. He apologized and said: "I don't mean to be rude and interrupt your dance, but I'm leaving and I have got to give these [promotional materials for an upcoming event] to you, y'all dance so damn good. You have got to come to this. There is going to be a great DJ and we need dancers like you to be there."

Another example of this expression of competence and recognition came when Julie and I attended a private party held by one of the many Steppin' promotional groups. The first time we came off the floor, a large man walked right up to us and said, "Hey, my man, you two are cool—you can definitely hang." He reached out and slapped my hand for a handshake. He nodded his head and with a little laugh repeated, "You can definitely hang. I can tell you that." Still others have made casual remarks such as, "Yeah. All right, y'all step!" or "Y'all step y'all asses off" as we have left the dance floor or when striking up conversation with us at the bar. Finally, one particularly memorable comment was made by a bouncer who followed us outside the club one night as we left. While I thought we might have left something behind or somehow done something wrong, he leaned out the door and called to us, "Hey, y'all done good in there. Come on back anytime."

In this way, a more radical conceptualization of race has nothing to do with skin color, but rather with people's practices, which are more important than their visible social category of race. If we were just two other African American dancers in the club, we certainly would not get the same level of attention, because the social understanding of race would be transparent: black bodies dancing well are completely congruous with our embedded racial schemes. People might still respect and appreciate our dancing skills, but the surprise and shock that results from the incongruity of white bodies and the seamless practice of Steppin' would disappear. Here we are doing this African American cultural practice, not in the refuge of an all-white space on the North Side, but in an all–African American venue. People's racial expectations are further complicated because this performance of dance is competent and thus earns appreciation and respect from that community.

This sense of respect comes not through our patronage of paying cover charges and buying drinks but as a result of our dancing; what is recognized in the way we dance is the cultural labor and dedication that we have undertaken to master an important cultural form within the African American communities of Chicago. As we became more and more aware of the way that people were responding to us, we grew more and more self-conscious.

As we entered a new club for the first time one night, my dance partner said to me:

> Why don't we go dance right away—before we get drinks, before we do anything else—just so we don't have to go through the whole process of everyone looking at us and wondering what we're doing here. That way we can just get it out of the way and relax.

As a result, we made an effort to establish our presence as dancers as soon as possible to avoid people responding to us suspiciously through the traditional racial categorizations.

One way this form of respect has been consistently demonstrated is that promoters always make sure we have the latest information on their parties and are up-to-date on the inner-circle knowledge, such as the best or trendiest spots to dance or when and where the best parties are being held. One promoter approached us at a dance at the International Brotherhood of Electrical Workers, of which one of the Steppers was a member, and introduced himself. "You and your lady dance real good. Here's a plugger for our next set. We would like you to come. My name's Steve. What's yours?" At another event, another promoter said, "I'm throwing a set next week and I want you to come to it. We do a real nice job. You'll like it." In the recognition of our dancing, there is a sense of mutual respect that drives much of this acknowledgment; respect for the dance is respect for the people, and this brings respect back to us in return. In the case of Steppin', we obviously could not learn to dance like this in a vacuum or abide by the normative and aesthetic codes of the community, which was all acknowledged and articulated through the way other Steppers interpreted our dancing.

After a while, people were inviting us to their private parties. One woman we had seen as a regular on Tuesday nights at the club 3G's invited us to her birthday party downtown at a non-Steppin' club. The week before the party we saw her out, and she reminded us: "Y'all are comin' to my party, right? At Chromium? I remember I gave you a plugger last time—it's going to be a real good time. You should definitely come out." As we became regulars, this sense of respect normalized us in the community, and bouncers and event greeters would acknowledge us on the way in or out with a "Hey, you're back, all right" or "Hey, thanks for stopping in. See you next time." While these comments are trivial in the sense that many patrons are greeted and thanked when entering and exiting the clubs, our normalization was instantiated through our very unexceptional status as regulars on the scene.

The construction of race is predicated on its practice; race must be enacted and constantly reproduced.[22] It is here through the normalization of fixing performance with the body that race becomes essentialized (Fanon 1991; Hall 1996a, 1996b). The physiology or explicit racial marking of the body as skin color must be remapped as the traditional racial identities of African American and white are transgressed through bodily knowledge and practice. Identity based in practice enables us to examine the difference between the racialized cultural form and the racialized body of the actor in practice. When racialized bodies and the practice of racialized cultural forms are no longer congruous, race as a social category of analysis is no longer useful in defining identity. Therefore, we must turn to understand the centrality of practice in defining the significance of racial identity.

CONCLUSION

When people see us dance, it confuses their expectations of how "white" racially marked bodies are supposed to "do" African American culture. One cannot merely "pick up" Steppin' by watching or reading about it. Steppin' is not a commodity that one can purchase, like a CD or an article of clothing; it requires bodily knowledge, time, and practice. Embodied knowledges, because of the labor required for their mastery, reveal a depth of experience that is not immediately available for self-fashioning. One must invest a significant amount of time and bodily labor into Steppin' in order to learn it. This embodied expressive practice requires cultivation and years of training that are neither easy nor arbitrary. The practice of Steppin' is more than just dance knowledge and skill; it involves ethical, aesthetic, and cultural dispositions of values and tastes.

Racial commonsense is so powerful that we continue to read the body on the surface, with its tangible visibility of "color," as a way to try to ground the reality of race. It is almost impossible to imagine ourselves outside of this visual mapping; this racial marking is part of our racial epistemology and almost inseparable from who we are. We have a practical commonsense trust in the objectivity of observation and accept these visual cues as truth when it conforms to our expectations, to the degree that we assume that these bodily fictions are naturally part of the flesh of the body. Where visible racial marking serves as the primary basis for classifying identity, this certainly can just as easily be undermined.

The case of the white Steppers, when understood through the model of embodied cultural practice, provides a way to understand how the body can be reracialized. Because of the failure of explicit skin color models to map racial differences, a new theory of race that is based on the body in terms of labor and practice is necessary.

The body is both symbolic and material and does not serve "one" purpose. The body as symbolic raw material shows how bodies are marked on and worked on; they are never predetermined biological facts. The body is groomed, dressed, and sculpted by social labor and social processes, which invest it with meanings and values.[23] These processes socialize the body into a signifier of social meanings. Practices of the body in everyday life serve as a site where collective identity is created, asserted, and negotiated. The body as symbolic material is malleable and can be metaphorically African American or white. Putting the white body in styles that are white and putting the African American body in styles that are African American conforms to our racial commonsense. But when we change this order and put a white body in a style that is African American, as in the Steppers example, or in hip hop with the case of Eminem, we no longer treat that body within the usual categories and expectations of the commonsense logic of race.[24] In these cases, the white body is not "playing" or pretending, but is African American through its competence in the practice. These are rare exceptions, in which white people are able to transcend the logic and aesthetic of whiteness and cultivate alternative values and aesthetics. In these cases, there is more than just an appreciation of African American culture and tastes enjoyed from a distance; there is a cultivated and embodied relationship with these practices. It is the cultural labor that allows one to move beyond playing African American to actually embodying these cultural practices and enacting them according to the logic of the specific local community in which they are situated. The shift of focus from racial skin color to practice is a shift from the superficial and trivial to something deeper—culture and knowledge. The visual indicators of race evade the crucial question of racial formation and instead rely on the absolute and static notions of race as essential and marked by skin color.

The practice model of race breaks down our commonsense understandings of race and our deterministic and essentialist ideas of racial groups and essences that are supposedly inherent in bodies. In addition, practice undermines the grounds for racial difference based on arguments of authenticity, naturalness, and biology. The practice model allows us to illuminate the mechanisms by which racial markings occur and are naturalized. By understanding the mechanisms that naturalize difference, we are able to gain a point of leverage to break the essentialism of race and differentiate between whiteness and white people, blackness and black people.

The bodily model of practice emphasizes not only the locality of the body in practice but also the competence of that practice. The convergence of the practice, the body, and competence must all be accounted for in order to reracialize the body. Cultural practice is not an idea, but rather knowledge and a mode of embodiment demonstrated by competence within a community of culture. The bodily labor of cultivating the dance, its style, motion, rhythm, and movement, is a competence that can be demonstrated only in practice. Through bodily practice we can understand how practice and labor are the underlying components of the body, identity, and race.

The bodily practice model does not mean that theorizing racialized identities should focus only on individuals and local situations; in no way does the individual example of the white Steppers change the structural relationships of race in the larger society. The white bodies are still "white," but this does not prevent their integration into the Steppers' world. The African American Steppers, by reracializing the white dancers, have transcended the boundaries of racial difference. But this suspension of racial categories is fleeting. These transgressions have little social structural impact on whiteness and African Americanness as governing racial mythologies or on the organization of these social structures, and does not change the fact that when the white Steppers leave the club, they are perceived as white by society at large, as the dominant commonsensical racial schemes come back into play. The ability to inculcate these practices within any individual body does not necessarily imply that these practices are acts of resistance, or guarantees any political effectiveness. However, this particular sociological understanding of race as a category of practice destabilizes our doxic racial schemes and normalized racial boundaries and opens up possibilities for a sense of agency that *can* be political and used to challenge and struggle against the authority of our assumed racial foundations that structure societies in racial dominance.[25] Just because the body is "white" does not mean one must subscribe to or perpetuate the logic of whiteness.

By theorizing the relations between bodies, practices, cultures and race, we can retheorize race not as prefabricated entities or racial groups "on paper," but as distinctive and distinguishing sets of cultural practices, competences, and dispositions.[26] In addition, we can show that just because the body is "white" does not mean that one must subscribe to or perpetuate the logic of whiteness. Through these transgressions, we can show that it is possible to train and cultivate the body in an alternative direction, in which its new practices, competences, and dispositions override its ostensive racial identity and lead it to be reracialized or in fact deracialized. Through this extension, as well as through the problematizing of race, culture, and identity that Ellison affords us, we can begin to see how our racial imagination imposes nothing but limitations and overrides the individual qualities and particular cultural, historical and contextual experiences out of which our identities are constituted.

For the sake of symmetry, and to point out the ever-laughing Ellisonian

irony of our everyday existence when it comes to living out that construction of racial identity, we should here take listen to an ongoing refrain: as
Ellison told us, our search for a foundation or a guarantee as to what race
really "is" may be nothing more than a never-ending joke upon ourselves
that we will never come to an answer, but will continuingly act out for each
all the while denying the laughter that we all share. And as Ellison would
prod us into asking—if only both sides knew they were really laughing with
each other and not at each other—from what might this shared joke upon
us all possibly spring?

LEAD OUT: LEARNING HOW TO MAKE LIFE SWING

So B, when you write all of this up, how are you going to account for yourself in all of this? How do you think you fit into all of this? Because you're technically white like they are. How will you explain the difference between you and them? What are you going to say?

Tanarra

Without the presence of Negro American style, our jokes, tall tales, even our sports would be lacking in the sudden turns, shocks and swift changes of pace (all jazz-shaped) that serve to remind us that the world is ever unexplored, and that while a complete mastery of life is mere illusion, the real secret of the game is to make life swing. It is its ability to articulate this tragic-comic attitude toward life that explains much of the mysterious power and attractiveness of that quality of Negro American style known as "soul." An expression of American diversity within unity, of blackness with whiteness, soul announces the presence of a creative struggle against the realities of existence.

Ralph Ellison (1995a, 109–10)

Coming to terms with Ralph Ellison's remarks on culture is not as straightforward as it may appear. While on the surface this statement seems transparent in describing the African American aesthetic or style that has come to inform all aspects of our cultural life, such a simplistic interpretation would violate the complexity of Ellison's thought and miss the subtle irony embedded within these words. This style, known as "soul," is defined not in exclusive terms but in fundamentally hybrid terms. The term's definition lies in the tension of diversity within unity, blackness within whiteness. If the secret of life is "to make life swing" as Ellison says, therein lies the Ellisonian reversal: the jazz-shaped nature of American society is that of a complex, syncopated rhythm and texture that was born out of the very plurality of groups that gave rise to that sound and feel. It is a carefully chosen metaphor for Ellison; jazz was the unbounded metaphor of creativity and possibility, and no form represents that truly hybridized world more so than swing.

While the ongoing pursuit of dance mirrored my own carnal-sociological project, I often wondered where one ended and the other began; ultimately they were one and the same. When I undertook the sociological aspect of the project, I had set out to go beyond mere cognitive approaches to ethnography and instead acquire a practical embodied knowledge of dance through my own lived experience. Had I developed the bodily consciousness and practical mastery of the dance necessary to obtain the analytical tools to understand how culture and racial essentialism, that is, racial mythologies simultaneously become embodied through mechanisms of inculcation, transmission, and translation (Wacquant 2003)? Would I know it if I felt it? Would I know it if I saw it? To ask these questions was to take pause and reflect on the theoretical and methodological framework I was utilizing. This afforded an opportunity to revisit the book's driving Ellisonian question: the contradiction between the centrality of African American culture in American society and the simultaneous marginality of African American people.[1] This tension was there from the outset of the project and still lingers on to this day. It started with one of my very first interviews. After a barrage of questions and a stroll across the grounds of a dance camp I was attending, Steven Mitchell full stopped, looked at me, and shook his head. He said:

> Man, all these years I've been doing this and no one has ever asked me these things. I mean I've thought about them, but no one has ever asked me. And here you come out of nowhere and start asking me all these questions and it's just so much, I mean I don't know what to think. I mean if you were black, but you're not. I mean here comes this white guy? I just don't know what to think about all this.

Steven's words brought my initial enthusiasm into a tailspin. Had I thought through the racial implications of this project? Had I considered how I would go about this? Was my race going to be a barrier to my research? What role would my racial marking play in this study? What role was I to play in mapping out white racial domination or in perpetuating it? Steven's befuddlement over what to say led me to puzzle over just how was I going to go about this study. What was at stake here? How would I arrive at an answer to that question? Steven's words echoed a question one of my best friends, Tanarra, posed to me after learning about what I was doing. She responded:

> So B, when you write all of this up, how are you going to account for yourself in all of this? How do you think you fit into all of this? Because you're technically white like they are. How will you explain the difference between you and them? What are you going to say?

I looked at her and wondered just that. In the end, just what was I going to say? That question, one of both personal and professional explanation, or self-disclosure, became one which has lingered with me to this day.

IMMERSION AND INITIAL QUESTIONS

•

Here I was, both a dancer and a sociologist, writing a study of the white engagement of African American culture—in this case, the Lindy Hop—and I could not help but think to myself: How was this or was this not about race? How was I different from the rest of the dancers in this community? I felt I was different; I thought that my racial politics and sociological interest in race and culture gave me a self-awareness and a social consciousness that necessarily made me more "sensitive" than everyone else. I could not be writing a study of white appropriation and perpetuating it at the same time. Could people tell the difference? And yet at the same time, how could I learn to dance in the same classes from the same instructors as everybody else and not be dancing the same way they did?

I went through numerous exercises and watched my movements in the mirror; I studied the shapes, the lines, the angles, the flow and style of each step, scrutinizing every inch of myself. Each mistake, each flaw brought me to a halt, to correct, refine, and repeat until the movement was corrected. Yet my steps still seemed awkward and constrained. My movements lacked the fluidity and ease that great dancers have. The difference between my dancing and the ideal was painful to recognize. Then, suddenly, I stopped and stared straight ahead. Looking at myself in the mirror, I began to feel myself as a dancer as if for the first time. A sudden and strange realization came over me as I stood there: I felt my body as both the sensing subject in motion and the object of my own analysis looking at my reflection. Despite my reflexivity and conscious intention to chronicle this white appropriation of the dance while keeping myself outside of that perpetuation, I realized that there was no difference in the way the other white Lindy Hoppers danced and the way that I did. I was not exceptional despite my reflexivity or self-awareness; I was part and parcel of the same socialization and embedded in the same context of the Lindy Hop world. This was not a matter of what I thought or what I intended; I had embodied the dance just as they had. I had embodied the same racial mythologies in my very motions. I kept thinking about what Tanarra had said. "What are you going to say?"

•

DECONSTRUCTING LINDY HOP:
ETHNOGRAPHIC DISCUSSION

•

The nighttime humidity had steamed up the windows of the studio; the air was so dense that it was difficult to breathe. The combination of the summer heat wave and the lack of air conditioning made the room a sauna; I had already worked my way through two T-shirts and had now soaked through a third. But John was letting me use the studio for free that night, and I could not turn down an opportunity to work in a space with mirrors and sound equipment. So on a Thursday night, just past 9:30 p.m., rather than work on my dissertation which I had recently begun to write, I was there at the studio, working through my steps, practicing figures, and, most important, working on my styling. The fluorescent lamps cast an omnipotent glare, illuminating every inch of the room. My eyes were focused ahead on the eight-foot-high mirrors that lined the entire wall of the studio, reflecting every movement; each step, each shift in weight, was shown back to me unmediated. I had been told by a great Lindy Hop master that the best way to improve your dancing is to practice in front of a mirror because it helps you get comfortable with seeing and feeling yourself dancing, as well as allowing you to correct mistakes in posture, alignment, and style. So there I was, alone in the studio with my harshest critic staring back at me. My self-consciousness about my dancing made working out in front of the mirror that much more painful, because I could not escape my own reflection. But my insatiable desire to master the elusive art of the Lindy Hop kept me in the studio long after the other dancers had left for the night. Getting comfortable with my own body? How was that supposed to happen?

Tannara's words—"What are you going to say?"—kept echoing through my head. I turned the music up louder, as if it could drown out her voice. With thirty minutes left before the studio closed, I tried my best to block out these thoughts and focus only on myself—my body, the music, and the dance. I realized that the way I was dancing had nothing to do with my consciousness or my attitude: it had everything to do with my body. This was not about the superficial epidermis of my white racial marking, but the internalized racial schemas that shape the way we interpret and understand the world. It wasn't an understanding, it was a feeling; a feeling of that process of moving my body through space that I hadn't felt before. This was a process of becoming comfortable; this wasn't about a dancer's level of consciousness, this was going on without the slightest self-awareness. But for how long? Had this happened before? What was this? Was this some sort of pivotal moment in defining my dancing? Was this some sort of "break-through" in my research? Were they one and the same? "What are you going to say?"

This transformative ethnographic moment was not about raising my racial awareness or bringing to consciousness my own previously concealed white identity; rather, it was about the unearthing of the dance in and through my body. More than just seeing myself locked in a struggle to learn to dance, I felt my own body in a struggle to move, to breathe, to feel the dance. All the lessons, all the practice, all that deliberate focus, whatever it was something was happening. Like hearing the syncopation for the first time, or being able to isolate the drums or the bass line as you hear the music, it was like finding your feet underneath you gliding along without focusing, just feeling in the moment. Again, "What was I going to say?" What would I say to those who have never danced before, who have never undertaken a craft like dance? How was I going to convey this epiphany? What was I going to say? If carnal sociology was supposed to lead me to understanding some sort of ongoing social processes, how was this not just my own self-involved process of learning to dance? How was I going to explain this?

Leaving the studio that night, I wondered to myself: How will I put into words something I was feeling about how learning to dance came through a series of racialized social structures that I could feel? How do you get someone to hear the pulse of the music? To hear the changes? To hear the bass and the drums working off each other to build that swelling feeling that makes dancing alive? How do you get them to hear the horns and feel "the swing"? Then again, maybe this wasn't about *how* to do anything. Maybe Lindy Hop, like jazz, isn't about *how* at all. Maybe they are like Ellison says "the real secret of the game." But like Tanarra said, "What are you going to say?"

•

CARNAL ETHNOGRAPHY

By looking at the labor necessary to inculcate the dance into the body of a dancer, through an analysis of the main components of partner dancing (choreography, leading and following, improvisation, and style), we can make explicit the processes of bodily labor that make up the "natural" dancer, who appears to move spontaneously and effortlessly to the music. In examining these components, I look at their embodied practice as well as how dancers verbally understand and articulate their acquisition of these components that make up the Lindy Hop, in order to get at both their physi-

cal enactment and how that embodiment is understood. After realizing my
own complicity, I started to scrutinize myself, becoming more reflexive
about watching my own dancing and the dancing of others.

In the end, I learned to dance twice—once with an uncritical approach
of learning formal rules and patterns, and the second through a carnal approach to understanding my body and its embodiment of dance. This insight, while possibly appearing to be something one could undertake by
observation or rule following alone, became the crucial turning point in
understanding the dance from the inside out. In this way it is not simply
the conscious identification of these racial mythologies that frees us from
them, as if we could mentally discard them, but to understand how they
must be reworked through the very ways we move and understand the
world through our bodies.[2]

Through undertaking my own journey in learning to dance, I began to
discern what I, and the other Lindy Hop dancers, perpetually misunderstood. What appears to be the most natural and instinctual of human activities is in fact a highly cultivated and disciplined process of cultural inculcation. By demythologizing dance in relation to race and the body, I gained
new insight into the intersection of race, culture, and the body. No one is
a natural dancer; one becomes a good dancer only through acquired skill
and training not through inherent racial marking. In doing so, we move
past previously discussed racial models by highlighting the contingency
of all cultural practices and their enactment. There is no necessity to bodies dancing in any particular manner, rather only practices that get misrecognized and enacted as natural to some groups and not others through
the symbolic power of the dominant racial mythology. Focusing on the
embodiment of racial mythologies, rather than the structural or intention
oriented approaches to race, suggests the need for an alternative analysis of
how cross-cultural engagement is mediated and enacted.

Acquiring the corporeal schemas of dance provided me with a bodily
awareness not only of the practical logic of the dance, but of interpreting
bodily movements more generally. As I observed myself and other dancers during years of training, I slowly came to realize how symbolic power
and violence are embedded in the very ways that white society interprets,
internalizes, and enacts African American cultural forms like the Lindy
Hop. As I continued to practice and cultivate my dancing in light of my
new understanding, I began to see the process by which my body became
that of a dancer. Inculcating the components of dance into one's body, especially a body that had no previous dance training, is an arduous process.
By watching this process unfold over time and marking the stages and steps
of accomplishment along the way, I began to see how much bodily labor

was necessary to learn the dance. Using my own body as the case study, I experienced the limits of how much and how quickly one can accumulate this bodily knowledge and the amount of practice required before it appears natural, as if one can spontaneously and naturally dance gracefully and effortlessly. Only by working back and forth between my own learning curve and watching and asking others about how they felt about their own progress could I see how this racial mythology dominated the way they gauged what they thought and had not thought about in terms of how well they would be able to learn how to dance.

CONCLUSION

Without a carnal approach, the Lindy Hop would have appeared as just another subculture of people blowing off steam in nightclubs and not as a microcosm of how race operates in contemporary American society. Through crossing back and forth from theory to fieldwork, I slowly came to see that what appears innocuous or neutral on the surface has enormous symbolic power in the reproduction of racial mythologies as they continue to go misrecognized in their real effects. While one can come to understand the racial dynamics of the Lindy Hop cognitively, my own lived experience of these dynamics opened up a new insight into the intersections of the body, culture, and race. Learning to dance enabled me to read the body symbolically in terms of how the dance is taught, and danced, and what these movements mean within the wider historical context of the white engagement with African American cultural forms. This new understanding provided insight into how the perpetuation of racial mythology and racial essentialism occurred without conscious awareness. In this way the carnal-analytic model exposes the symbolic power and violence of the dominant racial mythology and its effects without falling into the logic of the trial.

By drawing on the interconnection between cultural practices and racial mythologies, we can examine how white bodies learning to dance the historically African American Lindy Hop simultaneously inculcate how both a practical knowledge of dance and racial mythologies get refracted into the dancers' bodies, through the schemata of cognitive, emotional, and bodily labor. As the dance movements and steps are learned, this learning is always wrapped up in racial myths of blackness and whiteness. By illuminating this racial mythology at work, we can understand how everyday cultural practices like the Lindy Hop are articulations of material and symbolic contexts that are not immediately self-evident to us in their effects. While the carnal-analytic model does not provide the ultimate model for examining the intersections of race, culture and the body, it does provide new and fruitful racial insights into rethinking and questioning everyday cultural practices and cross-cultural engagement taking us beyond the essentialism of cultural appropriation.

After my epiphany that night in the studio, I spent the next three years doing everything I could to master the dance; I practiced, took classes and private lessons, and traveled to dance camps for intensive workshops. Through my carnal realizations I was able to identify the inscripted racialized social structures in my body and undertake a "thoroughgoing process of counter-training" by which I was able to form a new orientation to the dance. Only after this realization and reworking of my own body was I finally able to account for myself. The following scene, reconstructed from my fieldnotes, was the ultimate culmination of this undertaking.

•

Julie and I were taking a class taught by Steven Mitchell and his partner, Virginie Jensen. There were over thirty couples in the class. Everyone had partnered up in a circle around the instructors. Julie and I had separated ourselves from the rotation of dance partners so that we could work on our dancing together. The entire class was practicing the routine of figures that were presented at the beginning of class; now we were in the process of drilling the steps into our bodies. As we practiced to the music that was playing over the loudspeakers, out of the corner of my eye I saw Steven watching us, as he moved from the center of the circle to our side of the room. When the practice session ended, he asked us to come to the center of the room and demonstrate the routine we had all just learned. I was petrified. Steven was incredibly critical, and I could not remember ever hearing of a student demonstrating for his classes who was not used as an example of what not to do. I had felt so good when I was dancing the routine . . . was I that off? Was I doing it that poorly? Why pick on us? There must have been someone else in the room he could choose. Terrified of making a fool of myself in front of him, I made my way to the center of the room with Julie. Steven looked at me, smiling, and said, "Just do exactly what you were doing. Don't change a thing. Relax and just do what you do." He started the music and we danced the routine. When we finished, Steven nodded at us and said, "Exactly." He then motioned to me by pulling his arm to his stomach and clenching his hand into a fist, a gesture of approval. He turned to address the class. "That's what I'm talking about. Did you see that? Did you feel that? Could you see the way they were just one together with the music, how connected they were, how effortless it was? There was no excess. There was no restraint. That's what I want the rest of you to aim for."

Thrilled by Steven's compliment, I approached him after class and asked him to elaborate on why he had us demonstrate for his class. He looked at me and said,

> You moved me out there. You really did. Everyone was dancing and I looked over and I saw you guys and I could just see it, I could feel it. You've taken what we've shown you and made it your own. That really moved me; that's why I had you demonstrate for the class. You took it somewhere else because you made it your own. That's the key—not just copying what we do, but taking in what we give you, to take it in and turn it into your own expression, to make the dance yours. We can show you the steps, but we can't help you make it yours. That's up to you, and that's what you've done.

Steven smiled and excused himself; he had to rush off and teach another class. As I stood there, his words still hanging in the air, I no longer heard Tanarra's voice. At that moment, I knew I was finally able to answer her question: "What are you going to say?" I didn't have to say a word. I was learning to make life swing.

•

CONCLUSION: TOWARD NEW TERRITORY

It ain't where you're from, it's where you're at.

Eric B and Rakim

What is more, our unwritten history is always at work in the background to provide us with clues to how this process of self-definition has worked in the past. Perhaps if we learned more of what has happened and *why* it happened, we'll learn more of who we really are. And perhaps if we learn more about our unwritten history, we won't be so vulnerable to the capriciousness of events as we are today. And in the process of becoming more aware of ourselves we will recognize that one of the functions of our vernacular culture is that of preparing for the emergence of the unexpected, whether it takes the form of the disastrous or the marvelous.

Ralph Ellison (1995a, 144)

Rather than rehashing the overall argument of *American Allegory*, this concluding section takes the opportunity to both draw out the specific theoretical and sociopolitical contributions made, and to push the ideas presented here forward for future discussion. Drawing on Ellison's metaphor of heading out for new territory, these concluding thoughts also point to new ground upon which to more effectively grapple intellectually and politically with the overall sociological concerns that animate the book as a whole. By exploring how and why cultural appropriation in four of its dominant conceptualizations—as structural domination, commodification, cultural autonomy, and colonization—is inadequate to frame contemporary Lindy Hop dancers, it also offsets any misreading that would construe the project as one that elides macro-structural issues of racial inequality or one that celebrates cross-cultural engagements as remedies for America's ongoing racial conflicts. In addition, by bringing to light some of the undeveloped progressive outcomes at work in the process, we return to the themes of historical revisionism and the displacement of racial-cultural meanings that have been problematized throughout the narrative in hopes of moving the discussion forward. In doing so, this forces us to confront current theorizations of the politics of race, as well as the need to turn to a more generative alternative in the work of Ralph Ellison. Finally, coming full circle, we return to our point of entry, carnal sociology, and what it offers us in terms of rethinking our practical and political dispositions toward the allegory that these American dance forms ultimately instantiate.

Before turning to the more theoretical discussions, it is necessary to consider the practical impetus for this discussion. The politics of cross-cultural engagement are not just something documented on the dance floor. The same dynamics are also at play at conferences, in formal responses from journal reviewers, informally among colleagues, and with my own students, as I was met with enthusiastic acceptance of the themes of cultural appropriation that I was exploring. Yet when I begin revealing my new insights about the practice and enactment of race that resulted from my engagement with the Steppin' scene, I am met with fierce resistance. While everyone seems to be comfortable with the social construction of race and performance as an implicit part of any social theory of race, the thought of white people working against or even transcending the logic of white racial domination is clearly deemed inappropriate or methodologically "problematic."

Even within the sociology of race subfield, the underlying sentiment is that I am using "the right theories" on "the wrong people"; any complicating of the extant social relationship between white racial domination and white people is seen as either a celebration of white racial domination or a desperate search for "exceptional" white heroes. With the notable exceptions of hip-hop artist Eminem and basketball player Larry Bird (the two seminal examples in crossover arguments), it is argued that while white appropriation is a fact, even the most transgressive examples of white resistance to white racial domination are, in the end, just narcissism on the part of whites, or a way to avoid the guilt resulting from their history of white racism.

I am even confronted with the charge that my own work is part of a neo-colonial agenda in which white academics, like white dancers, are selfishly and shamelessly plundering black culture. Others argue that white people are just using "blackness" as a way to spice up white life, which is devoid of excitement and passion. Some argued that I was using my white identity in the African American Steppin' community in order to get African American people's approval and validation, as a way to assuage my own feelings of white guilt.

Finally, a West Coast practitioner of ethnographic "commonsense" criticized my work in a journal by asking and answering the following: "Just how does the use by whites of racial tropes to understand inadequacies in their dancing produce or support racial domination? Most obviously it supports jobs for black dance instructors like the author." Despite being sociologists, they were just as likely to appeal to racialized commonsense and racial my-thologies as were those outside of the academy less formally trained in the rigorous methods of the social sciences. Although many of these themes have echoed throughout contemporary scholarship, confronting them in face-to-face discussions made the issues not only academic, but personal as well.

These encounters, which became commonplace over the years, left me with the either/or position of capitulating to the dominant criticism that all whites are racist and do nothing but appropriate and exploit, or denying the very critical project I am engaged in by defending white people through ar-guments of exceptionalism. Given that the Lindy Hop craze is now over and the dance has receded from the public spotlight back into a small yet vital subculture, what can we gain from reflecting on the trajectory of this cul-tural form and the politics of cross-cultural engagement? Moreover, what can the case of the Lindy Hop tell us about something more general about American society in terms of race, culture, and identity?

In the case of the Lindy Hop revival, as well as other forms of white cross-cultural engagement with African American cultural forms such as blues, jazz, and hip hop, it has traditionally been argued that white cultural appropriation is a fact.[1] Even the most transgressive examples of white re-sistance to white racial domination are, in the end, considered narcissism on the part of whites, or a way to avoid the guilt resulting from the history of white racism.[2] The scholarly literature suggests four dominant paradigms through which this cross-cultural engagement could be analyzed—struc-tural domination, commodification, cultural autonomy, and colonization—all of which define white interaction with African American cultural forms as cultural appropriation. However, these paradigms logically fall into a ra-cial essentialism and a moral assessment of guilt or innocence, rather than analytic critique or help us explain how racial domination can be generated and perpetuated through the racial mythologies embedded in everyday cul-tural practices. In order to draw out the full import of what *American Al-legory* has to offer both theoretically and sociopolitically, it is necessary to highlight this approach in relation to current models of racial and cultural identity that theorize cross-cultural engagements. It is to five of these ac-counts of cultural appropriation I now turn. In doing so, I will present each of these camps in a compressed form without drawing out the nuances of any one author in great detail. As concluding remarks, my goal is not to advance an extended textual exegesis of these issues here; rather it is to en-gage these discussions, in light of the Lindy Hop, as a springboard for future debate.

STRUCTURAL ACCOUNTS OF CULTURAL APPROPRIATION

Several scholarly works, most prominently Richard Delgado's book *Critical Race Theory* and Ian Haney-Lopez's book *White by Law*, seek to explain this cross-cultural engagement through structural relations of power: economics, law, or simply via "white skin privilege."[3] This structural domination produces cultural appropriation because it enables whites to momentarily imagine themselves as African American or "acting black," the reverse of which is a privilege African Americans cannot enjoy because of regimented structural boundaries. By viewing cultural interaction in terms of structural relations of domination and subordination, appropriation always racializes and essentializes the structural positions of whites as the dominators and nonwhites as their victimized subordinates.

This structural determination of race and racism projects an assigned racial identity according to skin color whereby racial groups and their members easily fit into racially assigned categories. Thus, assuming these structural relations between races and appropriation leads to a monolithic mode of participation in the Lindy Hop, if white identity is the exploitative colonizer, then all participating whites are guilty of cultural appropriation because of their structural position in society. Accordingly, we base our evaluation not on people's performance of a cultural practice, but on their racial status and structural position alone. The structural guarantee of appropriation reinscribes the very essentialism that traps us in these naturalized conceptions of race that we seek to overcome on two fronts. First, tautologically, it assumes that all white performances are exploitative because they are white. Second, the structural model guarantees the qualities and characteristics of a particular group by their very structural position, in that culture becomes what is assigned to an already pre-existing identity.

Because culture is defined strictly in structural relations, it is acontextual and never examines the specificity of those relationships in context or the intentions, competences, or orientations of the actors.[4] Cultural practices and performances of identity are too complex and contradictory to simplistically assume that all white people appropriate African American culture or participate in it the same way or, conversely, that all African Americans do not exploit or commodify the Lindy Hop. By trying to account for the differences in structural power between racial groups, appropriation reduces all African Americans and all whites to one-dimensional groups with uniform attitudes and identities and limits the possibilities and diversity of what African American or white identity can be. Structural accounts of appropriation maintain a strategic essentialism whereby racial domination operates through skin color. However, this "skin privilege," which is independent of culture, cannot explain why whiteness as a system of racial domination is so powerful, resilient, and pervasive. If domination is defined by structural relations alone, then appropriation doesn't serve to perpetuate domination, since that domination is already been established. As a result, to theorize the nexus of racial-cultural intersections, and the way they serve to support or undermine domination, we must break with the logic of white racism and instead investigate the mechanisms that structure societies.

COMMODIFICATION ACCOUNTS OF CULTURAL APPROPRIATION

In addition to essentializing identity, the appropriation paradigm sometimes reduces culture to commodities as is the case of the work of Deborah Root's *Cannibal Culture* and Bruce Ziff's and Pratima Rao's edited volume *Borrowed Power: Essays on Cultural Appropriation*. By theorizing culture as a thing, a style, or a fashion that can be consumed, the paradigm of appropriation no longer treats culture as a way of life, but instead as a detached thing available in the marketplace to be used, utilized, and consumed regardless of cultural logic or interpretation.[5] By reducing culture to consumer goods, all cross-racial interaction is reduced to a simplistic consumption of goods as a substitute for real human interaction. Consequently, the paradigm of commodification takes culture out of its context and distorts its embedded connection to larger social and cultural processes. In the end, appropriation transforms all culture into nothing more than a consumer good, adrift in the marketplace without any identity beyond its racialized owners and those who appropriate them in consumption.

Theorizing the Lindy Hop as a commodity assumes a one-dimensional conceptualization of culture. Culture is for consumption, but it can be legitimately enjoyed only by the group that produces those commodities. Rather than looking at the specific context of human interaction, or the specific materialist conditions and the modes of production in which they emerge, the commodification of culture decontextualizes and essentializes culture by implicitly or explicitly assuming racial identity to be an effect of race. Ironically, scholars such as Walter Benn Michaels have used such an assumption to critique cultural appropriation and have asked: "But why does white men's learning to sing and dance like blacks counts as stealing black culture?" For Michaels, this must mean we assume that one racial group— "black"—has a right to "their culture," which is "violated" by whites who take up those practices. For Michaels, since culture is what one does, it is ultimately unnecessary to contest anyone else's adoption of a cultural practice, unless one has a essentialized notion of the link between those cultural practices and one's precultural (racial) identity, which would define who has a "right" to such practices. Therefore, Michaels concludes, that cultural appropriation depends upon the "racialist idea that cultural identity is a function of racial identity" and that "without recourse to the racial identity that (in its current manifestations) it repudiates, it makes no sense." Maintaining this argument requires an ultimate foundation of identity that must be presocial and prehistorical so that we can first "know who we are," which for Michaels is to know "which race we are," so that then "we can tell which culture is ours."[6]

While seemingly undermining cultural appropriation as a racial logic, his arguments reinforce the very commodification of culture that supports it. Accordingly, you must either perform stereotyped cultural practices associated with a racial group that makes you a member or with whom you have an essentialist biological-racial connection. If you are African American, it is either because you break-dance and wear cornrows in your hair or because this is part of your identity by birth. By reducing culture to race, and in doing so turning culture into objects that we identify with or have, we generalize a particular cultural practice to an entire group of people, as if everyone who is "naturally" African American logically identifies with break dancing as "theirs." Alternatively, we commit the intellectual fallacy that participation in a particular cultural practice or identification alone confers racial status. Such acontextual conceptualizations do not explain structural positions or the external imposition of racial and cultural categories upon peoples or practices by which they are categorized. Without taking into account the very social processes of which racial categories and racial domination are constitutive, in that the social is both determined and determining, such a misunderstanding of the workings of race and culture can occur. Extending this marketplace logic creates a bizarre and narrow world where culture becomes a set of things or objects to possess or let go of, upheld by rigid monolithic identities grounded in racial essentialism. The commodification of culture and the theorization of identity as biological and prehistorical, as if culture were an effect of race and not a constitutive of identity, valorizes the very ground of racism that we seek to overcome (Hall 1996).

AUTONOMOUS ACCOUNTS OF CULTURAL APPROPRIATION

The outcome of theorizing race and culture through the prism of cultural appropriation is that one must necessarily conceptualize cultural forms and racial identities as separate, autonomous, and easily identifiable entities. Each racial group produces its own distinct and easily recognizable cultural forms. In terms of African American culture, jazz and blues are easily identifiable because they are "black" art forms. These cultural forms are separate from "Latin" salsa or "white" classical music because they are marked as "black." In this case, the defense against appropriation cultivates a politics of racial preservation based on cultural autonomy. For instance, as a defense against white domination, a particular group will downplay the mixed element that contributes to its identity. The appropriation model furthers the misconception that each cultural form is considered pure and autonomous because it originates from a distinct racial background. The argument with this model is that if a cultural form is labeled "black," one must be African American to participate in that form. Consequently, anyone who is not African American is necessarily not authentic and cannot make anything but inauthentic derivations or parasitic copies. As represented in the work of LeRoi Jones' classic *Blues People* and more recently in Greg Tate's *Everything but the Burden*, "authenticity" is used for "strategic essentialism," whereby dominated groups work to preserve a sense of autonomy by carving out an essentialized identity.[7] Like the biological models that precede appropriation as fundamental guarantees of identity, authenticity becomes the unimpeachable transcendental category by which appropriation is explained. Culture accordingly is not a set of relations defined within a larger social context, but an a priori status fixed by phenotypical or rather "authentic" categories of race.

If we analyze culture strictly within the appropriation model, then cultural forms like the Lindy Hop must be generated without any interracial contact or influences from other groups. Therefore, appropriation either reduces multiculturalism to a set of isolated differences set side by side, like a salad bar of cultural choices to be sampled. For instance, a white middle-class individual may try Japanese food or learn how to dance the Lindy Hop, but his involvement with those cultures ends there. Because he never directly interacts with anyone from that culture, his level of involvement is individualistic. The Lindy Hop, like all other cultural forms, is a product of many diverse and varied cultural practices that congeal into one particular practice. The Lindy Hop contains movements from African dance, European ballroom, and American folk dances. Similarly, the music that accompanies the Lindy Hop is a product of the intertwined music from Africa, Europe, and America. Reducing the Lindy Hop to a simplified origin and identity not only diminishes its complexity, but it also negates the very basis of the cultural form.

COLONIZATION ACCOUNTS OF
CULTURAL APPROPRIATION

Because of the historical struggle between racial groups, cultural forms become a way to fix or certify racial identity and exclusive ownership. In the case of the Lindy Hop, whitewashing and commodification have become strategies for dislodging the Lindy Hop from its African American cultural context for white ownership and gain. Cultural appropriation arguments try to defend the purity of African American identity against these tactics of white colonization.

As a result, the appropriation model explains white interactions with African American culture as the desire to "eat the other" where whites appropriate and colonize other cultures for their own fulfillment and satisfaction (hooks 1992b). The idea of cultural colonization, as exemplified in the work of David Roediger and Noel Ignatiev, presupposes a vacuous and autonomous white society that somehow is devoid of culture or unable to manufacture pleasures internally.[8] Accordingly, whites have to seek out identity in the richness of others' cultures to offset their own impoverishment. While this desire may be for domination, or alternatively to praise the value of other cultures as positive, resistive, or liberating, it still re-essentializes whiteness as normality and blackness as distinct, apart, and different. By focusing on the desire of whites to appropriate and consume the other because of the other's "difference" and "exotic flavor," we maintain the normality and neutrality of whiteness as the category against which everything else is measured. By treating whites as devoid of culture, the colonization model reinscribes essentialism, not only by reifying culture into objects to be consumed, but by treating white culture as null and void. By misrecognizing the constructed nature of social difference, the colonization model essentializes both the colonizer and the colonized.

While these approaches lead to a racial essentialism on the macro level, they do however help illuminate the interconnection between bodily practices and the dominant mythology of racial differences. While cultural practices like dance may appear to be separate from the dominant racial mythology, they are in fact intimately interrelated. In the case of African Americans, the black body has traditionally been mythologized as innately and essentially exotic, sexual, expressive, and naturally rhythmic. This sense of blackness is constructed as exterior to whiteness, where the white body is marked by its rationality, restraint, and rigidity. As a result, African Americans are seen as natural dancers, while whites are considered naturally awkward and arrhythmic. This dominant racial mythology has served historically to reinscribe positions of domination and subordination through the naturalizing of certain competencies and attributes as "black" and "white."[9]

This racial mythology underlies a long tradition in whiteness studies in conceptualizing white people and the white body as emotionally and culturally vacuous.[10] From the days of minstrelsy, to Elvis Presley and rock-'n'-roll, to the wiggers and Eminems of today, white society has always imitated and emulated African American cultural forms.[11] whites have used, borrowed, and appropriated African American culture as a surrogate vehicle to express their own rebellion, sexuality, and pleasure denied due to the repressive nature of white society.[12] As a result, these cross-cultural engagements afford whites an opportunity to transcend, however fleeting, the repression of white society.

Charges of cultural appropriation, where one group has taken the property of another without warrant, or historical revisionism, where whites have revived the dance and rewritten history to erase the African American cultural influence, become facile ways to cast moral judgments as intellectual debate. To do so perpetuates the very anti-intellectualism that bolsters the naturalization of the racial mythologies that become embedded in our cultural practices; moreover, it fails to engage the larger allegory in the study of expressive cultural practices, in the subject of dance itself. Dance provides a way to consider the issue of American identity in relation to the maelstrom of categories—race, culture, history, politics—through which we attempt to conceptualize and articulate it. Since those categories necessarily never capture the complete picture or tell the whole story, we turn to metaphors like dance to represent an aspect of that larger whole. Accepting that appropriation or revisionism can assist us in understanding that allegory is an intellectual fallacy. To make an assessment of dance, as in culture, is to consider that our criteria for evaluation are as much aesthetic as rational, and to consider that assessment as much in terms of possibilities as in conclusions.

UNDERDEVELOPED OUTCOMES

Despite the seeming pervasiveness of contemporary racial domination, the representation and connotations associated to cultural forms is never complete; they are always locked in a hegemonic struggle to secure control and win consent of a particular point of view. Cultural forms are not static entities, but living processes in motion with dominant, residual, and emerging practices (Williams 1977, 143–46). As a result, white cross-cultural engagement does not always seamlessly reproduce racial domination. Following

Ellison's undermining of the conflation of race and culture, and the inter-twinedness of blackness and whiteness, new unrealized possibilities may also be emerging in the proliferation of the engagement of cultural forms across our perceived racial boundaries. I now turn to two of these: positive representation and cultural preservation. I conclude this section with a dis-cussion of why the possibilities for alternatives remain unfulfilled.

POSITIVE REPRESENTATION

With the explosion of the Lindy Hop in white America, white youth adopted another genre of African American culture, one that was different from to-day's mass-media popular culture that is dominated by images of gangstas, pimps, ghetto violence, and crass materialism. We need look no further than the nearest shopping mall to see whites imitating African American hip-hop culture by wearing stereotypical excessively baggy jeans and large costume jewelry, displaying the accompanying gangsta attitude and using the latest ghetto slang. As whites revel in the fantasy of being a hardcore gangster as seen in music videos, the ghetto becomes a mythologized and romanticized place of urban excess and pleasure, while at the same time, African Americans become pathologized.[13]

The Lindy Hop revival offers a very different contemporary represen-tation of African American expressive culture. In some ways it is a white enactment of African American culture that surpasses the negative stereo-types of African Americans in contemporary media as criminals, preda-tors, and menaces to society. Instead, the Lindy Hop is a representation of African American culture that articulates the resiliency and creativity of African American inner-city life (Gilroy 1994; Hall 1996; Kelley 1996; West 1993). The Lindy Hop could be considered an inversion of what other white subcultural movements have embraced and used from African American culture. In the stereotypes of African Americans that have dominated American history, beginning with the Sambo and Zip Coon figures of the past and continuing with today's gangster thugs, African Americans are portrayed as hypersexualized, excessive, barbaric, foolish, unintelligent beings, whereas in its best manifestations the Lindy Hop articulates a rep-resentation of African American culture that is stylized, glamorous, edu-cated, and sophisticated (Baker 1998; Turner 1994). Rather than continu-ing the tradition of denigration, practitioners of the Lindy Hop cultivate a positive representation of blackness based on creativity, social interac-tion, and refinement, a world of etiquette and sociability through partner dancing. Reaching into the past, Lindy Hoppers transcend the aspects of hip-hop culture that emphasize depravity or decadence, and take hold of a productive cultural form associated with social uplift and transcendence (Kelley 1996). This discord between the positive representation of African Americans and the negative typologies that are generated through other modalities of this cross-cultural embrace—minstrelsy, commodification, and whitewashing—offers fertile terrain for alternative possibilities for cross-cultural engagement.

CULTIVATION OF CULTURE

Ironically, despite the racial domination that is produced through white engagement with the Lindy Hop, the white embrace of the dance simultaneously keeps the heritage and practice of the dance alive as an embodied knowledge. If cultural practices are not reinforced they can be lost, and once no one remembers how to execute them they die off and become cultural relics, artifacts in a museum or abstract ideas of past cultural forms. The history of the Lindy Hop is unaffiliated with any canonized cultural institution and therefore generates little official cultural interest. As a result, vernacular forms like the Lindy Hop must be constantly cultivated by practitioners in order to sustain them as viable cultural practices. The cross-cultural embrace of the dance actually afforded a lifeline for the Lindy Hop, as it had faded from American society to the point of near extinction. There is more to dance than just steps; there is also an embodied aesthetic, normative, and ethical expression. At stake in the cultivation of embodied cultural forms like the Lindy Hop is what Raymond Williams referred to as "culture as an entire way of life" (Williams 1977). Without the conscious effort of securing and cultivating the dance, a distinct cultural self-expression of American cultural history may be lost and forgotten. If the Lindy Hop dies, so too does a rich, artistic part of African American culture.

It is only through the new generation of Lindy Hop dancers that this specific cultural form has been sustained. This is a seminal contribution made by the Lindy Hop scene; whereas Steppin' is an outgrowth of the Lindy Hop and does carry on many of its artistic and cultural traits, it is still a much simpler dance with a smaller vocabulary and more limited range of physical expression. While the Steppers are keeping the tradition of African American partner dance alive, they are not cultivating that entire history. We cannot look only to the Steppers to tap into that historical knowledge of the Lindy Hop or to replace the aesthetic of the Lindy Hop with Steppin'; the two are not interchangeable.

Through the cross-racial practice of the Lindy Hop, new identities and new modes of cultural exchanges can be formed and could lead to new understandings. By embracing the Lindy Hop, people learn and embody a unique cultural practice, which in turn offers the possibility of raising awareness of a racial group and its particular history. By learning to dance the Lindy Hop, whites have the opportunity to learn about an oppressed group—not about its domination and subordination, but about its resiliency and creativity. This type of interaction with a cultural form provides new avenues of communication and identification over shared cultural interests across racial lines and traditional boundaries. In today's overwhelmingly defensive and segregated society, the cross-cultural embrace of the Lindy Hop is keeping this particular African American cultural form alive, cultivating its technique and history. This cultivation generates discordance with the dominant racial order and opens up new possibilities for cross-cultural engagement.

Highlighting these "positive" racial representations opens up both the intentional and unintentional consequences of cross-cultural engagement. Whether those involved consciously think about these issues or not, whether they have cultivated a historical knowledge of the dance, their symbolic effect occurs with or without that awareness. These performances of identity also force us to return to issues of connecting bodies, practices, cultural forms, and racial identities. Just as whites in the immediacy of their engagement with the Lindy Hop could act out or speak in ways that perpetuated the denigration and erasure of the dance, here, as we can see, they are just as likely to celebrate and make visible and draw attention to the dance's aesthetic. As a result, the nexus of cultural practices, embodiment, and performance as it links to racial associations is always a contingent, open-ended situation. Without doubt the dominant structures and institutions of society lend themselves to a cultural reproduction that leads to inequality. However, to dismiss those possibilities of cross-cultural engagement as mere "moments" or ephemeral gestures is to lose the very power behind this perspective—that the "in the moment" expression of a cultural practice, whether informed or uninformed, can just as easily undermine stereotypes as it can uphold them. By linking the contingency of performance to the contingency of institutions, we may begin to open up a connection that could have greater purchase that previously imagined. To begin such a project, we must first bring our sensitivity to bear on these "in the moment" enactments, before we can begin to cultivate their enactments towards more progressive ends.

DOMINATING THE DOMINANT

Reflecting back on Ellison's remark that "if whites only knew how black they really were," they would have a much different orientation to race in American society. These words allow us to reflect back on the dominant themes throughout this study, as well as serve as an entry point into understanding why the aforementioned possibilities of the Lindy Hop remain partly uncultivated (Ellison 1995a). For many whites, the Lindy Hop affords a new form of cultural expression. Since partnered social dancing is not an everyday practice in most white communities, the Lindy Hop offers a new arena of creative expression and social interaction. As a creative and dynamic practice, African American culture is a space in which whites can find gratification by expressing themselves in ways normatively denied them. African American culture offers them both pleasure and a vehicle for enacting that pleasure.

However, the true potential of the Lindy Hop remains unrealized because the dominant racial dispositions that are inscribed in its participants dominate whites as well as non-whites. As a result, the primary outcome of the cross-cultural embrace of the Lindy Hop generates the symbolic and material violence of minstrelsy, whitewashing, and commodification and serves to secure and perpetuate the established racial order.

The dominant mythologies of blackness and whiteness that serve to dominate non-whites are embodied by whites and serve to dominate them as well. These dispositions are inscribed in bodies; they are not perpetuated consciously, but are embedded in the very schemas of perception and appreciation through which we make sense of the world. They, therefore, go unrecognized. The system of white racial domination not only produces domination over African Americans through the production of symbolic power and violence, but those same mythologies circumscribe the cultural and artistic expressive possibilities for whites. Learning to dance, especially learning bodily movement that may be foreign to one's racial group, whether Lindy Hop, salsa, or the waltz, taps into deep racial mythologies about the naturalness of the body, culture, and race. The white body, inscribed by the dominant racial order, fights its ability to be inculcated in "non-white" ways. Just as whiteness and blackness become essentialized, the myths of black bodies as natural dancers with an innate rhythmic sense, and white bodies as awkward and stiff, reinscribe the very racial paradigms that keep the essentialized archetypes of the body, race, and culture circulating in the racial imagination. As a result, white cultivation of the dance is undermined as whites constantly struggle with their bodily "comfortableness" or discordance with the proper practice of the dance. The result is a self-defeating belief that no matter how they try, they will never be "authentic Lindy Hop dancers" because they are white, not black (Bourdieu 2000b, 157).

These mythologies affect the ways that the dance is inculcated and enacted and circumscribe the possibilities of what whites can be and do, in terms of not just the Lindy Hop but all cultural forms and practices. Limiting the possibilities of the body means limiting the possibilities of the larger social world. Because we learn bodily, experiencing other cultures physically and learning them corporeally opens up possibilities for new understandings, expressions, and alternative social relations. The closing off of these possibilities, which occurs through the essentialization of race, culture, and the body, delimits the range and depth of embodied knowledge. A fully realized cross-cultural engagement opens up a new sense of possibility that is unrestrained by racial and ethnic essentialism and can move us out of the confines of racial domination. Understanding how whites themselves are dominated in the perpetuation of racial domination may force whites to confront the misrecognition that furthers their own subordination. When the Lindy Hop is cultivated in its alternative possibilities, the dance can become a resource for breaking with the mechanisms of racial domination, rather than a commodity to be casually consumed (Hall 1996).

CONFRONTING THE POLITICS OF RACE

Scholars who have grappled with the problems of whiteness have offered their own models for breaking from whiteness and theorizing white antiracist politics. The most important of these models have been the *race traitor* of Noel Ignatiev's and the *neo-abolitionist* of David Roediger.[14] Both models call for a white psychological identification with categories other than whiteness—preferably blackness—in an attempt to transcend the problem of whites perpetuating racial domination (Ignatiev and Garvey 1996). This cognitive shift from white to non-white offers an image of progressive whites acting in antiracist ways, but it ultimately falls back into the essentialized logic of appropriation. Embracing blackness as a saving and redemptive power re-essentializes the inherent good and evil in these monolithic categories and reinforces the racial imagination of essential racial difference (Day 1993, 1994; Garon 1995; Rubio 1993, 1994). This parceling out of guilt and innocence means that both the race traitor and the neo-abolitionist positions presume to draw a line between the former white self as villain and the new post-white (honorary black) self as hero (Hill 1998).

The race traitor and neo-abolitionist models, while radical in their aspirations, fail adequately to reflect upon their own racial assumptions and, as a result, undermine their own aspirations for racial critique and antiracist politics. Domination is part of the very social organization of our society and cannot be escaped simply by trading places; it is not something that can be accepted or rejected, as if one simply could choose to be racist or non racist.[15] As a result, there is no clear way to separate the race traitor or neo-abolitionist from the cultural appropriator. In both cases, identification ends up being white fantasy and romanticized patronage, as whites arbitrarily decide to identify as black or white based on desire and consequence. The racial cross-dressing associated with these positions only increases the self-importance of whites who believe that something significant is occurring in their cultural embrace alone and simultaneously allows non-white skeptics to justify their charge that all white attempts at cross-racial mixing are only psychological.

Specifically, working through the race traitor and neo-abolitionist models reveals three seminal problems in theorizing white antiracist politics. First, any discussion of African American cultural forms and the participation of white actors in them is subject to the charge of narcissism. Given the systematic racial inequality that defines contemporary American society, white politics appears self-involved when whites attempt to join non-whites in overcoming the "race" problem (Moon and Flores 2000). While narcissism is not the best place to start, any attempt at undermining white racial domination must come from whites. In contemporary society, the burden is on white people to reach out and take the initiative; with the failure of the civil rights movement and the continuing disparities in income, education, and incarceration rates, African Americans remain suspicious of and jaded by white society's gestures toward equality (Boyd 2004). Today the problems of integration and inequality persist not because African Americans gave up on this political project, but because white racial domination as a system of social organization blocked its realization. As a result, whites must now undertake the necessary labor to build bridges across the racial divide.[16] In order to undermine the power of white racial domination, it is necessary to have both an external critique by non-whites and an internal deconstructive approach in which white racial domination is attacked from the inside. This is not narcissism in the form of the Great white Hope coming to save race relations, but rather the rearticulating of white identity in nonessentialist and relational ways to form political and social coalitions. If white racial domination is to be undermined, whites themselves must be a reflexive starting point to engage and deconstruct the mechanisms of white racial domination.

Second, any critique that offers an individualistic approach to politics immediately appears to be conservative and not progressive by design. Conservatives have historically used individualism to deny the structural effects of power and inequality in society by placing responsibility on individuals rather than on the structural distribution of resources. Individualism has been invoked most effectively in the form of role models as positive figures of social reform, from whom individuals who desire to transcend their current status can learn by example. There are rare examples of success: someone from the projects who ascends to the middle class, a basketball player from the ghetto who makes it to NBA stardom. Accordingly, success or failure lies with the individual's own hard work and perseverance rather than the socioeconomic contexts or historical conditions within which he is situated. The use of role models serves to maintain the status quo rather than to provide a point of entry by which whites can engage, conceptualize, and act in antiracist ways toward social structural as well as cultural change.

Although it appears conservative in orientation, one should add, the individualistic nature of the role model must not be completely abandoned; it can be used strategically to undermine white racial domination. Because race appears to be such an abstract and immense problem, with no place for the individual to make a difference, it is precisely here at the level of the individual that we must engage in politics and offer a point of entry for others. We must avoid the twin traps of falling into conservative acontextual individualism or dismissing individualism as inherently conservative, or we forfeit the opportunity to forge a strategic point of engagement to enact social change.

Third, any theorization in which whites act in antiracist ways or attempt to transcend the conditions of white racial domination must confront the problem of volunteerism (Winant 1996). Volunteerist political models, such as the race traitor and neo-abolitionist, assume that racial categories are arbitrary, rather than historically embedded relations of power. The choice of racial cross-dressing allows whites to use African American culture as a self-serving vehicle for their own self-expression and rebellion—without any understanding, contact, or interaction with real African Americans (Lott 1993, 1995). Those who "play black" always retain the luxury of going back to the safety of white privilege when they tire of their instrumental use of African American culture. By contrast, it is never possible for African Americans to choose to "play white" or leave their "blackness" behind in American society (Deloria 1997). While it is necessary to avoid theorizing race as arbitrarily constructed, as if people could choose their racial identity, we must avoid also theorizing race as completely deterministic, with no possibility of movement against the abolition of white racial domination.

The alternative model of performance that I offered with the Steppin' example, of course, runs into its own limitations, which is necessary to acknowledge and address. While the Steppers' performance and bodily labor offer an example for others to emulate and an opportunity to cultivate cross-cultural practices, these very role models could perform with no racially conscious agenda, or they could even perform culture "correctly" with racist sentiments. While role models are necessary as examples for whites to emulate, these performers or their performances may not necessarily engage in antiracist politics. If performance is detached from a commitment to engage in social change, the role models could be just as essentialist and racist as those who perform in an inappropriate and minstrel-like way. One of the most disheartening aspects of the Lindy Hop scene that I confronted in the initial stages of my research was that even the most talented people teaching and promoting the dance were unaware of or unconcerned with issues of racial domination. While their labor had enabled them to master the dance, many desired nothing more than their own material reward. While bodily labor is the necessary ground from which to engage and open cross-racial dialogue and cross-cultural participation, in no way does this alone guarantee antiracist politics. In fact, as I discovered, competence can be a great mask for racism. Conversely, it is necessary to ground any future politics in bodily labor, because without the labor, racial mixing remains disembodied and purely psychological, without any investment or commitment.

ELLISONIAN HISTORY AND HYBRIDITY

The central Ellisonian question that drove this study was the simultaneous centrality of African American culture and the marginality of African Americans as people. While Ellison did not have a systematic theory of race or culture, his essays link together central themes that cut right to the heart of this paradox. In doing so, Ellison ushers in important ways to conceptualize the nexus of race, culture, identity, and society, as well as offers inspiration for realizing new possibilities of social interaction. Following Ellison, our central concern here is to address the notion of history and how it works itself out in different arenas of social life and social thought.

As cultural forms move in and out of public popularity like the latest trends or fads, practices such as the Lindy Hop become temporary centers of popular culture, where people participate in practices of which they have no cultural or historical knowledge. Although a cultural form like the Lindy Hop can be danced without any knowledge of its history, an Ellisonian alternative cross-cultural engagement must make the cultural history of the dance central to its cultivation. In order to be historically reflexive about the dance, to make sense of one's own position in relation to the racial-cultural identity of the dance, one must understand the historical conditions that gave rise to the Lindy Hop. By situating this cultural form within its historical production, we must address its African American history and appreciate the significance of the dance within that context. The Lindy Hop emerged in a time when segregation and racial violence were the norm. This influenced the orientation and aesthetic of the dance and also explains why the Lindy Hop serves as a significant symbolic expression and cultural practice within African American culture. This process of historicizing the cultural form also enables us to examine the mode of cross-cultural engagement that defines the Lindy Hop in contemporary society. Since the days of slavery, African American cultural forms have been historically embraced by whites within a context structured by racial domination. This has set a precedent for how whites interact and participate in more contemporary African American cultural forms. Knowing the history of the dance provides an understanding of what it meant to its participants at the time, as well as how it is linked to versions of the dance, like Steppin', that are currently danced in African American communities. Only by knowing the past can we carry the Lindy Hop on to the next generation of participants in a way that cultivates its heritage and connects it to an inclusive future.

As scholars have documented in other fields, we must have a rewriting of history: one that does not whitewash but rather documents and centralizes "marginalized" cultural contributions.[17] For Ellison, history is the process of identity, of learning what and why things happened as they did in order to be more aware of who we are. This process takes our vernacular culture as central to that understanding. It is our vernacular culture, defined by symbolic energy and expression that provides the basis for our way of life; the vernacular is the resource that we draw upon to articulate our agony and triumph of human life. It is this "unwritten history" that however obscured or repressed is always active in the shaping of events. For Ellison, "perhaps it is our need to avoid the discouraging facts of our experience that accounts for the contradiction between those details of our history which we choose to remember and those which we ignore or leave unstated" (1995a, 124) Our avoidance of our past and our shared culture leads us to a state of anxiety where we fall back onto a racial insularity. Thus studying the race and culture nexus of American society leads us to an irony; despite the overwhelming mixture of cultural and racial interaction that occurs in the embrace of trends and fads, one of the major problems plaguing contemporary American politics is the perception that between races, we fail to have common interests and shared concerns. While we may wear the same fashions, read the same books, idolize the same heroes in politics, sports and music, Ellison claims that this makes us "at once very, very unified, and at the same time, diversified. On many, many levels we don't know who we are, and there are always moments of confrontation where we meet as absolute strangers" (1994, 763). Because Americans tend to focus on the separate elements of culture, rather than the pluralistic unity that constitutes society, social life remains segregated and fragmented. Only by realizing the plurality in the unity of American society, as well as the unity in the plurality, the blackness in the whiteness and the whiteness in the blackness will we overcome these false divisions of racial separatism.

Through an Ellisonian concern with history, we can come to see how Ellison argued for the inherent hybridity of cultural life. By exploring the heterogeneous, interdependent culture of everyday life, Ellison's forces us to examine how we so often see race and culture as interchangeable. Through Ellison's critique we can begin to sever them and understand it is the very basis of cultural hybridity that we—all Americans—have forged our identities. It is the multiplicity of our different tastes, traditions, ways of life, and values that go into making up what we know as American that have been "ceaselessly appropriated and made their own—consciously, unselfconsciously, or imperialistically—by groups and individuals to whose own backgrounds and traditions they are historically alien" (1995a, 27). It was these very interchanges of cultural appropriation and misappropriation for Ellison that blended, mixed, and formed the American identity of all its people.

By denaturalizing the fusion of culture and race through historical critique we are able to neutralize the effects of naturalization, as a mode of political intervention (Bourdieu 2000b, 182). The act of historicizing the Lindy Hop, enables us to break from misrecognition and understand both the pervasiveness of racial domination and the significance of what is passing completely unnoticed in our everyday experience. History offers critical tools to break with racial domination that is central to the cultivation of a new racial politics (180). Whether it is Lindy Hop or hip hop, we have failed consistently to mobilize the white embrace of those forms into a more progressive multiracial politics. There is no way to force people to become invested in the history of the activity in which they participate; however, making history central to any cultural form does not detract from its pleasure. Rather, in this case history enhances the dance and prevents the detachment and ignorance that so often surrounds participation in popular culture. Although many may not embrace the history or develop it in any significant sense, making it available is the first step in generating interest and cultivating deeper appreciation. In the current iteration of the Lindy Hop, the dance is simply a fun social activity, divorced from any larger context of history and cultural labor that initially formed and cultivated the dance.

By illuminating the mechanisms of racial domination, we can begin to cultivate an approach to the cultural form that was previously unconsidered. This allows whites to be self-aware of their complicity and embeddedness in the dynamics of racial domination in society, and, simultaneously, allows them to break from perpetuating that domination in their everyday actions. In turn, the severing of white people from white racial domination affords non-whites a new non-essentializing mode of understanding white people. By understanding the basis of social dominance, we are able to form a new perspective that enables both whites and non-whites to understand how white people can participate in African American culture in new and progressive ways. Using Ellisonian history and hybridity as critical tools of interrogation, we can begin to theorize the un-theorized and make reflexive and self-conscious what has previously been misrecognized. By coming to terms with our truly hybridized past and present, our essentializing racial categories no longer hold sway over the ways that we can conceptualize ourselves and others.

THE POLITICS OF CARNALITY AND COUNTERTRAINING

By examining history and hybridity we can open up new understandings and possibilities of what race, culture, and identity are. However, because the racial order is inscribed in bodies in the form of durable, corporeal dispositions, symbolic violence cannot be overcome simply by raising consciousness or converting minds. Since the racial order is inscribed in our bodily dispositions, we must also undertake a countertraining of the schemata of perception and appreciation of the social world in order to break with the dominant racial order. By making our embodied corporeal dispositions central to the formation of an alternative model of racial politics, we can begin to countertrain the body into new alternative dispositions. Forming these dispositions will require new practices of education; it will also require countertraining the body through new modes of inculcating dispositions. An alternative racial politics must transform the system that produces and reinforces our racial dispositions in order to break with the dominant racial order (Bourdieu 2000b, 181). These two strategies of history and countertraining work reciprocally, each conditioning the other as they form critical tools for political intervention.

Adopting an alternative orientation to the Lindy Hop must begin, for example, with education and resocialization through a different paradigm. In the case of Steppin', in which the African American Steppers recognized and appreciated that the white Steppers could and did dance in their style, we can see "role models" for both blacks and whites. With appropriation— whitewashing, commodification, and minstrelsy—defining contemporary white participation in African American culture, the rare positive example of whites performing African American culture "correctly" offers an alternative articulation of white identity for both African Americans and other whites. For African Americans, this provides proof that whites can and will undertake the labor to properly appreciate African American culture by learning the dance and demonstrating this labor in an African American public sphere. For whites, this provides a template for emulation and a way to understand the significance of enacting cultural practices and the cultural labor required for their mastery. While the exemplars offer embodied examples of this new orientation, they are not possessors of some special knowledge; they are merely exemplars of a new racial paradigm and facilitators of a new white antiracist politics and mode of multicultural participation.

This alternative model of politics serves to inform not only cross-cultural engagement with the Lindy Hop, but all forms of cross-cultural engagement and antiracist struggle. This struggle seeks to undermine the material and symbolic mechanisms of white racial domination not only by addressing institutions, attitudes, and beliefs, but also by grappling with the schemata of perception and appreciation embodied in social agents (Wacquant 1995a, 1995b, 1997a, 2002b, 2003, 2004a). This "politics of habitus," as Wacquant has called it, that is, a politics of bodily awareness and reflexivity over our most subtle modes of socialization and indoctrination that are mediated through the multiples layers of our everyday embedded experiences. In order to do so, we must pay close attention to the "social production and modalities of expression" of racial proclivities (2004b, 8). This model offers new possibilities for the participants of the Lindy Hop as well as for all forms of cross-cultural engagement and antiracist struggles.

By undertaking a politics of the body in this way, through coming to understand how the racial imagination works to racialize our deepest dispositions, we can begin to break the naturalized dispositions and attributes that have been forgotten as historical constructions. It is here at the "politics of habitus" that our conceptual understanding of social life and our everyday experience of that intersect, by making what goes unnoticed as the ordinary and everyday basis of social interactions gives rise to often unanticipated and unintended modes of domination. As has been previously discussed, not all politics are amenable to intellectual persuasion or recognition. By locating the specific mechanisms by which power operates and manifests itself into relations of domination, we can address both conscious beliefs and subconsciously embodied dispositions; we can therefore begin to address how the dominant racial order operates through the double naturalization of our social structures and mental structures (Bourdieu 2004a, 10). By unearthing the embodiment of our racial relations we can begin to dismantle our complicity, which is no less perpetuating among the dominated than the dominant, in societies structured in racial domination.

Significant social change will not come from dance or cultural participation alone. The exemplars must work actively to connect this paradigm shift to larger social contexts and social concerns over racial inequality. They must promote this paradigm shift not only at the level of dancing or culture, but by using the specific context as a microcosm, illuminating the mechanisms of white racial domination that structure society as a whole. Exemplars must be constantly vigilant about their cultural practices and thwart the ever-present threats of commodification, minstrelsy, and whitewashing. These exemplars must educate, cultivate, expose, and break the mechanisms that generate racial domination by countertraining the body and thus opening it to new possibilities that can be durably inscribed. This alternative orientation must begin with those cultural translators who will step forward and be exemplars through the embodiment of politics in their very practice. As the exemplars apply the twofold strategy of historicization and countertraining to themselves as well as to their world, they become both tools and examples of critical intervention in practice. Whether in social dance, performance, or teaching, they must be reflexive about how they embody and enact their practice. Although using this new paradigm with the Lindy Hop alone may not help us transcend race—we cannot easily move outside the power dynamics of white racial domination—it may offer a new way of working within its confines for progressive political ends and new racial alliances. While the Lindy Hop may have faded back into a small subculture, the cross-cultural engagement that occurred left behind an object lesson for enacting racial politics through embodied intervention. This can be used as a model in other arenas of racial struggle in hopes of realizing an alternative racial future.

Undertaking this analysis overcomes the notion, which is cultivated by more academics than one may imagine, that this inquiry simply leads us to rid ourselves of our distinctions in bodily dispositions, that is, to either change how dispositions map onto the landscape of bodies, or to keep lines of distinction intact but learn to cross them. Following this, many may misconstrue this project as seeking to maintain racial boundaries only on respectful terms, a position of "respectful cultural pluralism" that attempts to avoid defining identity in terms of race but actually does the opposite. As a result, some insightful critics go overboard in their attempts to call into question academic commitments to social constructionism vis-à-vis racial categories and making identity the central claim in the social arena.[18] However, these arguments fall back into tautologies of what they are trying to critique. Any position that makes race and culture interchangeable or as structural equivalents at best misunderstands their analytical and practical separation and at worst trivializes them as epiphenomenal to more pressing real-life concerns.[19]

Maintaining a commitment to the social construction of racial and cultural categories, we are able to come to understand how all notions of identity, whether racial, cultural, societal, are mutable forms that ultimately have no clear boundaries. In addition, this forces us to confront how even those most taken-for-granted assumptions about identity are never static or stable, never something already formed or already there. Identity is always a product of context, history, language and experience that can only come through lived experience, never irreducible to racial categories. Throughout this analysis I have sought to deconstruct our notion of racial categories, all the while presuming them at the same time as a way to posit those categories as place holders. For lack of other language, they are used to designate difference, and yet simultaneously play with them as the constructed fictions they are. For both there is no contradiction; a nonessentialist multiculturalism does not pressure and reinforce existing boundaries, rather it opens up the possibilities of becoming who we are.

In this becoming, which is always a state of motion and transformation, by seeing the blackness in whiteness and the whiteness in blackness, is part of the very process of erasing those very notions. For even as we speak them, they become the very hurdles we seek to overcome as they have prevented us from fully realizing what lies beyond them. As Ellison reminds us, it is in our unwritten history, in our vernacular culture, that we find the clues to our self-definition. It is in the vernacular that the unexpected can occur and it is in the vernacular that new territory can emerge for us to explore. It is toward this new territory that we must go.

This brings us back to our initial riddle that started this inquiry. What exactly did Ellison mean when he spoke of the riddle that "perhaps the symmetrical frenzy of the Lindy-hop conceals clues to great potential powers"? Maybe, this riddle comes to be much closer to home than we might have initially imagined. In this era of colorblindness and multiculturalism, where we as a society are simultaneously as together as we are apart, we are constantly looking for a new story to explain to ourselves who and what we are. Perhaps the symbolism of two dancers balanced together in motion suggests something more than meets the eye. Perhaps the symmetrical frenzy of the Lindy Hop is at the heart of the vernacular culture of which Ellison spoke. Perhaps the allegory of the Lindy Hop tells us the story.

NOTES

Prologue

1. See Diawara 1994, Dinerstein 2003, Haley 1964, Kelley 1996, Miller and Jensen 2001, and Stowe 1994 for accounts of the Savoy Ballroom.
2. De Certeau 1984, Fiske 1994, Kelley 1996, Radano and Bohlman 2001, and Scott 1990.
3. The literary technique of allegory plays a formative narrative and analytical role in the work of cultural anthropologist James Clifford. For Clifford: "Allegory draws special attention to the narrative character of cultural representations, to the stories built into the representational process itself. It also breaks down the seamless quality of cultural description by adding a temporal aspect to the process of reading. One level of meaning in a text will always generate other levels.... Allegory prompts us to say of any cultural description not "this represents, or symbolizes, that" but rather "this is a (morally charged) *story* about that" (Clifford 1986, 100).

    Accordingly, Clifford argues that ethnographic writing itself is allegorical, "at the level both of its content (what it says about cultures and their histories) and of its form (what is implied by its mode of textualization)," and as a result, ethnographic texts are necessarily allegorical which changes the ways that they can be they can be "written and read." Following Clifford's allegorical emphasis, *American Allegory* offers its own self-reflexive presentation as yet another layer of the ongoing story of race and American identity of which it is both constitutive and product.

Lead In

1. The collected essays of Burawoy et al. (2000) were instrumental in organizing multiple international fieldsites.

Introduction

1. The terms "Swing dance" and "Lindy Hop" can be used interchangeably, unless noted otherwise.

2.   For an overview of the reemergence of the Lindy Hop and retro culture more gener-
     ally in the late 1990s see Penner 1999 and Vale and Wallace 1998.

3.   In the year 2000 when I attended the Herrang Lindy Hop dance camp in Herrang,
     Sweden, there were dancers from twenty-six different countries as diverse as Tur-
     key, Singapore, India, Switzerland, France, and Norway, to name but a few.

4.   For discussions of the Harlem Renaissance in relation to art, music and politics, see
     Dinerstein 2003; Douglas 1995; Emery 1988; Erenberg 1981, 1998; Haskins 1990;
     Huggins 1971; Hutchinson 1995; Lewis 1979; Malone 1996; Martin 1994; Osofsky
     1966; Stearns and Stearns 1994; and Watson 1995.

5.   For detailed exegesis on African American dance and the multiplicity of sociopo-
     litical expressions it manifests, see Dinerstein 2003; Emery 1988; Gottschild 1996,
     2002, 2003; Hazzard-Gordon 1990; Malone 1996; and Stearns and Stearns 1994.

6.   Gilroy 1993; Hall 1992; Hall and Du Gay 1996; Hutchinson 1995; Kelley 1996, 1998;
     Lewis 1979; Malone 1996; Miller and Jensen 2001; Stearns and Stearns 1994.

7.   For a sociopolitical analysis of the closing of the Savoy, see Gold 1994.

8.   While beyond the scope of this analysis, the categories of "authenticity" and "ori-
     gins" would prove vital in future research to draw out the ways that racial-cultural
     identities are manifested, contested, and redefined both conceptually and spatially
     (both physically and institutionally). These categories would also prove useful in
     alternative trajectories of analysis around issues of institutionalization by which in-
     vention or reinvention distance cultural practices from their historical-contextual
     spaces of emergence. In this way the historical notion of the dance as "revived" can
     then be seen as just as formidable a ground for the dance's origin as much as any
     other "origin," as it opens the notion of cultural forms to the processes of having
     many beginnings. For helpful discussions of the concept of authenticity and origins
     see Grazian 2005; Hobsbawm and Ranger 1983; Johnson 2003; Peterson 1997.

9.   For the complexities of discussing issues of race in the American context see
     Bonilla-Silva 2001; Crouch 1995; Fiske 1994; Hacker 1992; Lasch-Quinn 2001; Ratliff
     2001; Williams 2006, 2008, 2011.

10. The literature on whiteness and "whiteness studies" has become a burgeoning field
     in the last two decades, such that it is beyond the scope of this manuscript to do it
     justice. Among the works most instrumental for the crafting of this project were
     Allen 1994, 1997; Bay 2000; Bonilla-Silva 2001; Dyer 1997; Feagin and O'Brien 2003;
     Fine 1997; Frankenberg 1993, 1997; Gallagher 2003; Haney-Lopez 1998; Hartigan
     1999; Ignatiev 1995; Ignatiev and Garvey 1996; Lipsitz 1998; Roediger 1991, 1994,
     2002; and Wellman 1993.

11. For exceptional studies in these areas that motivated my work see Frankenberg
     1997; Hartigan 1999; Jackson 2001.

12. Due to the specific historical developments in the city of Chicago, the lingering ef-
     fects of segregation have maintained a black/white binary, albeit in more nuanced
     ways. For other contemporary ethnographic studies that highlight these nuances
     see Grazian 2005; Lloyd 2005; Pattillo 2008; Pattillo-McCoy 2000; Wacquant 2004a.

13. For key discussions of the use of cultural practices within the African American

community see Coleman 2005; Gilroy 1993, 1994; hooks 1992a, 1992b, 1994; Lott 1995; Root 1998; Tate 2002; Ziff and Rao 1997.

14. For a more elaborate discussion of Ellison's thoughts in his own words, see Hersey 1974.

15. For an excellent analysis of this duality of expression in terms of music, see William Roy's recent work (2010) on folk music and racial classifications.

16. Ellison's comments about the counterfeiting of identity, as a mode of revealing the social construction of ethnoracial categories, can be seen in light of John Jackson's (2005) ethnographic work *Real Black: Adventures in Racial Sincerity*. In both cases, invocations of authenticity, when coupled with race, can be analytically related to notions of sincerity, as a way of parceling out the supposedly real and unreal, the frame and the reframed, the original and the duplicate, in the articulations of racialized embodiment. For Jackson, sincerity and authenticity have very different ways of imagining identity. Therefore, racial *sincerity* should not be confused with racial *authenticity*, since sincerity exemplifies a distinct mode of rendering identity, solidarity, and reality in relation to race. For Jackson, sincerity is a way of discussing the subjects internally defined personal styles and ways of doing that highlights the "ever-fleeting 'liveness' of everyday racial performances" (18). By contrast, authenticity can be seen as an externally imposed notion of how race, culture, and identity should be expressed and comported. For Ellison, as for Jackson, sincerity provides a way to discuss issues of race and identity while jettisoning the either/or logic of authenticity. In doing so, sincerity allows one to capture the ways that race both matters and is always subject to the fluidity of social life and the multiplicity of contexts within which it is experience.

17. I take this term from Radano and Bohlman 2001, 5. The concept of the racial imagination runs throughout Radano's work, from which I draw heavily, especially his magisterial work *Lying Up a Nation: Race and Black Music* (2003).

18. Rather than taking for granted Ellison's position outside of the academy of sociology, as proxy for the African American "authenticity" of black cultural practices, I draw upon Ellison's analytic differentiation between race and culture, as well as his historical-cultural commentary in the American context. In doing so, Ellison provides the conceptual framework through which to assess the dominant racialized logic through which we perceive the world and how that logic mythologizes our everyday culture. As a scholar of the vernacular on the one hand, and a trained musician on the other, Ellison grappled with the Lindy Hop, and questioned the echoes of multiple identities heard in jazz. Ellison asks us to call out our racial categories as fictions and to question our American identity from the inside out. For a series of excellent essays that cover Ellison's interest in vernacular culture see Bentson 1987, as well as Neal's "Ellison's Zoot Suit" in Hersey 1974. For an interesting take on Ellison's writings on jazz, see Porter 2001.

19. Ellison 1995b, 123. On another occasion Ellison wrote: "I don't deny that these sociological formulas are drawn from life, but I do deny that they define the complexity of Harlem. They only abstract it and reduce it to proportions which the sociologists

can manage. I simply don't recognize Harlem in them, and I certainly don't recognize the people of Harlem whom I know" (1994, 730).

20. For a reading where Ellison does have a sociological imagination, see Doane 2004. Doane's title on the surface appears to be in radical contradiction to my own assessment of Ellison. However, Doane's "Sociological Imagination" is taken not from Ellison's nonfiction work, rather his reading offers a Hegelian, Marxist, and Freudian reading of Invisible Man by highlighting the concepts of alienation, freedom, and unconsciousness as thematic frameworks.

21. Other scholars, including social scientists, have made similar arguments. However, to dismiss Ellison as being somehow "outside" of the debates about everyday practices and vernacular assumptions of race due to his lack of "canonical status" as a sociologist or academic is a long-standing strategy by which to exclude African American "thinkers" from more proper "social scientific" concerns and debates. To do so would be to fall into the same myopic disciplinary concerns that Ellison is here criticizing. This long-standing history can be seen throughout the discipline of sociology by scholars such as Baker 1998; Daynes and Lee 2008; Holloway 2006; Jones 1971; Kelley 1996, 1998; Ladner 1973; Lyman 1971; Mckee 1992; Saint-Arnaud 2009; Warren 2003; Williams 2006, 2008, 2011.

22. For an excellent analysis of the connection between race and culture along similar lines, see Lee Baker's excellent work (1998).

23. Ellison argues: "What I am suggesting is that when you go back you do not find a pure stream; after all, Louis Armstrong, growing up in New Orleans, was taught to play a rather strict type of military music before he found his jazz and blues voice.... Talk about cultural pluralism! It's what we have to come to grips with as we are and what we want to add to the ongoing definition of the American experience.... It is very difficult in the country to find a pure situation. Usually when you find some assertion of purity, you are dealing with historical, if not cultural ignorance" (Ellison 1994, 447).

24. The principles that Wacquant (2002b) lays out concretize "Pierre Bourdieu in the field" and have, in turn, had a practical influence upon the ways I have designed and carried out my own research on race/body/culture.

25. Loïc Wacquant has developed and codified the project of carnal sociology in numerous books and articles from early articles such as "The Social Logic of Boxing in Black Chicago" (1992) up through his monograph Body and Soul (2004a). This work has garnered much attention, to which he has clarified and elucidated his work in symposium rejoinders "Shadowboxing with Ethnographic Ghosts" and in responses to special issues of journals dedicated to its discussion "Carnal Connections." Furthermore, Wacquant has discussed his intellectual project extensively in two synthetic overviews that detail the methodological, theoretical, and empirical aspects of ethnography, urban marginality, and ethnoracial domination that span his entire corpus in "The Body, the Ghetto, and the Penal State" (2009) and "Habitus as Topic and Tool" (2011).

26. Wacquant's project of a carnal sociology engages the literature surrounding the sociology of the body. For a discussion of the sociology of the body, see Burkeitt 1999;

Butler 1990, 1993; Csordas 1995; Falk 1994; Frank 1991; Freund 1998; Howson and Inglis 2001; Nettleton and Watson 1998; Schilling 1993, 2001; Turner 1984; Wacquant and Hughes 2003; Williams and Bendelow 1998.

27. For discussions of autoethnography and its application for sociological analysis, see Bochner and Ellis 2002, Ellis 2004, Gatson 2003, Holt 2003, Meneley and Young 2005, Reed-Danahay 1997, Spry 2001, and Vidal-Ortiz 2004.

28. In this way a formal analysis of the rules of dancing, or the instructions of how to go about doing particular steps or patterns will not be sufficient for understanding the practice of the dance, nor will mere observation allow us to understand the anxiety and tension that the dancers undertake consciously or unconsciously, in the ways that race gets refracted through culture in learning how to dance.

29. Stoller's main concern is on how "non-western" modes of representation are not strictly textually based and that the neglected senses are crucial to experience and "central to the metaphoric organization of experience" (1997, xv–xvi).

30. For a more extended discussion of this conceptualization and craft of writing, see Wacquant 2011, 90.

31. For recent inquiries taking up the carnal challenge of practical initiation as a means of ethnographic inquiry, see Auyero and Swistun 2007; Buchholtz 2006; Crossley 2004; Desmond 2007; Hancock 2005, 2007, 2008, 2009; Lande 2007; McRoberts 2004; Purser 2009; Scheffer 2008; Thiel 2007. Others have engaged in simillar work, though not specifically self-identifying as carnal sociology, around crafts such as the work of Harper 1987, Katz 1999, O'Connor 2005, Pagis 2010, and Sennett 2008. This approach goes beyond those who have adopted Wacquant's project, and yet limited their use of carnal sociology to discussions of practical knowledge and its role in describing the dynamics of a particular social world, and as a means to group membership.

32. For a detailed analysis of cognition on racial categorization, see Brubaker, Loveman, and Stamatov 2004; Loveman 1999a, 1999b. See also Bourdieu and Wacquant 1992, Brubaker and Cooper 2000, Jenkins 1994, and Wacquant 1997b. For studies of group formation through racialization see Ignatiev 1995, Omi and Winant 1994, and Roediger 1991.

33. For extended discussions of misrecognition, see Bourdieu 1977 and 1990a.

34. As Bourdieu argues: "The whole truth of collective magic and belief is contained in this game of two-fold objective truth, a double game played with truth, through which the group, the source of all objectivity, in a sense lies to itself by producing a truth whose sole function and meaning are to deny a truth known and recognized by all, a lie that would deceive no one, were not everyone determined to be mistaken" (1990a, 234).

35. For a detailed account of how Wacquant uses this approach, see Wacquant 1997b.

Chapter 1

1. This analysis builds off Wacquant's study of boxing. See Wacquant 1992, 1995a, 1995b, 1998a, 1998b, 2004a.

2. For an exploration of this theme in African American dance, see Comaroff 1985, Desmond 1997, Hazzard-Gordon 1990, and Savigliano 1995.

3. Certainly this material could be read through the framework of Bourdieu's habitus (1990a, 53), as it shares the concerns with embodied knowledge and construction of expertise. However, while this chapter discusses the process of becoming a dancer, its primary focus is not on the habitus in the way Wacquant makes it central to his work. For an explanation of how Wacquant explicates his own radicalization of Bourdieu's "habitus" see my article "Following Loïc Wacquant into the Field" (Hancock 2009). See also Wacquant's (2011) compact recapitulation of the genealogy and functions of this oft-misunderstood concept.

4. The notion of "mastery" discussed here resonates with Houston Baker's discussion of the differences between "the mastery of form" and "the deformation of mastery" (Baker 1987, 1989). For Baker, these distinctions are presented in order to argue for the distinctive character and history of Afro-American expressive culture. Mastery of form refers to ways in which a writer works to assimilate into the dominant tradition in order to be recognized. For Baker, mastery of form implies a mask which allows for the appearance of orthodoxy, wherein the true subversive nature of the performance is concealed. The paradigmatic example Baker draws on is the minstrel show. While white audiences were presented with a "minstrel show," black audiences and performers were actually engaged in strategies of survival or in processes of "negotiating the economics of slavery" (Baker 1989, 15). The deformation of mastery, by contrast, refers to the refusal of, or an attack on, the dominant tradition through form and content which "secures territorial advantage and heightens a group's survival possibilities" (50). For Baker, one must simultaneously engage in both the mastery of form and the deformation of mastery in order to forge a unique and recognized self. While initially useful to make superficial distinctions at the level of racial difference, Baker's categories do nothing to help us understand the cultivation and comportment of those individuals in relation to those forms. As a result, the complexities of race in relation to cultural expression, break down into a simplistic racial essentialism and absolutism that conflate race with culture and culture with race. Instead, following Ellison, we can see how both mastery of form and the deformation of mastery have nothing to do with race and everything to do with the practical mastery of the cultural form in question.

5. Film footage of the famous dancer Shorty George Snowden captured in the 1929 film *After Seven* documents the Swing Out emerging from the partnered version of the Charleston.

6. The Lindy Hop world consists of three hierarchical tiers that apply to the teachers and performers. The international tier is occupied by the very elite masters of the dance that travel across the globe. The national tier refers to experts that travel the United States, but are not at that elite level. The local tier refers to those dancers that teach and perform only in their own cities.

7. This quotation is taken from a videotaped interview with Steven Mitchell (Herräng dance camp videotape, 1993).

8. This aspect of embodied knowledge of dance resonates with Bourdieu's statement

that "Having acquired from this exposure a system of dispositions attuned to these regularities, it is inclined and able to anticipate them practically in behaviors which engage a *corporeal knowledge* that provides a practical comprehension of the world that is quite different from the intentional act of conscious decoding that is normally designated by the idea of comprehension" (2000b, 135).

9. Bourdieu theorizes "the feel for the game" accordingly, "The feel for the game is being in the zone, about the practical master able to anticipate the rhythms and actions of the game, the continuity with detached reflection of how to act and respond to what is going on in the game. It follows from the practical sense" (1990a, 75).

10. Bourdieu defines this practical sense of self-monitoring as "the reflection in situation and in action which is necessary to evaluate instantly the action or the posture just produced and to correct a wrong position of the body, to recover an imperfect movement" (Bourdieu and Wacquant 1992, 131).

11. For an extended use of this metaphor in relation to practical understanding, see Bourdieu and Wacquant 1992, 128.

12. Despite what some critics may argue, it is not important whether dance is learned "formally" in classrooms like Lindy Hop dancers in Chicago or "informally" like salsa dancers in the favelas of Rio. Dance requires teaching and learning. While the learning environment may differ, the result does not; one must learn how to dance. Those who argue otherwise fall into the very mythologies of "naturalism" attached to informal learning and race that this project seeks to undermine. Just like other forms of bodily knowledge, from using chopsticks to fixing a leaking pipe to dancing the Lindy Hop, it can be "brandished" or shown, just by using that knowledge in a particular situation that demands it.

13. For an excellent parallel analysis of how jazz musicians who have never played together can join without rehearsal in a coordinated musical collaboration with a successful performance (through repertoires, skill sets of listening and adapting in interpreting the other, and other competences by which one becomes a jazz musician), see Faulkner and Becker 2009. Just like musicianship, dance is enacted by those partners involved and both must operate synchronously for it to be done "right." For other studies of jazz and improvisation that motivated this analysis, see Berliner 1994, Keil and Feld 2005, Monson 1996, and Murphy 1990.

Chapter 2

1. For a discussion of armor as a racial defense, see Warren 2003, 77, and West 1993, 15–16.

2. For analysis of the African forms in African American dance, see Asante and Welsh-Asante 1989; DeFrantz 2002; Emery 1988; Friedland 1995; Gottschild 1996; Hazzard-Gordon 1990; Malone 1996; Ross 2010; Stearns and Stearns 1994; Welsh-Asante 1993.

3. Lott 1995; Radano 2001, 2003; Roediger 1991, 2002; Rogin 1996; Toll 1974; and Turner 1994.

4. Boyd 1997, 2004; Fusco 1995; George 1988, 1992; hooks 1992b, 1994; Jones 1963;

Lipsitz 1997; Lott 1995; Maira 2002; Michaels 1997; Root 1998; Tate 2002; and Toll 1974.

5. I take this term from Radano and Bohlman as "the shifting matrix of ideological construction of difference associated with body type and color that have emerged as part of the discourse network of modernity" (2001, 5). In building on this notion of the racial imagination I also draw on the work of Bourdieu 1990a, 1991b, 2000a, 2000b; Hall 1996a, 1996b; and Radano 2001, 2003.

6. This operates in parallel to how Bourdieu defines the mechanisms by which gender is constructed and naturalized. Bourdieu writes, "The work of transformation of bodies, which is both sexually differentiated and differentiating and which is performed partly through the effects of mimetic suggestion, partly through explicit injunctions and partly through the whole symbolic construction of the view of the biological body (and in particular the sexual act, conceived as an act of domination, possession), produces systematically differentiated and differentiating habitus. The masculinization of the male body, and the feminization of the female body, immense and in a sense of interminable tasks which, perhaps now more than ever, always demand a considerable expenditure of time and effort, induce a *somatization* of the relation of domination, which is thus naturalized. It is through the training of the body that the most fundamental dispositions are imposed, those which make a person *inclined and able* to enter into the social games most favorable to the development of manliness—politics, business, science, etc." (2000a, 55).

7. Scholars such as Baker (1998), Lott (1995), hooks (1992b, 1994), Radano (2001, 2003), and Roediger (1991, 2002), have all explored this topic in their respective areas. The social construction of race parallels Bourdieu's analysis of gender. In particular, racial differences, like gender differences, reinforce "the prevailing system of classification by making it appear grounded in reality Which since it helps produce that reality and since incorporated social relations appear natural not only in the eyes of those whose interests they serve by the prevailing classification, when properties and movements of the body are socially qualified, the most fundamental social choices are naturalized and the body with its properties and its movements is constituted as an analogical operator establishing all kinds of practical equivalences among the different divisions of the social world." See Bourdieu 1990a, 71.

8. Baker (1998), Gilroy (1993, 1994, 1997), Martin (2002), O'Meally (1998), Radano (2001, 2003), and Ramsey (2000, 2003), have all argued against the cultural-racial conflation that occurs in the analysis of African American cultural forms, specifically here music.

9. Radano 2001, 471. For further analyses of the coupling of blackness and rhythm see also Radano 2003.

10. See Radano 2001, 2003 for a detailed exegesis of this issue.

11. The racial imagination operates akin to Bourdieu's theory of symbolic power—the ability to control the schemas of perception and appreciation that are constitutive of the ways we apprehend and conceptualize the world, won through social conflict and struggle—produces symbolic violence. For Bourdieu, symbolic power operates by es-

tablishing arbitrary social and cultural distinctions and valuations that become mis-recognized as the legitimated and taken-for-granted assumptions of the social order. Symbolic power results in a symbolic violence where the socialization of the very cat-egories of thought, the basis of our social understanding, remains hidden even to our self-conscious reflection. Bourdieu argues that this process is a "two-fold naturaliza-tion" embedded simultaneously in the social order and in socialized bodies facilitated by the fact that it goes on almost automatically and therefore legitimates the dominant social order without need for propaganda or covert manipulation since the world ap-pears self-evident and commonsensical. For discussions of symbolic power, symbolic violence and misrecognition see: Bourdieu 1991b, 167–70; 2000a, 35; 2000b, 181.

12. Bourdieu 1990a, 71–72. Also see Mercer 1994 and Radano 2003.

13. Kyra Gaunt's (2006) work on how black girls come to understand black womanhood through ongoing vernacular training in popular dance styles and musical games, such as double-dutch, illuminates the body-conscious musicality as "learned musi-cal blackness." This informal socialization of socializing of girls into the local so-cial practices of black urban life provides an excellent point of cross-fertilization between dancing bodies and racialized ones. Most important in Gaunt's analysis, is the way that she highlights how the "rules of black social identity" are at work be-yond the obvious dance floor and music video culture and embedded in much more "trivial maneuvers" such as in the games girls play (Gaunt 2006, 14). For additional studies that link ethnography and performance to issues of dance, see amongst oth-ers: Albright 1997; Browning 1995, 1998; Buckland 1999; Delgado and Muñoz 1997; Desmond 1997, 2000; Dils and Cooper Albright 2001; Goellner and Murphy 1994; Hanna 1987; Lepecki 2004; Lewis 1995; Ness 1992; Reed 1998; Spencer 1986; Taylor 1998; Thomas 1995; Thomas and Ahmed 2004.

14. Several scholars have used Bourdieu's notion of cultural capital in the theorization of symbolic boundaries between groups and how they are constructed through inclusion and exclusion. See Hall 1992; Lamont 1994, 1999; Lamont and Fournier 1992; Lamont and Lareau 1988; and Lareau and Horvat 1999.

15. See, e.g., Conley 2001; Frankenberg 1993, 1996, 1997; Fusco 1995; Garon 1995; Ge-rard 2001; Grazian 2005; Ignatiev and Garvey 1996; Perry 2001; Roediger 1991, 1994, 1999, 2002; Rogin 1996; Spivak 1998; Tomlinson 1991; Turner 1994; Wald 2000; Young 2008; and Ziff and Rao 1997.

16. Gubar 1997; Lott 1995; Roediger 1991, 1994, 1999, 2002; Rogin 1996; and Wald 2000. For a critique of this position see Radano 2001, 2003.

17. Gubar 1997; Lott 1995; Radano 2001, 2003; Roediger 1991, 1994, 1999, 2002; Rogin 1996.

18. These modes of engagement are not particular to the Lindy Hop, but are underlying frameworks that inform the ways that whites generally engage African American practices.

19. See Gubar 1997; Lhamon 2000; Lott 1995; Mahar 1999; Roediger 1991; Rogin 1996; Saxton 1975, 1998; and Toll 1974.

20. For an excellent analysis of this, see Gabriel 1998.

Chapter 3

1. See de Certeau 1984; Fiske 1993; Ross and Rose 1994; and Scott 1985, 1990.

2. Because I am a white ethnographer, embedded and embodied in this particular white social dance world as a teacher, dancer, and performer, my ability to get at the discourses of the Lindy Hop was quite easy. Yet while as a white interviewer I had a special "insider" position within which to work, I never felt that I was gaining any "hidden" or "secret" racial knowledge of whites' "real" attitudes, of beliefs they would have kept secret from non-whites. The idea that such secret beliefs exist merely re-essentializes racial difference and assumes that there is always something that whites are *really* saying to other whites, concealed in politically correct language or euphemisms. In fact, I wasn't interested in what whites thought of other racial groups or in any individual prejudices; I was interested in the discourses through which they conceptualized the Lindy Hop and the consequences they had for understanding the intersections of race, culture, and society. For a discussion that takes up these issues of the privilege of white racial knowledge and the white interviewer, see Fine 1997, Frankenberg 1993, Nakayama and Martin 1999, Perry 2001, Roediger 2002, and Twine and Warren 2000.

3. I interviewed and discussed the Lindy Hop with all levels of dancers, performers, DJs, and instructors. Through mapping that landscape I selected the discourses that were pervasive across social positions within that world.

4. By moving toward a paradigm of racial domination we can understand how agents reproduce racial inequality without the need for deciphering intentions (prejudice or discrimination) or by relying on simple structural models of racial essentialism (structural racism).

5. I take this term from Radano and Bohlman 2001, 5.

6. For a discussion of the logic of trial, see Wacquant 1997b.

7. See Blauner 1992; Bonilla-Silva 2001, 2003; Brown et al. 2003; Feagin and O'Brien 2003; Frankenberg 1993; Gallagher 2003; Lipsitz 1998; Wellman 1993.

8. Bourdieu's arguments about the power of language as a tool through which social and political beliefs, practices, ideologies, subject positions, and norms can all be mediated and instantiated; see Bourdieu 1977, 1991a, 1991b. For Bourdieu, discourse is not something an individual has or creates; rather it is a product of socialization into the dominant meanings that reinforce commonsense. In this way discourse is at once an expression of the individual and the social world in which he lives. As a result, discourses operate like habitus below the level of consciousness and work through to structure and interpret the world around us.

9. For Bourdieu, symbolic systems of categories and classifications are the stakes in the power struggle between groups. See Bourdieu and Wacquant 1992, 12–14.

10. For a discussion of reverse racism or racism against whites, see Bonilla-Silva and Doane 2003; Gallagher 1999, 2003; and Lipsitz 1998.

11. This position is different than Bonilla-Silva's theory of "racism without racists" since his paradigm is one of justifications for racism. Bonilla-Silva's approach is still locked in the racist/non-racist duality. Instead, by moving toward a paradigm of ra-

cial domination, we can understand how these discourses reproduce racial inequality without the explicit or even tacit complicity of actors with "racism." By bypassing outdated models of racial inequality defined by intention (prejudice or discrimination) or essentialism (structural racism) we can move past arguments mired in the logic of the trial which parcel out guilt and innocence.

12. Baker 1998; Gottschild 1996, 2002, 2003; hooks 1992b; Lott 1995; and Turner 1994;.

13. For an excellent contemporary study of how racial/musical spaces are defined by identity investments and those who come to hold more influence over a particular space, see Grazian's 2005 study of blues clubs which served as a model for thinking through these issues.

14. For ethnographic studies that detail the complexities of racial binaries and in group variations in African American urban life see Anderson 1976, 1992, 2000; Drake and Cayton 1945; Du Bois 1994; Duneier 1994, 2000; Jackson 2001, 2005; Pattillo 2008; Pattillo-McCoy 2000; and Wilson 1980, 1987, 1997. This internal variation problematizes the relations between race and culture by offering other layers of stratification by which multiple cultures exist within any one racial category. These internal variations also further undermine notions of cultural ownership both within and between racial groups.

15. For several studies of collective memory that animate these questions, see Blight 2001, Connerton 1989, Gundaker 1998, Halbwachs 1980, Handler 1991, Hobsbawm and Ranger 1983, Kammen 1991, Lipsitz 1990, Lowenthal 1985, and Olick 2007.

16. For a discussion of the historical roots of the Lindy Hop, see Dance 2001, DeFrantz 2002, Emery 1988, Malone 1996, Miller and Jensen 2001, Penner 1999, Stearns and Stearns 1994, and Vale and Wallace 1998.

17. It should be noted that from a purely corporeal and embodiment standpoint, the fixation on race obscures the inculcation and performance of the dance which requires knowledge of race, culture of history.

18. See Gubar 1997, Guillory and Green 1998, Lhamon 2000, Lott 1995, Rogin 1996, and Toll 1997.

Chapter 4

1. This resonates with Suttles's experiences in *The Social Order of the* Slum, in which he discusses his interactions with people in the neighborhood. At first he thought people were prejudiced or inhospitable, but he then came to realize that he was simply out of place. His mere physical presence there was very unexpected (1970, 47–51).

2. While this "social" observation of the differences between the white North Side and the black South Side may strike the reader as superficial, more in-depth analysis of these differences in more specific sociological studies can be found in Hirsch 1998, Massey and Denton 1998, and Wilson 1997.

3. There have been other offshoots from the Lindy Hop, such as West Coast Swing and the Hustle, that were picked up in the white community.

4. For two excellent videos on Steppin' see Chi-Sounds Records 1997, 1999. For a dis-

cussion of DC Hand dancing see Frazier 2000, and for an overview of the multiple
forms Steppin' takes in different regions, see Lindsay 2000.

5. See Hancock and Garner 2011; Hirsch 1998; Massey and Denton 1998; Wacquant
    1992, 1998b, 2003, 2004a; Wilson 1980, 1987, 1997.

6. I define whiteness, following Bonilla-Silva (1997, 2001, 2003), Frankenberg (1993),
    Hartigan (1999), Lott (1993, 1995), and Roediger (1991, 2002), in particular, as the
    invisible, normative, unspoken—commonsense—assumptions about the normal-
    ized operation of the racial organization of society by which white values, ideas,
    aesthetics, preferences, and privileges are made to appear natural and the basis of
    the social order.

7. In *Black Picket Fences*, Mary Pattillo-McCoy discusses how working and middle-class
    African Americans often engage in "code switching" between formal American
    English and vernacular African American English as a way of establishing commu-
    nity. Garner and Rubin (cited in her footnote) found in their sample of black lawyers
    that nearly all use black English in more comfortable and familiar surroundings.
    Similarly to Pattillo-McCoy, I attempt to reconstruct the pronunciation of the ver-
    nacular language with which people talked to us. In addition to more accurately
    representing the people we met and interviewed, their use of black English when
    speaking to us also reflected our status as insiders. They spoke to us as they did with
    others in the Steppin' scene.

8. Whiteness studies sometimes deploy a distinction between social and sociological
    understandings of race. In doing so, it often conflates the two positions. One of the
    recent advancement in whiteness studies has been the theorizing of the heteroge-
    neity and complexity of the relationship between blackness and African American
    people. However, as John Hartigan has pointed out, whiteness studies have failed
    to do the same for whiteness and whites, because this same distinction serves to
    muddle the clarity of whiteness as a system of racial domination.

9. Gilroy argues that hip hop represents the blackest of African American expressions.
    Given the overwhelming influx of non–African Americans into the hip-hop com-
    munity as artists and participants since Gilroy published that statement seven years
    ago, that label could now be applied to Steppin'. For Gilroy's remarks see Gilroy
    1997.

10. For this tradition of resistive practices, see hooks 1992b, 1994; Kelley 1996; Lipsitz
    1997; Mercer 1994, and Rose 1994.

11. This ethnographic methodology draws upon Paul Willis's *The Ethnographic Imagina-
    tion*, in which he argues that it is critical for the ethnographer to be there in order
    to understand the nonverbal meanings of dress, style, bodily dispositions, ways of
    walking, talking, gesture, and posture that are the basis of meaning-making in ev-
    eryday life while simultaneously framing these meanings within a larger analytical
    framework. See Willis 2001.

12. Dance classes are held before all DJ sets at clubs or before parties. In addition there
    are over a dozen competing instructional dance companies that offer lessons, at lo-
    cations as diverse as dance studios to community colleges.

13. For discussions of African American practices structured through the call and re-
    sponse dynamic, see Caponi 1999; Gottschild 1996, 2003; and Malone 1996.

14. See the CD liner notes for *Steppin' Out* (Rhino Records 2001).

15. See, e.g., Caponi 1999, Gilroy 1993, Hall 1996b, Kelley 1996, and Malone 1996 for
    discussions of expressive practices and African American culture.

16. This is in no way an argument for the transcendence of race. Rather, it points di-
    rectly to the power of the racial imagination and the reality of the racialized body
    in relation to its engagement in cultural practices. The reracializing or recategori-
    zation of the bodies in question is strictly circumscribed and limited to the realm
    of the dance floor alone, and operates with decreasing significance as one moves
    from the dance floor to the socializing areas, to the exiting of the club and beyond.
    The cultural practice of dance attenuates racialized differences within the specific
    spatiotemporal confines of the club, but does little to impact the larger structures
    of ethno-racial domination which imbue those different racial categories with their
    meanings. For a developed critique against such misconstrued notions, see Wac-
    quant 2005a.

17. Again I draw upon Willis's ethnographic method of emphasizing the importance of
    the connection between language and the material world to illuminate why these
    expressions carry such weight in this context.

18. Here we can see how the racialization of the body comes through a multiplicity of
    actions and behaviors. In the case of the Steppin' scene, it is an analysis of the com-
    plexities of white bodies engaging black cultural practices in relation to other racial-
    ized actions in both the arenas of dance and outside those arenas. This occurs not
    only through the dance, but through knowledge of fashion, language, negotiating
    the territories of finding the proper clubs on the proper nights, familiarity with
    music, and so on, that go well beyond the bounds of "just dancing." In this way a
    myriad of sociocultural practices signify a body as a racial anomaly and not as a
    cannibalistic racial threat.

19. Viewing race through the lens of practice does not mean that race is erased or that it
    no longer has any social meaning; rather through the competence of culture prac-
    tices race as a category becomes unimportant in defining identity.

20. A key aspect of ethnographic inquiry is the ways that identity of the ethnographer,
    the informants, or social spaces may be temporarily suspended, fluctuate, or be
    redefined depending on the audience, the purpose, and the circumstances in the
    course of building extended intimate relationships. For an account of the mutabil-
    ity of identities in relation to carnal sociology, see Wacquant 2005a. It is necessary
    to note here that this is in no way to claim that I "became black" or that my racial
    identity was magically transformed as I danced, nor did this situation create an in-
    dividual exceptionalism by which I was them able to write about the Steppin' scene
    as an African American.

21. A long-standing debate within music circles is whether or not white musicians can
    "play" jazz in the same way as black musicians. This debate resonates across other
    cultural arenas, such as sports and dance. Fred Moten's work on music serves as a

forceful critique of this racial-cultural fluidity. For Moten, blackness is a metaphysical essence that links all black performances and expressions (Moten 2003). Moten dismisses white performative mastery of African American dominated cultural forms with his discussion of the "white hipster." For studies that call into question the idea of autonomy in musical works and instead emphasize the historical and social contingency of knowledge, music, competence, and society, see Gaunt 2006; Monson 1996; Radano 1993, 2001, 2003; Taylor 1992; Tomlinson 1991; and Walser 1993, 1995.

22. Bourdieu 1990a, 2000b; Butler 1993, 1994, 1997; Goffman 1959, 1967; Wacquant 2003.

23. For a discussion of this idea of the cultivation of the body, see Bourdieu 1990a, 2000b. For a discussion of the black body and its cultivation in cultural styles, see Hall 1996 and Mercer 1994.

24. See Boyd 1997, 2004; Bozza 2003; Briggs and Colby 1999; Daws 1998; Roediger 2002; and Ross 1996 for discussions.

25. For examples of politics grounded in performance, see Butler 1993, 1994; Gubar 1997; and Lott 1995.

26. For a discussion of this type of positioning in terms of class, see Bourdieu 1990b, 1987.

Lead Out

1. For a discussion of the Lindy Hop in relation to African American dance, see Adjaye and Andrews 1997; DeFrantz 2002; Emery 1988; Gottschild 1996, 2002, 2003; Haskins 1990; Hazzard-Gordon 1990; Malone 1996; Miller and Jensen 2001; and Stearns and Stearns 1994.

2. For a detailed analysis of cognition on racial categorization, see Brubaker, Loveman, and Stamatov 2004; Loveman 1999a, 1999b. See also Bourdieu and Wacquant 1992, Brubaker and Cooper 2000, Jenkins 1994, and Wacquant 1997b. For studies of group formation through racialization, see among others, Ignatiev 1995, Omi and Winant 1994, and Roediger 1991.

Conclusion

1. See Roediger 1994 for the most damning statement that whiteness is, and thus most whites are, nothing but oppressive.

2. Bonnett 1996a, 1996b; Dyer 1997; Fine 1997; Frankenberg 1997; Giroux 1997; Hill 1998; Karenga 1999; Kincheloe et al. 1998; Kolchin 2002; and Rothenberg 2002.

3. See Crenshaw et al. 1995, Delgado 1995, Delgado and Stephanic 1997, Feagin 2000, Haney-Lopez 1998, Kincheloe et al. 1998, McIntosh 1989, Perry 2001, Rothenberg 2002, and Wildman 1996.

4. Colorblind racism as a model of ideology also functions this way when applied to culture. See Bonilla-Silva 1997, 2001, 2003, and Bonilla-Silva and Doane 2003.

5. See Appadurai 1988; Briggs and Colby 1999; Chin 2001; Cutler 1999; Deloria 1997;

Dent and Wallace 1999; Featherstone 1991; Gallagher 1999, 2003; Hall 1997; Halter 2002; hooks 1992a, 1992b, 1994; Lury 1996; Maira 2002; McClintock 1995; McCracken 1991; Miller 1987, 1998; Perry 2002; Root 1998; Wood 1997; and Ziff and Rao 1997.

6. See Michaels 1995, 129, 142, 15. Michaels discusses his position on the relationship between race and culture in a number of different articles and books (Michaels 1992, 1994, 1995, 1997). While it is beyond the scope of this chapter to fully reckon with Michael's arguments, his account of distinguishing race from culture ends in a highly contentious conclusion that "the modern concept of culture is not a critique of racism; it is a form of racism" (1995, 129). Michaels's critique of multiculturalism cuts across all four of the forms of appropriation discussed here, since he argues that our current concerns with issues of "culture" are really, in fact, issues of "race." My engagement with Michaels comes not from his dismissals of social constructionism, but rather through his framing of culture as "not as the things you love to do but as the things you love to do because they are your culture" (120). While Michaels does refer to culture as "beliefs and practices" elsewhere, he still conceptualizes them not as constitutive of our identity, but as objects, or property derived from what "should properly go with the sort of people we happen to be" (1992, 683). As a result, his dismissal of contesting cultural practices is based on the wrongheaded assumptions that cultural practices are simply transitory and disposable and that their significance is only in the momentary engagement with them. The ironic nature of Michaels's argument, especially in the case of *Our America*, is that his literary interpretations of nativism, modernism, and pluralism, which he deftly chronicles in the literature of the 1920s, become ahistorical when extended to a discussion of contemporary cultural practices. In doing so, where the shifting contexts within which our categories of race and culture operate in relation to the material conditions of their production, Michaels jettisons the role history plays in relation to multiple dimensions of cultural practices both past, present, and future. For a review of *Our America* that speaks to this historical dynamic, see Sollors 1999. For excellent critique of Michaels's position in relation to schools of theory, see Gordon and Newfield 1994.

7. See Boyd 1997, 2004; George 1988, 1992; Gilroy 1997; Jones 1963; Lipsitz 1997; Maira 2002; Michaels 1997; Tate 2002. For a critique of this position through the model of hybridity, see Canclini 1995; Flores 2000; Kalra and Hutnyk 2003; Modood and Werbner 1997; and Sollors 1997.

8. See, e.g., Conley 2001; Frankenberg 1993, 1996, 1997; Fusco 1995; Garon 1995; Ignatiev and Garvey 1996; Perry 2001; Roediger 1991, 1994, 1999, 2002; Rogin 1996; Spivak 1998; Stephens 1991, 1992, 1999; Tomlinson 1991; Turner 1994; Wald 2000; and Ziff and Rao 1997.

9. Baker 1998; hooks 1992a, 1992b, 1994; Lott 1995; Radano 2000, 2003; and Roediger 1990, 2002.

10. Gubar 1997; Lott 1995; Radano 2000 2003; Roediger 1991, 1994, 1999, 2002; and Rogin 1996.

11. See, e.g., Conley 2001; Frankenberg 1993, 1996, 1997; Fusco 1995; Gallagher 2003;

Garon 1995; Ignatiev and Garvey 1996; Perry 2001; Roediger 1990, 1994, 1999, 2002; Rogin 1996; Spivak 1998; Tomlinson 1991; Turner 1994; Wald 2000; and Ziff and Rao 1997.

12. Deloria 1997; Fusco 1995; hooks 1992b, 1994; Lott 1995; Radano 2000, 2003; Roediger 1991, 1994, 1999, 2002; Rogin 1996; Wald 2000.

13. See Boyd 1997, 2004; and Kelley 1996. In addition, see the recent proliferation of this theme in recent popular movies such as *White Boyz*, *Bringing Down the House*, *Barbershop*, *8 Mile*, *Black and White*, and *Malibu's Most Wanted*.

14. For the abolition of whiteness, see Roediger 1991, 1994, 2002. For the race traitor model, see Ignatiev and Garvey 1996. For whiteness as demonized and the necessity to choose against it, see Haney-Lopez 1998 and McLaren 1997. For movement from racist to antiracist, see Clark and O'Donnell 1999. For whiteness defined and essentialized as white skin privilege, see Delgado and Stefancic 1997, Haney-Lopez 1998, McIntosh 1989, Rothenberg 2002, and Wildman 1996. For a good overview of these positions and a critique, see Gallagher 2000, Giroux 1997, Kolchin 2002, and Warren 2003.

15. Bonnett 1996a, 1996b; Flores 2000; Winant 1994; and Yudice 1995

16. Delgado 1995; Feagin and O'Brien 2003; Feagin and Vera 1995; Helms 1990, 1992; and Kivel 1996.

17. Fishkin 1995, Lipsitz 1997, Lott 1995, Roediger 2002, and Sundquist 1993.

18. For a particularly charged and well-reasoned critique of social construction of race see Michaels 1992, 1994, 1995, 1997.

19. For an excellent critique of Michaels's position see Warren 2003.

REFERENCES

Adjaye, Joseph K., and Adrianne R. Andrews. 1997. *Language, Rhythm, and Sound: Black Popular Cultures into the Twenty-First Century.* Pittsburgh, PA: University of Pittsburgh Press.

Adshead-Lansdale, J. 1999. *Dancing Texts: Intertextuality in Interpretation.* London: Dance Books.

Albright, Ann Cooper. 1997. *Choreographing Difference: The Body and Identity in Contemporary Dance.* Middletown, CT: Wesleyan University Press.

Allen, Theodore. 1994. *The Invention of the White Race.* Vol. 1. New York: New Left Books.

———. 1997. *The Invention of the White Race.* Vol. 2. New York: New Left Books.

Aloff, Mindy. 1999. "Rediscovering an Old Dramatic Partner: Dance." *New York Times,* October 3, 26.

Anderson, Elijah. 1976. *A Place on the Corner.* Chicago: University of Chicago Press.

———. 1992. *Streetwise: Race, Class, and Change in an Urban Community.* Chicago: University of Chicago Press.

———. 2000. *Code of the Street: Decency, Violence, and the Moral Life of the Inner City.* New York: W. W. Norton.

Appadurai, A. 1988. *The Social Life of Things: Commodities in Cultural Perspective.* Cambridge: Cambridge University Press.

Asante, Molefi Kete, and Kariamu Welsh-Asante, eds. 1989. *African Culture: The Rhythms of Unity.* Trenton, NJ: World Press.

Auyero, J., and D. Swistun. 2007. "Confused Because Exposed: Towards an Ethnography of Environmental Suffering." *Ethnography* 8:123–44.

Auyero, Javier. 2001. *Poor People's Politics: Peronist Survival Networks and the Legacy of Evita.* Durham, NC: Duke University Press.

Baker, Houston, Jr. 1987. In Blues, Ideology, and Afro-American Literature. Chicago: University of Chicago Press.

———. 1989. *Modernism and the Harlem Renaissance.* Chicago: University of Chicago Press.

Baker, Lee D. 1998. *From Savage to Negro: Anthropology and the Construction of Race, 1896–1954*. Berkeley: University of California Press.

Batchelor, Christian. 1997. *This Thing Called Swing: A Study of Swing Music and the Lindy Hop*. London: The Original Lindy Hop Collection Press.

Bay, Mia. 2000. *The White Image in the Black Mind: African-American Ideas about White People, 1830–1925*. New York: Oxford University Press.

Bentson, Kimberley. 1987. *Speaking for You: The Vision of Ralph Ellison*. Washington, DC: Howard University Press.

Berliner, Paul F. 1994. *Thinking in Jazz: The Infinite Art of Improvisation*. Chicago Studies in Ethnomusicology. Chicago: University of Chicago Press.

Black, Les, and John Solomos. 2000. *Theories of Race and Racism: A Reader*. New York: Routledge.

Blauner, Bob. 1992. "Talking Past Each Other: Black and White Languages of Race." *American Prospect* 10:55–64.

Blight, David. 2001. *Race and Reunion: The Civil War in American Memory*. Cambridge, MA: Belknap Press.

Bochner A. P., and C. Ellis. 2002. *Ethnographically Speaking*. Walnut Creek, CA: Altamira Press.

Bonilla-Silva, Eduardo. 1997. "Rethinking Racism." *American Sociological Review* 62 (3): 456–79.

———. 2001. *White Supremacy and Racism in the Post–Civil Rights Era*. Boulder, CO: Lynne Reiner.

———. 2003. *Racism without Racists: Color-Blind Racism and the Persistence of Racial Inequality in the United States*. Lanham, MD: Roman and Littlefield.

Bonilla-Silva, Eduardo, and Ashley W. Doane. 2003. *White Out: The Continuing Significance of Racism*. New York: Routledge.

Bonnett, Alastair. 1996a. "'White Studies': The Problems and Projects of a New Research Agenda." *Theory, Culture and Society* 13:145–55.

———. 1996b. "Anti-Racism and the Critique of 'White' Identities." *Journal of Ethnic and Migration Studies* 22 (1): 97–110.

Bourdieu, Pierre. 1977. *Outline of a Theory of Practice*. Cambridge: Cambridge University Press.

———. 1987a. *Distinction: A Social Critique of the Judgment of Taste*. Cambridge: Harvard University Press.

———. 1987b. "What Makes a Social Class? On the Theoretical and Practical Existence of Groups." *Berkeley Journal of Sociology* 32:1–18.

———. 1990a. *The Logic of Practice*. Stanford, CA: Stanford University Press.

———. 1990b. *In Other Words: Essays on Reflexive Sociology*. Stanford, CA: Stanford University Press.

———. 1991a. "Identity and Representation." In *Language and Symbolic Power*. Cambridge: Harvard University Press.

———. 1991b. *Language and Symbolic Power*. Cambridge: Harvard University Press.

———. 2000a. *Masculine Domination*. Stanford, CA: Stanford University Press.

———. 2000b. *Pascalian Meditations*. Stanford, CA: Stanford University Press.

Bourdieu, Pierre, and Loïc Wacquant. 1992. *An Invitation to Reflexive Sociology.* Chicago: University of Chicago Press.

Boyd, Todd. 1997. *Am I Black Enough for You?* Bloomington: Indiana University Press.

———. 2004. *The New HNIC: The Death of Civil Rights and the Reign of Hip Hop.* New York: New York University Press.

Bozza, Anthony. 2003. *Whatever You Say I Am: The Life and Times of Eminem.* New York: Crown.

Briggs, Adam, and Paul Colby. 1999. "I Like My Shit Sagged: Fashion, 'Black Musics' and Subcultures." *Journal of Youth Studies* 2 (3): 337–52.

Brown, Michael K., Martin Carnoy, Elliott Currie, Troy Duster, and David B. Oppenheimer. 2003. *Whitewashing Race: The Myth of a Color-Blind Society.* Berkeley: University of California Press.

Browning, Barbara. 1995. *Samba: Resistance in Motion.* Bloomington: Indiana University Press.

———. 1998. *Infectious Rhythm: Metaphors of Contagion and the Spread of African Culture.* New York: Routledge.

Brubaker, Rogers, and Frederick Cooper. 2000. "Beyond Identity." *Theory and Society* 29 (1): 1–47.

Brubaker, Rogers, M. Loveman, and P. Stamatov. 2004. "Ethnicity as Cognition." *Theory and Society* 33:31–63.

Buchholtz, L. 2006. "Bringing the Body Back into Theory and Methodology." *Theory and Society* 35:481–90.

Buckland, Theresa. 1999. *Dance in the Field: Theory, Methods and Issues in Dance Ethnography.* Basingstoke: Palgrave Macmillan.

Burawoy, Michael. 2000. *Global Ethnography: Forces, Connections, and Imaginations in a Postmodern World.* Berkeley: University of California Press.

Burawoy, Michael, Joseph A, Blum, Sheba George, Zsuszsa Gille, Teresa Gowan, Lynne Haney, Maren Klawiter, Steven H. Lopez, Sean O Riain and Millie Thayer. 2000. *Global Ethnography: Forces, Connections, and Imaginations in a Postmodern World.* Berkeley: University of California Press.

Burkeitt, I. 1999. *Bodies Thought: Embodiment, Identity, and Modernity.* London: Sage.

Burns, Ken, dir. 2000. *Jazz: A Film by Ken Burns.* PBS Home Video.

Butler, Judith. 1990. *Gender Trouble: Feminism and the Subversion of Identity.* London: Routledge.

———. 1993. *Bodies That Matter: On the Discursive Limits of "Sex."* New York: Routledge.

———. 1994. *Gender Trouble.* New York: Routledge and Kegan Paul.

———. 1997. *Excitable Speech: A Politics of the Performative.* New York: Routledge.

Canclini, N. G. 1995. *Hybrid Cultures: Strategies for Entering and Exiting Modernity.* Minneapolis: University of Minnesota Press.

Caponi, Gena Dagel. 1999. *Signifyin,' Sanctifyin,' and Slam Dunking: A Reader in African American Expressive Culture.* Amherst: University of Massachusetts Press.

Chi-Sounds Records. 1997. *Let's Get to Steppin.'* Video.

———. 1999. *Steppin' Around the World.* Video.

Chin, Elizabeth. 2001. *Purchasing Power: Black Kids and American Consumer Culture.* Minneapolis: University of Minnesota Press.

Clark, Christine, and James O'Donnell, eds. 1999. *Becoming and Unbecoming White: Owning and Disowning a Racial Identity.* Westport, CT: Begin and Garvey.

Clifford, James. 1986. "On Ethnographic Allegory." In *Writing Culture: The Poetics and Politics of Ethnography*, ed. James Clifford and George E. Marcus, 98–121. Berkeley: University of California Press.

Coleman, Elizabeth B. 2005. *Aboriginal Art, Identity and Appropriation.* Aldershot: Ashgate.

Comaroff, J. 1985. *Body of Power, Spirit of Resistance: The Cultural History of a South African People.* Chicago: University of Chicago Press.

Conley, D. 2001. *Honkey.* New York: Vintage.

Connerton, Paul. 1989. *How Societies Remember.* New York: Cambridge University Press.

Crenshaw, Kimberly, Neil Gotanda, Gary Peller, and Kendall Thomas. 1995. *Critical Race Theory: The Key Writings that Formed the Movement.* New York: New Press.

Crossley, N. 2004. "The Circuit Trainer's Habitus: Reflexive Body Techniques and the Sociality of the Workout." *Body and Society* 10 (1): 37–69.

Crouch, Stanley. 1995. *The All-American Skin Game, or, the Decoy of Race.* New York: Vintage.

Csordas, T. J. 1995. *Embodiment and Experience: The Existential Ground of Culture and Self.* Cambridge: Cambridge University Press.

Cutler, Cecilia A. 1999. "Yorkville Crossing: White Teens, Hip Hop and African American English." *Journal of Sociolinguistics* 3 (4): 428–42.

Dance, Stanley. 2001. *The World of Swing: An Oral History of Big Band Jazz.* Boston: DaCapo Press.

Daws, Martin. 1998. "Wiggers and Wannabes: White Ethnicity in Contemporary Youth Culture." *Left Curve* 22:82–87.

Day, Christopher. 1993. "Gangsta' Rap: Live on the Stage of History." *Race Traitor: Journal of the New Abolitionism* 2:29–38.

———. 1994. "Out of Whiteness." *Race Traitor: Journal of the New Abolitionism* 3:55–61.

Daynes, S., and O. Lee. 2008. *Desire for Race.* Cambridge: Cambridge University Press.

De Certeau, Michel. 1984. *The Practice of Everyday Life.* Berkeley: University of California Press.

DeFrantz, Thomas F. 2002. *Dancing Many Drums: Excavations in African American Dance.* Madison: University of Wisconsin Press.

Delgado, Celeste Fraser, and José Esteban Muñoz. 1997. *Everynight Life: Culture and Dance in Latin/o America.* Durham, NC: Duke University Press.

Delgado, Richard. 1995. *Critical Race Theory: The Cutting Edge.* Philadelphia: Temple University Press.

Delgado, Richard, and Jean Stephanic, eds. 1997. *Critical White Studies: Looking Behind the Mirror.* Philadelphia: Temple University Press.

Deloria, Phillip. 1997. *Playing Indian.* New Haven, CT: Yale University Press.

Dent, Gina, and Michele Wallace. 1999. *Black Popular Culture.* New York: New Press.

Desmond, Jane. 1997. *Meaning in Motion: New Cultural Studies of Dance (Post-Contemporary Interventions).* Durham, NC: Duke University Press.

———. 2000. "Terra Incognita: Mapping New Territory in Dance and 'Cultural Studies.'" *Dance Research Journal* 32 (1): 43–53.

Desmond, Matt. 2007. *On the Fireline.* Chicago: University of Chicago Press.

Diawara, Manthia. 1994. "Malcolm X and the Black Public Sphere: Conversionists vs. Culturalists." In *Social Theory and the Politics of Identity*, ed. Craig Calhoun Basil, 215–30. Cambridge, MA: Blackwell.

Dils, Ann, and Ann Cooper Albright. 2001. *Moving History/Dancing Cultures: A Dance History Reader.* Middletown, CT: Wesleyan University Press.

Dinerstein, Joel. 2003. *Swinging the Machine: Modernity, Technology, and African American Culture between World Wars.* Amherst: University of Massachusetts Press.

Doane, Randall. 2004. "Ralph Ellison's Sociological Imagination." *Sociological Quarterly* 45 (1): 161–84.

Douglas, Ann. 1995. *Terrible Honesty: Mongrel Manhattan in the 1920s.* New York: Farrar, Strauss and Giroux.

Drake, St. Clair, and Horace R. Cayton. 1945. *Black Metropolis: A Study of Negro Life in a Northern City.* New York: Harper and Row.

Du Bois, W. E. B. 1994. *The Souls of Black Folk.* New York: Dover Publishing.

Duneier, Mitchell. 1994. *Slim's Table: Race, Respect, and Masculinity.* Chicago: University of Chicago Press.

———. 2000. *Sidewalk.* New York: Farrar, Strauss and Giroux.

Dyer, Richard. 1997. *White.* New York: Routledge.

Ellis, C. 2004. *The Ethnographic I: A Methodological Novel about Autoethnography.* Walnut Creek, CA: AltaMira Press.

Ellison, Ralph. 1974. "A Completion of Personality: A Talk with Ralph Ellison." In *Ralph Ellison: A Collection of Critical Essays*, ed. John Hersey, 272–301. Englewood Cliffs, NJ: Prentice-Hall.

———. 1994. *The Collected Essays of Ralph Ellison.* Edited by John Callahan. New York: Random House.

———. 1995a. *Going to the Territory.* New York: Vintage Books.

———. 1995b. *Shadow and Act* (reissue). New York: Vintage Books.

———. 1999. "American Culture Is of a Whole: From the Letters of Ralph Ellison." Edited by John Callahan. *New Republic*, March 1, 45–63.

Emery, Lynne Fauley. 1988. *Black Dance: From 1619 to Today.* 2nd rev. ed. Hightstown, NJ: Princeton Book Company Publishing.

Erenberg, Lewis A. 1981. *Steppin' Out: New York Nightlife and the Transformation of American Culture, 1890–1930.* Chicago: University of Chicago Press.

———. 1998. *Swingin' the Dream: Big Band Jazz and the Rebirth of American Culture.* Chicago: University of Chicago Press.

Fab Five Freddy. 2003. "The White Hot Steppers." *Vibe* Magazine, June 2003, 112–20.

Falk, Pasi. 1994. *The Consuming Body.* London: Sage.

Fanon, Frantz. 1991. *Black Skin, White Masks.* New York: Grove Press.

Faulkner, Robert R. and Howard S. Becker. 2009. *"Do You Know . . . ?" The Jazz Repertoire in Action*. Chicago: University of Chicago Press.

Feagin, Joe. 2000. *Racist America: Roots, Realities, and Future Reparations*. New York: Routledge.

Feagin, Joe, and E. O'Brien. 2003. *White Men on Race: Power, Privilege, and the Shaping of a Cultural Consciousness*. Boston: Beacon.

Feagin, Joe, and Hernan Vera. 1995. *White Racism: The Basics*. New York: Routledge.

Featherstone, M. 1991. *Consumer Culture and Postmodernism*. London: Sage.

Fine, Elizabeth C. 2003. *Soulstepping: African American Step Shows*. Urbana: University of Illinois Press.

Fine, Michelle. 1997. *Off White: Readings on Race, Power, and Society*. New York: Routledge.

Fishkin, Shelly. 1995. "Interrogating 'Whiteness,' Complicating 'Blackness': Remapping American Culture." *American Quarterly* 47 (3): 428–66.

Fiske, John. 1993. *Power Plays Power Works*. London: Verso.

———. 1994. *Media Matters: Everyday Culture and Political Change*. Minneapolis: University of Minnesota Press.

Flores, Juan. 2000. *From Bomba to Hip Hop*. New York: Columbia University Press.

Foster, Susan Leigh. 1988. *Reading Dancing: Bodies and Subjects in Contemporary American Dance*. Reprint. Berkeley: University of California Press.

———. 1995. *Corporealities: Body, Knowledge, Culture, Power*. London: Routledge.

Fountain, John W. 2001. "Admiring the Art of Steppers." *Illinois Entertainer*, December 11, 5.

Fraleigh, S. H., and P. Hanstein. 1999. *Researching Dance: Evolving Modes of Inquiry*. London: Dance Books.

Frank, A. W. 1991. "For a Sociology of the Body: An Analytical Review." In *The Body: Social Process and Cultural Theory*, ed. M. Featherstone, M. Hepworth, and B. S. Turner, 36–102. London: Sage.

Frankenberg, R. 1993. *White Women, Race Matters: The Social Construction of Whiteness*. Minneapolis: University of Minnesota Press.

———. 1996. "'When We Are Capable of Stopping, We Begin to See': Being White, Seeing Whiteness." In *Names We Call Home: Autobiography on Racial Identity*, ed. B. Thompson and S. Tyagi, 3–17. London: Routledge.

———. 1997. *Displacing Whiteness: Essays in Social and Cultural Criticism*. Durham, NC: Duke University Press.

Frazier, Kim L. 2000. *D.C. Hand Dance: Capitol City Swing*. Washington, DC: Morris Publishing/Scriptural Foundations.

Freund, Peter E. S. 1998. "Bringing Society into the Body: Understanding Socialized Human Nature." *Theory and Society* 17 (6): 839–64.

Friedland, LeeEllen. 1995. "Social Commentary in African-American Movement Performance." In *Human Action Signs in Cultural Context: The Visible and the Invisible in Movement and Dance*, ed. Brenda Farnell, 136–57. London: Scarecrow Press.

Fusco, Coco. 1995. *English Is Broken Here: Notes on Cultural Fusion in the Americas*. New York: New Press.

Gabriel, John. 1998. *Whitewash: Racialized Politics and the Media*. London: Routledge.

Gallagher, Charles A. 1999. "Researching Race, Reproducing Racism." *Review of Educa-tion/Pedagogy/Cultural Studies* 21 (2): 165–81.

———. 2000. "White Like Me? Methods, Meaning, and Manipulation in the Field of White Studies." In *Racing Research, Researching Race: Methodological Dilemmas in Critical Race Studies*, ed. F. W. Twine & J. W. Warren, 67–92. New York: New York University Press.

———. 2003. "Color-Blind Privilege: The Social and Political Functions of Erasing the Color Line in Post-Race America." *Race, Gender and Class* 10 (4): 22–37.

Garon, P. 1995. "White Blues." *Race Traitor: Journal of the New Abolitionism* 4:57–66.

Gatson, S. N. 2003. "On Being Amorphous: Autoethnography, Genealogy, and a Multi-racial Identity." *Qualitative Inquiry* 9:20–48.

Gaunt, Kyra D. 2006. *The Games Black Girls Play: Learning the Ropes from Double-Dutch to Hip-Hop*. New York: New York University Press.

George, Nelson. 1988. *The Death of Rhythm and Blues*. New York: Pantheon.

———. 1992. *Buppies, B-Boys, Baps, and Bohos: Notes in Post-Soul Black Culture*. New York: HarperCollins.

Gerard, Charley. 2001. *Jazz in Black and White: Race, Culture, and Identity in the Jazz Community*. Westport, CT: Greenwood Press.

Gilroy, Paul. 1993. *The Black Atlantic: Modernity and Double-Consciousness*. Cambridge: Harvard University Press.

———. 1994. *Small Acts: Thoughts on the Politics of Black Cultures*. London: Serpent's Tail.

———. 1997. "'After the Love Has Gone': Bio-Politics and Ethno-Politics in the Black Public Sphere." In *Back to Reality? Social Experience and Cultural Studies* ed. A. McRobbie, 83–115. Manchester: Manchester University Press.

Giroux, Henry. 1997. "White Squall: Resistance and the Pedagogy of Whiteness." *Cultural Studies* 11 (3): 376–89.

Goellner, Ellen W., and Jacqueline Shea Murphy, eds. 1994. *Bodies of the Text: Dance as Theory*. New Brunswick, NJ: Rutgers University Press.

Goffman, Erving. 1959. *The Presentation of Self in Everyday Life*. New York: Anchor.

———. 1967. *Interaction Ritual: Essays on Face to Face Behavior*. New York: Pantheon.

Gold, Russell. 1994. "Guilt of Syncopation, Joy, and Animation: The Closing of Har-lem's Savoy Ballroom." *Studies in Dance History* 5:50–64.

Gordon, Avery, and Christopher Newfield. 1994. "White Philosophy." *Critical Inquiry* 20 (4): 737–57.

Gottschild, Brenda Dixon. 1996. *Digging the Africanist Presence in American Performance: Dance and Other Contexts*. Contributions in Afro-American and African Studies. Westport, CT: Greenwood.

———. 2002. *Waltzing in the Dark: African American Vaudeville and Race Politics in the Swing Era*. New York: Palgrave Macmillan.

———. 2003. *The Black Dancing Body: A Geography from Coon to Cool*. New York: Pal-grave Macmillan.

Grauer, Rhoda. 1993. *Dancing*. New Worlds, New Forms, vol. 5. 13/WNET in associa-tion with RM Arts and BBC-TV. Videocassette.

Grazian, David. 2005. *Blue Chicago: The Search for Authenticity in Urban Blues Clubs.* Chicago: University of Chicago Press.

Gubar, Susan. 1997. *Racechanges: White Skin, Black Face in American Culture.* New York: Oxford University Press.

Guillory, Monique, and Richard C. Green. 1998. *Soul: African American Power, Politics, and Pleasure.* New York: New York University Press.

Gundaker, Grey. 1998. *Keep Your Head to the Sky: Interpreting African-American Home Ground.* Charlottesville: University Press of Virginia.

Hacker, Andrew. 1992. *Two Nations: Black and White: Separate, Hostile, Unequal.* New York: Ballantine Books.

Halbwachs, Maurice. 1980. *The Collective Memory.* Translated by Francis J. Ditter Jr. and Vida Yazdi Ditter. New York: Harper and Row.

Haley, Alex 1964. *The Autobiography of Malcolm X: As Told to Alex Haley.* New York: Ballantine Books.

Hall, J. R. 1992. "The Capital(s) of Culture: A Nonholistic Approach to Status Situations, Class, Gender and Ethnicity." In *Cultivating Differences: Symbolic Boundaries and the Making of Inequality*, ed. Michele Lamont and Marcel Fournier, 257–88. Chicago: University of Chicago Press.

Hall, Perry A. 1997. "African-American Music: Dynamics of Appropriation and Innovation." In *Borrowed Power: Essays on Cultural Appropriation*, ed. Bruce Ziff and Pratima V. Rao, 31–51. New Brunswick, NJ: Rutgers University Press.

Hall, Stuart. 1996a. "Cultural Identity and Cinematic Representation in Black Cultural Studies." In *Black British Cultural Studies: A Reader*, ed. A. Baker Houston Jr., Manthia Diawara, and Ruth H. Lindeborg, 210–22. Black Literature and Culture series. Chicago: University of Chicago Press.

———. 1996b. *Critical Dialogues in Cultural Studies.* Edited by David Morley and Kuan-Hsing Chen. Comedia series. New York: Routledge.

Hall, Stuart, and Paul Du Gay. 1996. *Questions of Cultural Identity.* Thousand Oaks, CA: Sage.

Halter, Marilyn. 2002. *Shopping for Identity: The Marketing of Ethnicity.* New York: Schocken Books.

Hancock, Black Hawk. 2005. "Steppin' Out of Whiteness." *Ethnography* 6:427–62.

———. 2007. "Learning How to Make Life Swing." *Qualitative Sociology* 30 (2) : 113–33.

———. 2008. "Put a Little Color on That!" *Sociological Perspectives* 51 (4): 783–802.

———. 2009. "Taking Loic Wacquant into the Field." *Qualitative Sociology* 32 (1): 93–100.

Hancock, Black Hawk, and Roberta Garner. 2011. "From *Native Son* to *The New Chicago*: Segregation and the Windy City." *ASA Footnotes* 39 (2). http://www.asanet.org/footnotes/feb11/chicago_0211.html#top (accessed October 22, 2012).

Handler, Richard. 1991. "Who Owns the Past? History, Cultural Property, and the Logic of Possessive Individualism." In *The Politics of Culture*, ed. Brett Williams, 63–74. Washington, DC: Smithsonian Institution Press.

Haney-Lopez, Ian. 1998. *White by Law: The Legal Construction of Race.* New York: New York University Press.

Hanna, Judith Lynne. 1987. *To Dance Is Human: A Theory of Nonverbal Communication* Chicago: University of Chicago Press.

Harper, Doug. 1987. *Working Knowledge: Skill and Community in a Small Shop.* Chicago: University of Chicago Press.

Hartigan, John, Jr. 1999. *Racial Situations: Class Predicaments of Whiteness in Detroit.* Princeton, NJ: Princeton University Press.

Haskins, James. 1990. *Black Dance in America: A History through Its People.* New York: Thomas Y. Crowell.

Hazzard-Gordon, Katrina. 1990. *Jookin': The Rise of Social Dance Formations in African-American Culture.* Philadelphia: Temple University Press.

Helms, Janet E., ed. 1990. *Black and White Racial Identity: Theory, Research, and Practice.* Westport, CT: Greenwood Press.

———. 1992. *A Race Is a Nice Thing to Have: A Guide to Being a White Person or Understanding the White Persons in Your Life.* Topeka, KS: Content Communications.

Hersey, John, ed. 1974. *Ralph Ellison: A Collection of Critical Essays.* Englewood Cliffs, NJ: Prentice-Hall.

Hill, Mike 1998. *Whiteness: A Critical Reader.* New York: New York University Press.

Hirsch, Arnold R. 1998. *Making the Second Ghetto: Race and Housing in Chicago 1940–1960.* Chicago: University of Chicago Press.

Hobsbawm, Eric, and T. Ranger. 1983. *The Invention of Tradition.* Cambridge: Cambridge University Press.

Holloway, J. S. 2006. "The Black Scholar, the Humanities, and the Politics of Racial Knowledge since 1945." In *The Humanities and the Dynamics of Inclusion since World War II*, ed. D. A. Hollinger, 217–46. Baltimore: Johns Hopkins University Press.

Holt, N. L. 2003. "Representation, Legitimation, and Autoethnography: An Autoethnographic Writing Story." *International Journal of Qualitative Methods* 2 (1): 18–28

hooks, bell. 1992a. "Representing Whiteness in the Black Imagination." In *Cultural Studies*, ed. Lawrence Grossberg, Cary Nelson, and Paula Treichler, 338–46. New York: Routledge.

———. 1992b. *Black Looks: Race and Representation.* Boston: South End Press.

———. 1994. *Outlaw Culture: Resisting Representations.* New York: Routledge.

Howson, Alexandra, and David Inglis. 2001. "The Body in Sociology: Tensions Inside and Outside Sociological Thought." *Sociological Review* 49 (3): 297–317.

Huggins, Nathan Irving. 1971. *Harlem Renaissance.* Oxford: Oxford University Press.

Hutchinson, George. 1995. *The Harlem Renaissance in Black and White.* Cambridge: Harvard University Press.

Ignatiev, Noel. 1995. *How the Irish Became White.* New York: Routledge.

Ignatiev, Noel, and John Garvey. 1996. *Race Traitor.* New York: Routledge.

Jackson, John L. 2001. *Harlemworld: Doing Race and Class in Contemporary Black America.* Chicago: University of Chicago Press.

———. 2005. *Real Black: Adventures in Racial Sincerity.* Chicago: University of Chicago Press.

Jenkins, Richard. 1994. "Rethinking Ethnicity: Identity, Categorization and Power." *Ethnic and Racial Studies* 17:197–223.

Johnson, E. Patrick. 2003. *Appropriating Blackness: Performance and the Politics of Authenticity.* Durham, NC: Duke University Press.

Jones, LeRoi. 1963. *Blues People: Negro Music in White America.* New York: William Morrow.

Jones, R. S. 1971. "Black Sociology, 1890–1917." *Black Academy Review* 2:43–66.

Kalra, V., and J. Hutnyk. 2003. *Hybridity and Diaspora.* New York: Sage Publications.

Kammen, Michael. 1991. *Mystic Chords of Memory: The Transformation of Tradition in American Popular Culture.* New York: Knopf.

Karenga, Maulana. 1999. "Whiteness Studies: Deceptive or Welcome Discourse, An Interview." *Black Issues in Higher Education* 16 (6): 26–27.

Katz, Jack. 1999. *How Emotions Work.* Chicago: University of Chicago Press.

Keil, Charles, and Steven Feld. 2005. *Music Grooves: Essays and Dialogues.* Chicago: University of Chicago Press.

Kelley, Robin D. G. 1996. "The Riddle of the Zoot: Malcolm Little and Black Cultural Politics during World War II." In Kelley, *Race Rebels: Culture, Politics, and the Black Working Class*, 161–82. New York: Free Press.

———. 1998. "Check the Technique: African American Urban Culture and the Predicament of Social Science." In *Near Ruins: Cultural Theory at the End of the Century*, ed. Nicholas B. Dirks, 39–66. Minneapolis: University of Minnesota Press.

Kincheloe, Joe L. 1997. *About Face: Performing Race in Fashion and Theater.* New York: Routledge.

Kincheloe, Joe L., Shirley R. Steinberg, Nelson M. Rodriguez, and Ronald Chennault, eds. 1998. *White Reign: Deploying Whiteness in America.* New York: St. Martin's.

Kivel, P. 1996. *Uprooting Racism: How White People Can Work for Racial Justice.* Philadelphia: New Society Publishers.

Kolchin, Peter. 2002. "Whiteness Studies: The New History of Race in America." *Journal of American History* 89 (1): 154–73.

Ladner, Joyce A. 1973. *The Death of White Sociology: Essays on Race and Culture.* New York: Random House.

Lamont, Michele. 1994. *Money, Morals, and Manners: The Culture of the French and American Upper-Middle Class.* Chicago: University of Chicago Press.

———. 1999. *The Cultural Territories of Race: Black and White Boundaries.* Chicago: University of Chicago Press.

Lamont, Michele, and Marcel Fournier. 1992. *Cultivating Differences: Symbolic Boundaries and the Making of Inequality.* Chicago: University of Chicago Press.

Lamont, Michele, and Annette Lareau. 1988. "Cultural Capital: Allusions, Gaps and Glissandos in Recent Theoretical Developments." *Sociological Theory* 6 (2): 153–68.

Lande, B. 2007. "Breathing Like a Soldier: Culture Incarnate." *Sociological Review* 55:95–108.

Lareau, Annette, and E. M. Horvat. 1999. "Moments of Social Inclusion and Exclusion: Race, Class, and Cultural Capital in Family School Relationships." *Sociology of Education* 72 (1): 37–53.

Lasch-Quinn, Elisabeth. 2001. *Race Experts: How Racial Etiquette, Sensitivity Training, and New Age Therapy Hijacked the Civil Rights Revolution*. New York: W. W. Norton.

Lepecki, André. 2004. *Of the Presence of the Body: Essays on Dance and Performance Theory*. Middleton, CT: Wesleyan University Press.

Lewis, David Levering. 1979. *When Harlem Was in Vogue*. New York: Penguin Books.

Lewis, J. Lowell. 1995. "Genre and Embodiment: From Brazilian Capoeira to the Ethnology of Human Movement." *Cultural Anthropology* 10 (2): 221–43.

Lhamon, J. T. 2000. *Raising Cain: Blackface Performance from Jim Crow to Hip Hop*. Cambridge: Harvard University Press.

Lindsay, Beverly, prod. 2000. *Swing, Bop and Hand Dance*. WHUT, Howard University Television.

Lipsitz, George. 1990. *Time Passages: Collective Memory and American Popular Culture*. Minneapolis: University of Minnesota Press.

———. 1997. *Dangerous Crossroads: Popular Music, Postmodernism, and the Politics of Place*. New York: Verso.

———. 1998. *The Possessive Investment in Whiteness: How White People Profit from Identity Politics*. Philadelphia: Temple University Press.

———. 2006. *The Possessive Investment in Whiteness: How White People Profit from Identity Politics*. Philadelphia: Temple University Press.

Lloyd, Richard. 2005. *Neo-Bohemia: Art and Commerce in the Postindustrial City*. New York: Routledge.

Lott, Eric. 1993. "White Like Me: Racial Cross-Dressing and the Construction of American Whiteness." In *Culture of United States Imperialism*, ed. Amy Kaplan and Donald E. Pease, 474–95. Durham, NC: Duke University Press.

———. 1995. *Love and Theft: Blackface Minstrelsy and the American Working Class*. Oxford: Oxford University Press.

Loveman, Mara. 1999a. "Is Race Essential? A Response to Bonilla-Silva." *American Sociological Review* 64 (6): 891–99.

———. 1999b. "Making 'Race' and Nation in the United States, South Africa, and Brazil: Taking Making Seriously." *Theory and Society* 28:903–27.

Lowenthal, David. 1985. *The Past Is a Foreign Country*. Cambridge: Cambridge University Press.

Lury, Celia. 1996. *Consumer Culture*. New Brunswick, NJ: Rutgers University Press.

Lyman, S. M. 1971. *The Black American in Sociological Thought: A Failure of Perspective*. New York: G. P. Putnam's Sons.

Mahar, William J. 1999. *Behind the Burnt Cork Mask: Early Blackface Minstrelsy and Antebellum American Popular Culture*. Urbana: University of Illinois Press.

Maira, Sunaina. 2002. *Desis in the House: Indian American Youth Culture in New York City*. Philadelphia: Temple University Press.

Malone, Jacqui. 1996. *Steppin' on the Blues: The Visible Rhythms of African American Dance*. Urbana: University of Illinois Press.

Martin, Carol. 1994. *Dance Marathons: Performing American Culture in the 1920s and 1930s*. Jackson: University of Mississippi Press.

Martin, Charles D. 2002. *The White African American Body: A Cultural and Literary Exploration.* New Brunswick, NJ: Rutgers University Press.

Massey, Douglas S., and Nancy A. Denton. 1998. *American Apartheid: Segregation and the Making of the Underclass.* Reprint. Cambridge: Harvard University Press.

McClintock, A. 1995. *Imperial Leather: Race, Gender, and Sexuality in the Colonial Conquest.* New York: Routledge.

McCracken, Grant. 1991. *Culture and Consumption: New Approaches to the Symbolic Character of Consumer Goods and Activities.* Reprint. Bloomington: Indiana University Press.

McIntosh, Peggy. 1989. "White Privilege: Unpacking the Invisible Knapsack." *Peace and Freedom* (July/August): 10–12.

Mckee, J. B. 1992. *Sociology and the Problem: The Failure of a Perspective.* Urbana: University of Illinois Press.

McLaren, Peter. 1997. "Decentering Whiteness: In Search of a Revolutionary Multiculturalism." *Multicultural Education* 5:4–11.

McRoberts, Omar. 2004. "Beyond Mysterium Tremendum: Thoughts toward an Aesthetic Study of Religious Experience." *Annals of the American Academy of Political and Social Science* 595:190–203.

Mead, Lawrence M. 1986. *Beyond Entitlement: The Social Obligation of Citizenship.* New York: Free Press.

Meneley, A., and D. J. Young. 2005. *Autoethnographies: The Anthropology of Academic Practices.* Toronto: Broadview Press.

Mercer, Kobena. 1994. *Welcome to the Jungle: New Positions in African American Cultural Studies.* New York: Routledge.

Michaels, Walter Benn. 1992. "Race into Culture: A Critical Genealogy of Cultural Identity.". *Critical Inquiry* 18 (4): 655–85.

———. 1994. "The No-Drop Rule." *Critical Inquiry* 24 (4): 758–69.

———. 1995. *Our America: Nativism, Modernism, and Pluralism.* Durham, NC: Duke University Press.

———. 1997. "Autobiography of an Ex-White Man." *Transition* 73:122–43.

Miller, Daniel. 1987. *Material Culture and Mass Consumption.* Hoboken, NJ: Blackwell Publishers.

———. 1998. *Material Cultures: Why Some Things Matter.* Chicago: University of Chicago Press.

Miller, Norma, and Evette Jensen. 2001. *Swinging at the Savoy: The Memoir of a Jazz Dancer.* Philadelphia: Temple University Press.

Mills, C. Wright. 1959. *The Sociological Imagination.* New York: Oxford University Press.

Modood, Tariq, and Pnina Werbner. 1997. *Debating Cultural Hybridity: Multicultural Identities and the Politics of Anti-Racism.* New York: Zed Books.

Monson, Ingrid. 1996. *Saying Something: Jazz Improvisation and Interaction.* Chicago: University of Chicago Press.

Moon, D. G., and L. A. Flores. 2000. "Antiracism and the Abolition of Whiteness: Rhetorical Strategies of Domination among 'Race Traitors.'" *Communication Studies* 51:97–115.

Morris, G. 1996. *Moving Words: Rewriting Dance.* London: Routledge.

Moten, Fred. 2003. *In the Break: The Aesthetics of the Black Radical Tradition.* Minneapolis: University of Minnesota Press.

Murphy, John P. 1990. "Jazz Improvisation: The Joy of Influence." *Black Perspective in Music* 18:7–19.

Nakayama, Thomas K., and Judith N. Martin. 1999. *Essays in Whiteness: The Communication of Social Identity.* Thousand Oaks, CA: Sage.

Neal, Larry. 1974. "Ellison's Zoot Suit." In *Ralph Ellison: A Collection of Critical Essays*, ed. John Hersey, 58–79. Englewood Cliffs, NJ: Prentice-Hall.

Ness, Sally Ann. 1992. *Body, Movement, and Culture: Kinesthetic and Visual Symbolism in a Philippine Community.* Philadelphia: University of Pennsylvania Press.

Nettleton, S., and J. Watson. 1998. *The Body in Everyday Life.* London: Routledge.

North, Michael. 1998. *The Dialect of Modernism: Race, Language and Twentieth-Century Literature.* New York: Oxford University Press.

O'Connor, Erin. 2005. "Embodied Knowledge: The Experience of Meaning and the Struggle towards Proficiency in Glassblowing." *Ethnography* 6 (2): 183–204.

O'Meally, Robert G. 1998. *The Jazz Cadence of American Culture.* New York: Columbia University Press.

Olick, Jeffrey K. 2007. *The Politics of Regret: On Collective Memory and Historical Responsibility.* New York: Routledge.

Omi, Michael, and Howard Winant. 1994. *Racial Formation in the United States.* New York: Routledge.

Osofsky, Gilbert. 1966. *Harlem: The Making of a Ghetto.* Chicago: Elephant Paperbacks.

Pagis, Michal. 2010. "Producing Intersubjectivity in Silence: An Ethnographic Study of Meditation Practice." *Ethnography* 11 (2): 309–28.

Parker, Andrew, and Eve K. Sedgwick. 1995. *Performativity and Performance.* New York: Routledge.

Pattillo, Mary. 2008. *Black on the Block: The Politics of Race and Class in the City.* Chicago: University of Chicago Press.

Pattillo-McCoy, Mary. 2000. *Black Picket Fences: Privilege and Peril among the Black Middle Class.* Chicago: University of Chicago Press.

Penner, Degen. 1999. *The Swing Book.* San Francisco: Back Bay Books.

Perry, Pamela. 2001. "White Means Never Having to Say You're Ethnic." *Journal of Contemporary Ethnography* 30 (1): 56–91.

———. 2002. *Shades of White: White Kids and Racial Identities in High School.* Durham, NC: Duke University Press.

Peterson, Richard. 1997. *Creating Country Music: Fabricating Authenticity.* Chicago: University of Chicago Press.

Porter, Horace A. 2001. *Jazz Country: Ralph Ellison in America.* Iowa City: University of Iowa Press.

Purser, G. 2009. "The Dignity of Job-Seeking Men: Boundary Work among Immigrant Day Laborers." *Journal of Contemporary Ethnography* 38 (1): 117–39.

Radano, Ronald. 1993. "How to Get at the Elusive Meanings of Cultural Expressions that Refer to Racial Difference." *Jazz, Modernism, and the Black Creative Tradition: Reviews in American History* 21 (4): 671–76.

———. 2001. "Hot Fantasies: American Modernism and the Idea of Black Rhythm." In *Music and the Racial Imagination*, ed. Ronald Radano and Philip V. Bohlman, 459–80. Chicago: University of Chicago Press.

———. 2003. *Lying Up a Nation: Race and Black Music.* Chicago: University of Chicago Press.

Radano, Ronald, and Philip V. Bohlman, eds. 2001. *Music and the Racial Imagination.* Foreword by Houston A. Baker Jr. Chicago: University of Chicago Press.

Ramsey, G. P., Jr. 2001. "Who Hears Here? Black Music, Critical Bias, and the Musicological Skintrade." *Musical Quarterly* 85 (1): 1–52.

———. 2003. *Race Music: Black Cultures from Bebop to Hip-hop.* Berkeley: University of California Press.

Ratliff, Ben. 2001. "Fixing, for Now, the Image of Jazz." Review of the PBS/Ken Burns documentary *Jazz. New York Times*, January 7.

Reed, S. A. 1998. "The Politics and Poetics of Dance." *Annual Review of Anthropology*, 503–32.

Reed-Danahay, D. 1997. *Auto/ethnography: Rewriting the Self and the Social.* Oxford: Berg Publishers.

Rhino Records. 2001. *Steppin' Out.* CD. Warner Music Group.

Roediger, David. 1991. *Wages of Whiteness: Race and the Making of the American Working Class.* New York: Verso.

———. 1994. *Towards the Abolition of Whiteness.* Minneapolis: University of Minnesota Press.

———. 1999. *Black on White: Black Writers on What It Means to Be White.* New York: Schocken Books.

———. 2002. *Colored White: Transcending the Racial Past.* Berkeley: University of California Press.

Rogin, Michael. 1996. *Blackface, White Noise: Jewish Immigrants in the Hollywood Melting Pot.* Berkeley: University of California Press.

Root, Deborah. 1998. *Cannibal Culture: Art, Appropriation, and the Commodification of Difference.* Boulder, CO: Westview Press.

Rose, Tricia Black. 1994. *Noise: Rap Music and Black Culture in Contemporary America.* Middletown, CT: Wesleyan University Press.

Ross, Andrew. 1996. "Wiggaz with attitude (WWA)." *Artforum International* 35 (2): 25.

Ross, Andrew, and Tricia Rose. 1994. *Microphone Fiends: Youth Music and Youth Culture.* New York: Routledge.

Ross, Patricia. 2003. Reader response. *Vibe* (August): 43–46.

Ross, Frank Russel. 2010. *Soul Dancing! The Essential African American Cultural Dance Book.* Reston, VA: National Dance Association.

Rothenberg, Paula S. 2002. *White Privilege: Essential Readings on the Other Side of Racism.* New York: Worth.

Roy, William G. 2010. *Reds, Whites, and Blues: Social Movements, Folk Music, and Race in the United States.* Princeton, NJ: Princeton University Press.

Rubio, Phil. 1993. "Crossover Dreams: The 'Exceptional White' in Popular Culture." *Race Traitor: Journal of the New Abolitionism* 2:68–80.

———. 1994. "Can I Get a Witness." *Race Traitor: Journal of the New Abolitionism* 3:79–82.

Saint-Arnaud, P. 2009. *African American Pioneers of Sociology: A Critical History.* Toronto: University of Toronto Press.

Savigliano, M. 1995. *Tango and the Political Economy of Passion.* Boulder, CO: Westview Press.

Saxton, Alexander. 1975. "Blackface Minstrelsy and Jacksonian Ideology." *American Quarterly* 27 (1): 3–28.

———. 1998. "Blackface Minstrelsy, Vernacular Comics, and the Politics of Slavery in the North." In *The Meaning of Slavery in the North*, ed. David Roediger and Martin H. Blatt, 157–175. New York: Garland.

Scheffer, R. 2008. "Gaining Insight from Incomparability: Exploratory Comparison in Studies of Social Practices." *Comparative Sociology* 7 (3): 338–61.

Schilling, Chris. 1993. *The Body and Social Theory.* London: Sage.

———. 2001. "Embodiment, Experience and Theory: In Defense of the Sociological Tradition." *Sociological Review* 49 (3): 327–45.

Scott, Daryl Michael. 1997. *Contempt and Pity: Social Policy and the Image of the Damaged Black Psyche.* Chapel Hill: University of North Carolina Press.

Scott, James C. 1985. *Weapons of the Weak: Everyday Forms of Peasant Resistance.* New Haven, CT: Yale University Press.

———. 1990. *Domination and the Arts of Resistance: Hidden Transcripts.* New Haven, CT: Yale University Press.

Sennett, Richard. 2008. *The Craftsman.* New Haven, CT: Yale University Press.

Sollors, Werner. 1997. *Neither Black nor White Yet Both: Thematic Explorations of Interracial Literature.* New York: Oxford University Press.

———. 1999. "Our America: Nativism, Modernism, and Pluralism: Review." *Modern Philology* 96 (4): 550–52.

Sorensen, Jesper, V. Winding, and T. Ross, dirs. 1988. *Call of the Jitterbug.* Green Room Productions. Film.

Spencer, Paul. 1986. *Society and the Dance: The Social Anthropology of Process and Performance.* Cambridge: Cambridge University Press.

Spivak, Gayatri C. 1998. "Can the Subaltern Speak?" In *Marxism and the Interpretation of Culture*, ed. Cary Nelson and Lawrence Grossberg, 271–313. Urbana: University of Illinois Press.

Spry, T. 2001. "Performing Autoethnography: An Embodied Methodological Praxis." *Qualitative Inquiry* 7:706–32.

Stearns, Marshall Winslow, and Jean Stearns. 1994. *Jazz Dance: The Story of American Vernacular Dance.* 2nd ed. New York: DaCapo Press.

Stephens, Gregory. 1991. "Rap Music's Double-Voiced Discourse: A Crossroads for Interracial Communication." *Journal of Communication Inquiry* 15 (2): 70–91.

———. 1992. "Interracial Dialogue in Rap Music: Call-and-Response in a Multicultural Style." *New Formations* 16:62–79.

———. 1999. "'You Can Sample Anything': Zebrahead, 'Black' Music, and Multiracial Audiences." *New Formations.*39:113–28.

Stoller, Paul. 1997. *Sensuous Scholarship*. Philadelphia: University of Pennsylvania Press.

Stowe, David W. 1994. *Swing Changes: Big Band Jazz in New Deal America*. Cambridge: Harvard University Press.

Sundquist, Eric. 1993. *To Wake the Nations: Race in the Making of American Literature*. Cambridge: Harvard University Press, 1993.

Suttles, Gerald D. 1970. *The Social Order of the Slum: Ethnicity and Territory in the Inner City*. Chicago: University of Chicago Press.

Tate, Greg. 2002. *Everything but the Burden: What White People Are Taking Away from Black Culture*. New York: Broadway Books.

Taylor, J. 1998. *Paper Tangos*. Durham, NC: Duke University Press.

Taylor, Timothy. 1992. "His Name Was in Lights: Chuck Berry's 'Johnny B. Goode.'" *Popular Music* 11 (1): 27–41.

Thiel, D. 2007. "Class in Construction: London Building Workers, Dirty Work and Physical Cultures." *British Journal of Sociology* 58 (2): 227–51.

Thomas, Helen. 1995. *Dance, Modernity and Culture: Explorations in the Sociology of Dance*. New York: Routledge.

Thomas, Helen, and Jamilah Ahmed. 2004. *Cultural Bodies; Ethnography and Theory*. New York: Blackwell.

Toll, Robert. 1974. *Blacking Up: The Minstrel Show in Nineteenth Century America*. New York: Oxford University Press.

Tomlinson, John. 1991. *Cultural Imperialism: A Critical Introduction*. London: Pinter Publishers.

Turner, B. S. 1984. *The Body and Society*. Oxford: Basil Blackwell.

Turner, Patricia A. 1994. *Ceramic Uncles and Celluloid Mammies: Black Images and Their Influence on Culture*. New York: Anchor.

Twine, F. W., and John W. Warren. 2000. *Racing Research, Researching Race: Methodological Dilemma in Critical Race Studies*. New York: New York University Press.

Vale, V., and Marian Wallace. 1998. *Swing! The New Retro Renaissance*. San Francisco: V/Search Press.

Vidal-Ortiz, S. 2004. "On Being a White Person of Color: Using Autoethnography to Understand Puerto Ricans' Racialization." *Qualitative Sociology* 27:179–203.

Ware, Vron, and Les Back. 2002. *Out of Whiteness: Color, Politics, and Culture*. Chicago: University of Chicago Press.

Wacquant, Loïc. 1992. "The Social Logic of Boxing in Black Chicago: Toward a Sociology of Pugilism." *Sociology of Sport Journal* 7 (3): 221–54.

———. 1995a. "Pugs at Work: Bodily Capital and Bodily Labor among Professional Boxers." *Body and Society* 1 (1): 65–94.

———. 1995b. "The Pugilistic Point of View: How Boxers Think and Feel about Their Trade." *Theory and Society* 24 (4): 489–535.

———. 1997a. "The Prizefighter's Three Bodies." *Ethnos* 63 (3): 325–52.

———. 1997b. "Towards an Analytic of Racial Domination." *Political Power and Social Theory* 11:221–34.

———. 1998a. "A Fleshpeddler at Work: Power, Pain, and Profit in the Prizefighting Economy." *Theory and Society* 27:1–42.

———. 1998b. "Negative Social Capital: State Breakdown and Social Destitution in America's Urban Core." *Netherlands Journal of Housing and the Built Environment* 13 (1): 25–39.

———. 2002a. "Scrutinizing the Street: Poverty, Morality, and the Pitfalls of Urban Ethnography." *American Journal of Sociology* 107:1468–1532.

———. 2002b. "Taking Bourdieu into the Field." *Berkeley Journal of Sociology* 46:180–86.

———. 2003. "From Slavery to Mass Incarceration: Rethinking the 'Race Question' in the United States." *New Left Review,* 2d ser., 13:40–61.

———. 2004a. *Body and Soul: Notebooks of an Apprentice Boxer.* New York: Oxford University Press.

———. 2004b. "Pointers on Pierre Bourdieu and Democratic Politics." *Constellations* 11:3–15.

———. 2005a. "Carnal Connections: On Embodiment, Membership and Apprenticeship." *Qualitative Sociology* 28 (4): 445–71.

———. 2005b. "Shadowboxing with Ethnographic Ghosts: A Rejoinder." *Symbolic Interaction* 28 (3): 441–47.

———. 2009. "The Body, the Ghetto and the Penal State." *Qualitative Sociology* 32 (1): 101–29.

———. 2011. "Habitus as Topic and Tool: Reflections on Becoming a Prizefighter." *Qualitative Research in Psychology* 8:81–92.

Wacquant, Loïc, and Nancy Scheper-Hughes. 2003. *Commodifying Bodies.* London: Sage.

Wald, Gayle Freda. 2000. *Crossing the Line: Racial Passing in Twentieth-Century US Literature and Culture.* Durham, NC: Duke University Press.

Walser, Robert. 1993. "Out of Notes: Signification, Interpretation, and the Problem with Miles Davis." *Musical Quarterly* 77 (2): 343–65.

———. 1995. "Rhyme, Rhythm, and Rhetoric in the Music of Public Enemy." *Ethnomusicology* 39 (2): 193–218.

Warren, Kenneth. 2003. *So Black and Blue: Ralph Ellison and the Occasion of Criticism.* Chicago: University of Chicago Press.

Watson, Steven. 1995. *The Harlem Renaissance: Hub of African American Culture, 1920–1930.* New York: Pantheon.

Wellman, David T. 1993. *Portraits of White Racism.* 2nd ed. Cambridge: Cambridge University Press.

Welsh-Asante, Kariamu, ed. 1993. *The African Aesthetic: Keeper of the Traditions.* Contributions in Afro-American and African Studies series. Westport, CT: Greenwood Press.

West, Cornel. 1993. *Race Matters.* Boston: Beacon.

White, Shane, and Graham J. White. 1999. *White Stylin': African American Expressive Culture, from Its Beginnings to the Zoot Suit.* Ithaca, NY: Cornell University Press.

Wildman, Stephanie M. 1996. *Privilege Revealed: How Invisible Preference Undermines America.* New York: New York University Press.

Williams, Raymond. 1989. *Resources of Hope: Culture, Democracy, Socialism.* London: Verso.

———. 1977. *Marxism and Literature*. London: Oxford University Press.

Williams, S. J., and G. A. Bendelow. 1998. *The Lived Body: Sociological Themes, Embodied Issues*. London: Routledge.

Williams, Vernon J. 2006. *The Social Sciences and Theories of Race*. Urbana: University of Illinois Press.

———. 2008. "An Inclusive History of Sociology?" *Journal of African American Studies* 12:85–94.

———. 2011. "Was There a Distinct 'African American Sociology'?" *Western Journal of Black Studies* 35:39–43.

Willis, Paul. 2001. *The Ethnographic Imagination*. London: Polity Press.

Wilson, William Julius. 1980. *The Declining Significance of Race*. Chicago: University of Chicago Press.

———. 1987. *The Truly Disadvantaged: The Inner City, the Underclass, and Public Policy*. Chicago: University of Chicago Press.

———. 1997. *When Work Disappears: The World of the New Urban Poor*. New York: Vintage Books.

Winant, Howard. 1994. *Racial Conditions: Race, Theory, Comparisons*. Minneapolis: University of Minnesota Press.

———. 1996. "Behind Blue Eyes: Whiteness and Contemporary U.S. Racial Politics." In *Off White: Readings on Race, Power, and Society*, ed. Michelle Fine, Lois Weis, Linda C. Powell, and L. Mun Wong, 40–53. New York: Routledge.

Wood, Joe. 1997. "The Yellow Negro." *Transition* 73:40–66.

Wulff, Helena. 2007. *Dancing at the Crossroads: Memory and Mobility in Ireland*. New York: Berghahn Books.

Young, James. 2008. *Cultural Appropriation and the Arts*. Malden, MA: Blackwell.

Yudice, G. 1995. "Neither Impugning nor Disavowing Whiteness Does a Viable Politics Make: The Limits of Identity Politics." In *After Political Correctness*, ed. C. Newfield and R. Strickland, 255–81. Boulder, CO: Westview.

Ziff, Bruce H., and Pratima V. Rao. 1997. *Borrowed Power: Essays on Cultural Appropriation*. New Brunswick, NJ: Rutgers University Press.

INDEX